RANDOM
ACTS OF
MEDICINE

RANDOM
ACTS OF
MEDICINE

THE HIDDEN FORCES THAT
SWAY DOCTORS, IMPACT PATIENTS,
AND SHAPE OUR HEALTH

ANUPAM B. JENA, M.D., PH.D.
& CHRISTOPHER WORSHAM, M.D.

DOUBLEDAY  NEW YORK

Image on page 69 courtesy of private collection
Image on page 115 courtesy of Harvard University Press
All other images were generated using R software.

Jacket photograph © Yasu + Junko/Trunk Archive
Jacket design by John Fontana

Library of Congress Control Number 2022056219

ISBN: 978-0-385-54881-6 (hardcover)
ISBN: 978-0-385-54882-3 (ebook)

MANUFACTURED IN THE UNITED STATES OF AMERICA

1st Printing

To my wife, Neena, for her friendship and much more; to Annika and Aiden, who make every day end with a smile; and to my parents, Puru and Tripti, whose sacrifices made this life possible

To my wife, Emily, for her limitless love and support; to my boys Luke and Adam, for the joy they bring; to my brother Alex, for his friendship and trust; and to my parents, Jim and Donna, journalists whose influence fills these pages

CONTENTS

RANDOM
ACTS OF
MEDICINE

OUR LIVES ARE WOVEN IN A FABRIC OF CHANCE

CHANCE OCCURRENCES CHANGE the course of our lives all the time. Imagine the couple who meets in an airport when a blizzard cancels their flights. Or think of the entrepreneurs who happen to sit next to each other at jury duty and who hatch a business plan to start a company in the six hours it takes to be dismissed. Imagine the woman who misses the bus because a meeting ran late and who, on her walk home, happens to pass an animal shelter and adopts her new best friend.

These are unpredictable moments—chance waltzing into our lives when we least expect it. We can all probably think of times in our lives when we were led down alternate paths, both good and bad, thanks to chance. These phenomena go by many familiar names: randomness, luck, serendipity, kismet, happenstance, accidents, or flukes.

Chance can even play a role in life and death. A retiree collapses in the supermarket from a heart attack and is rushed to the hospital as paramedics perform CPR, but the ambulance is delayed due to scheduled road closures. He dies from the heart attack two weeks later. If he had collapsed the day before when the roads were clear, might he have survived? A child doesn't get a flu shot at his annual doctor's visit, because the vaccine is not yet available in his doctor's office. His parents never bring him back for a flu shot appointment. That winter, he catches influenza and spreads it to his grandmother, who ends up in the hospital. Had the flu shot been available at his annual visit, he likely would have received it. Would he and his grandmother still have gotten sick?

It's frightening to think about how random occurrences contribute to our health, life, and death. We all like to think that if we do the right things—eat well, wear a seat belt, quit smoking, take the medications our doctor prescribes—we can control what happens with our bodies and our lives.

This is no less true for doctors. We too like to think that the decisions we make for our patients—whether to prescribe them a drug, perform surgery, order a diagnostic test—are based only on science and carefully considered data, not on simple chance. The reality, though, is that medicine can be messy, complicated, and uncertain. There are many opportunities for randomness to affect the medical care we give and receive.

Most people tend to think in terms of "good luck" and "bad luck": the good luck of getting to the bus stop just as the bus arrives, or the bad luck of driving over a nail and getting a flat tire. But in everyday medicine, people are sent down paths of care by factors they may not think to consider—the doctor who happened to be working in the ER the day they sprained their ankle, or the patient they happened to share a waiting room with just prior to a routine doctor's visit. It's not "good luck" to sprain your ankle on a Tuesday or "bad luck" to sprain it on a Wednesday—it's as random as a roll of the dice. Yet the day a person sprains their ankle may determine which doctor happens to treat them in the ER, and thus the likelihood they're prescribed an opioid pain medication that could lead to long-term use. Because opioid-prescribing tendencies vary from doctor to doctor, as one important study demonstrated, the doctor you happen to see can have lasting repercussions. Similarly, it's not inherently "good luck" or "bad luck" to share a doctor's office waiting room with someone. But if that person happens to have a viral infection, a chance encounter could lead to a bout of the flu two weeks later, and especially for the very young and the elderly the flu is no laughing matter.

In this book, we're going to explore the hidden but predictable ways in which chance affects our health—and our health-care system. We're going to do it by diving into real research conducted by ourselves and others. We'll examine what happens to patients when the doctor they expect to see in an emergency can't be at the hospital—and why they might be better off with a substitute. We'll look at why meeting a surgeon just before a big birthday versus just after can affect major surgical decisions (and why this phenomenon can be explained by well-known grocery store pricing tactics). And in an era when health care is becoming increasingly politically polarized, we'll see whether the politics of the doctor who happens to care for you in the hospital matters for the care that you receive.

Beyond just making observations, we're going to look at what these occurrences can teach us about what works and what doesn't in health care today. Because while we can't remove randomness from our lives, we can learn from it—so we don't become victims of chance.

———

Economists, epidemiologists, and social scientists sometimes talk about "natural experiments." Natural experiments are "natural" because they occur without the influence of any manipulating hand. One person grows up in one zip code; another person grows up across the street, which happens to be in a different zip code. One baby is born into a season of drought; another is born during record monsoons. There is no researcher designing a study, no patients signing up to participate, no new medical intervention being intentionally tested. These are conditions for accidental experiments, science occurring in the wild.

Natural experiments run in contrast to what we might think of when we use the word "experiment." In medicine, randomized controlled trials—the gold standard of science, where researchers randomly assign subjects to either a treatment or a control group and then follow them into the future—are our most powerful and preferred tool for studying cause and effect. They are our best way of knowing whether an intervention really works. These are the studies that have been used for decades to prove the efficacy of the blood pressure drugs, cancer therapies, and vaccines we use today.

But randomized controlled trials aren't perfect. They can be logistically difficult, expensive to perform, take unreasonable amounts of time, or be flat-out unethical. Imagine you were interested in studying the effect of air pollution on human health. A scientist couldn't simply assign human test subjects to regions with different levels of air pollution and observe the results. Or imagine you wanted to study the long-term effects of screen time on children. Assuming you could surmount the complicated ethics of such a controlled study, you might still have to wait dozens of years to see results, at which point your study might have ceased to be relevant.

So researchers in some fields—economics in particular—have come to rely on natural experiments in their work. How so? Let's circle back to air pollution. You can't just purposefully expose people to air pollution, but what if scientists could isolate a naturally occurring event in which some defined groups of people were exposed to higher levels of air pollution than some other groups were—by nothing more than chance? Actionable conclusions could be drawn from those findings.

In one study, the Princeton economist Janet Currie and the UC Berkeley economist Reed Walker did precisely that. They showed that among families living near congested highway tollbooths in Pennsylvania and New Jersey, babies who happened to be born just before E-ZPass automatic payments were introduced were more likely to be born prematurely and with low birth weights than the babies born just after E-ZPass, when air pollution levels dropped alongside traffic congestion (since cars no longer needed to wait in long lines at tollbooths).

You might be unconvinced. What if there were other factors at play? What if the types of mothers living near the toll plazas were somehow different—older or younger, more or less healthy—before and after E-ZPass started? The researchers wondered the same thing. But their analysis didn't yield any major differences in the two groups, and the overall result was unchanged even after statistical adjustments were made for small differences in smoking, teenage pregnancy, education, race, and birth order (moms' second versus third baby). The researchers even considered whether the findings were driven by health-conscious prospective home buyers, who knew air pollution would be reduced in the area, being more likely to move into the neighborhood. If that actually occurred, the greater demand should have driven up housing prices. But they found no differences in housing prices near toll plazas before and after E-ZPass. They could only conclude that E-ZPass meant less air pollution, and thus improved birth outcomes in the vicinity.

Here's another natural experiment in a similar spirit, this time by the University of Illinois Urbana-Champaign economists Tatyana Deryugina, Nolan Miller, David Molitor, and Julian Reif and the Georgia State University economist Garth Heutel, who were interested in the health effects of air pollution on elderly patients. The researchers looked at the death rates of certain patients on days when the wind happened to be blowing polluted air *into* a certain area compared with days when the wind blew *away,* directing pollution elsewhere. Is there any purer example of the role of chance than, literally, which way the wind blows? Sure enough, the economists found convincing evidence ("statistically significant" evidence, they would say) that days with greater incoming air pollution led to higher hospitalizations and death among the elderly of that region.

In both instances, health outcomes were affected by chance—the mother who happened to deliver her baby after E-ZPass was introduced near her home, the elderly adults whose health outcomes were affected by the wind direction. But in both cases, the role of chance was measurable. This is more than just interesting data; it helps us rigorously quantify the effect of air pollution on our health, something no randomized controlled study could ever ethically achieve.

———

We are both practicing doctors, and so naturally we love a good randomized controlled study. But our backgrounds have given us a special affinity for natural experiments.

One of us, Anupam (who goes by his middle name, Bapu), studied economics and biology at MIT and completed his medical training and PhD in economics at the University of Chicago. That makes him a member of the very small group of doctor/economists in the world. Today he's a professor of health-care policy and medicine at Harvard Medical School and sees patients at Massachusetts General Hospital in Boston. Many of the stories and the studies that we'll tell you about in this book come from his own experiences as a doctor who, when treating patients, can't turn off the economist inside him. Bapu never planned to be a doctor and economist, though. That was chance, the result of a suggestion by an influential, eccentric professor at the University of Chicago who offhandedly suggested he consider doing a PhD in economics alongside medicine, instead of the biology PhD he had been considering. That suggestion hopefully wasn't a reflection of Bapu's promise as a biologist; either way, the rest is history.

The other of us, Chris, is a pulmonary and critical care doctor at Massachusetts General Hospital, and also a health-care policy researcher on the faculty of Harvard Medical School. Learning the basics of medicine from rural patients in New Hampshire as a medical student at Dartmouth, and later from many of Boston's historically underserved patient populations as a resident at Boston Medical Center and VA Boston, Chris completed his subspecialty and public health training at Harvard. He now does research into natural experiments in medicine while also treating patients in the intensive care unit.

Our experience as doctors has shown us that, for as much we'd love to see illness as something discrete—you isolate the culprit, identify it, hopefully treat it—the reality is that illness is extraordinarily complex. Sick patients under our care rarely present with only one problem. They can deteriorate without warning; we doctors often must act quickly, using imperfect information, to keep them alive.

In acute hospital care especially, hard scientific evidence on what to do in any given situation is often limited. We are frequently forced to rely on our knowledge of how the body works, our experience, and our instincts. Fortunately for all of us, this approach is often effective. Yet it leaves us vulnerable to chance in ways that doctors and patients may not realize, but that we can all learn from (at least when we try). This book—as well as our work as doctors and researchers—is devoted to the idea that examining the role chance plays in medicine can contribute to the health of our patients and the well-being of our communities.

———

The beauty of natural experiments that occur in medicine—and why they so excite us that we wrote a whole book dedicated to them—is not only that they have the power to let us uncover problems in our health-care system that cannot be readily answered with traditional research but that they point us toward potential solutions. You don't have to take our word for it. The study of natural experiments has been shown to be such a powerful tool that some of the pioneers of its modern use—David Card, Joshua Angrist, and Guido Imbens—were awarded the Nobel Prize in Economics in 2021. Their work has been credited with bringing about a so-called credibility revolution in the field, allowing the scientifically rigorous methods they helped develop to be applied to nearly every field of economics, including health economics.

While economics has had a heavy hand to play in the modern study of natural experiments, one of the first natural experiments ever studied was actually in medicine. It was such an influential study that many call the physician who wrote it, Dr. John Snow, the "father" of the field of epidemiology—the study of diseases within populations.

In 1854, London was suffering an outbreak of cholera, a diarrheal disease that would often lead to death from dehydration. At the time, it wasn't known how cholera was spread. Because the disease caused gastrointestinal symptoms, Snow hypothesized that patients who contracted the illness had ingested something that caused disease. When an outbreak occurred among people living in a specific neighborhood, he began to investigate. There were dozens of deaths concentrated in the area, but he found it curious that some neighbors were completely unaffected while others became sick. He studied those who became sick or died, and he found that they had drunk from a specific water pump—how Londoners got their water at the time. Meanwhile, healthy neighbors who were otherwise similar—

living in similar physical conditions, making a similar income, eating from similar food sources—happened to get their water from a different nearby pump, drawn from a different water supply. The water source could be the only culprit.

This was a natural experiment at work. The findings supported Snow's hypothesis that whatever was causing cholera was being ingested by sick patients. For further confirmation, Snow had the handle removed from the offending pump, preventing locals from getting their water there. The result? Cases of cholera declined.

As it turned out, the water supply at that pump had been contaminated by sewage from a household with an early infection. And because his experiment was "natural," he was able to establish cause and effect without ever seeing bacteria under a microscope or doing any of the modern tests we would rely on today. He simply collected data and analyzed it with an eye toward causality. We know now that Snow was right: *Vibrio cholerae* is the bacteria that causes cholera, and it's spread via ingestion of food or water contaminated by infected sewage.

Our health problems today are different in countless ways from those of Snow's time (though, clearly, infectious disease remains a threat). But striving to improve and prolong life, free from disease, remains a priority of modern medicine, and the natural experiment remains as powerful a tool now as it was in 1854.

———

The challenge in identifying and studying natural experiments in health care, or in the world more broadly, is that it's not always obvious when they're happening! (Part of why we remain gainfully employed.) It takes practice to find them hiding in the data—we're not all born with the instincts of John Snow. Indeed, the ways in which we've stumbled onto our studies have often been accidental, as much a product of chance as anything we discover in our research—a chance conversation with a spouse, a chance encounter while waiting in line for coffee, a chance experience with a patient or colleague.

Our hope with this book is to show you that there's much for us to learn from these natural experiments, as doctors and patients alike. We can expose the hidden forces in our health care that send two otherwise-similar people down very different paths of care, by chance alone. By examining those forces, we can identify their implications in the broader context of medicine and our daily lives. By the end of this book, you'll have a framework for thinking about how chance might be affecting your life—at the doctor's office, in the hospital, and beyond—and how we can use that knowledge to make ourselves healthier and happier, as individuals and as a community.

But first, we'll need to get a bit more comfortable with the language and concepts of natural experiments. In the next chapter, we'll take a quick look at the role chance plays in others' lives—presidents and pro football players, among them—to ease us into the subject. From there on out, we'll tell stories about our patients, ourselves, and our research. We'll show you how medical care can be accidental and how chance events create natural experiments that can help us navigate the gray areas of modern medicine. Some of these stories will apply to you, your parents, your kids, or your neighbors. Many will be just as relevant to your doctors (so feel free to leave an extra copy of this book in the waiting room at your next visit).

Because if there's one thing we've realized in our years-long study of chance, it's that doctors (including ourselves) can be just as blind to these hidden forces as anyone else. And who can blame us? If we were aware of them, they wouldn't be hidden.

—

Before moving on to the next chapter, there are a few key points that will be important to remember:

- **There's more to every research study.** In order to focus on the important aspects, we won't be discussing every aspect of every study we explore in this book. To be published in academic journals, research articles undergo a peer review and editorial process. When we share a study with you, we'll do our best to give our honest and succinct interpretation of what it means to us, keeping in mind that every research study must be taken in the context of others. If you're curious and want to learn more about any study we mention, we've put together an extensive bibliography so that you can look them up yourself.

- **Research is a team sport.** Most of the studies featured in this book were collaborations between multiple people and across multiple institutions. We think it's important for you to know who did the work we're talking about, but we don't have space in the main text to list every single person who helped with the studies we're discussing. Again, if you're interested in learning more, we'd point you to the bibliography at the end of this book.

- **We'll let you know who's talking.** You'll notice that we use the first-person voice to tell stories or describe research. Most of the time, "we" refers to both of us, but occasionally narration will shift to one of us, when telling a personal story or when describing research done by a group that didn't include both of us. To avoid confusion, we'll specify exactly whom we mean when we say "we" or "I," before returning to the both of us in a new section.

- **We have changed small details to protect privacy.** Whenever we tell stories about specific patients, we either change some of the small details or create "composite" stories that tell a representative story of what a typical patient might experience. Our goal is to paint realistic, insider pictures of what goes on in the walls of the hospital without violating the confidentiality that all patients are entitled to.

Now, with this in mind, let's dive into the natural experiments.

CHAPTER TWO

NATURAL EXPERIMENTS

IT WASN'T LONG into Barack Obama's presidency before people started noticing a subtle change in his appearance. The leader of the free world was going gray. Some wondered whether he had simply stopped dyeing his hair—after all, he was forty-seven when he took office, young for a president but certainly within the Just for Men demographic. Others assumed it was because of a phenomenon suggested by past presidents and researchers: that the burden of the presidency causes a person to age faster.

"With the stress of a financial meltdown, two wars, and a massive oil spill, can you blame Mr. Obama for the salt-and-pepper top?" quipped a CNN report from 2010, less than two years into his presidency. The CNN coverage of Obama's hair color continued at his barbershop in Chicago, where a customer pointed out that Obama was not alone. "Look on Bill Clinton, look on George Bush. It happened with them, so you know it's going to happen with this president as well."

Obama didn't dispute the point. A couple of years after leaving office, while speaking at a 2018 event in Indiana attended by the pro basketball player Victor Oladipo, he noted, "Ten years ago, I was campaigning for president. I had no gray hair at the time. . . . Victor Oladipo was showing me a picture of me and him together, and like, he looks the same [today]—but I don't. But you know what? I earned this gray hair."

Obama's implication is that while they are both ten years older than they had been in the photo, he *aged faster* than Oladipo over that ten-year stretch. But what does it mean to "age faster" than someone else? If aging is the process that ushers us from our births to our deaths, then aging faster must mean that we're accelerating toward our deaths at a greater rate. In other words, dying younger.

Now, let's say you were interested in knowing whether being president actually leads to faster aging, and thus earlier death. How would you figure this out?

The ideal way, as we've said, would be to run a randomized controlled trial. We would find a group of presidential hopefuls, then randomly make some of them president of the United States and some not, and then we would follow them into the future to see how long they live. We would need a reasonable sample size for the evidence to be compelling. Say, fifty presidents? We could then look at the differences in average life span between the people assigned to be president and those not assigned to be president. Any difference, we could then say, was caused by the accelerated aging of the presidency. We would know this to be true because randomization would ensure that no other variable was at play.

The alert (or even slightly conscious) reader will notice several problems with our proposed trial. First, the U.S. Constitution does not allow for random assignment of the president—even for science. Second, since there's only one president at a time, it could take a long time to do this study. Third . . . well, we won't keep going, you get the point—a randomized controlled trial simply can't answer this question.

But a natural experiment could.

For a natural experiment to take place, a chance occurrence must lead individuals down one of two paths—in this case, becoming president or not becoming president. Which path they take must be effectively random. This results in two groups: the group that was exposed to the presidency, and a control group made up of similar people who were not exposed to the presidency. If these groups are otherwise similar, then the experience of the control group should tell us what would have happened to the presidents had they *not* been elected.

The philosophical term for the concept of "what would have happened" is the "counterfactual" (with what actually happened being the "factual"). We won't bother you with too much jargon in this book, but the concept of the counterfactual is at the core of natural experiments and our study of chance in your health and health care. Since it can be hard to wrap your head around the idea, let's turn to an example provided by a classic 1980s movie.

At the beginning of the movie *Back to the Future,* we meet the teenager Marty McFly. He lives in 1985 in the home of his unhappily married parents, George, a wimp and a pushover, and Lorraine, who married George out of pity after her father hit him with his car in 1955. Through a series of chance occurrences, Marty takes a time machine to 1955, where he meets his parents as high school students. Marty ends up helping his teenage father stand up to the high school bully who torments him. In the process, Marty's mother ends up seeing his father in a whole new light. When Marty returns to 1985, he finds the course of his parents' lives completely changed: they are now deeply in love, his father confident and successful.

The movie ultimately presents us with two different timelines, each of which is counterfactual to the other. One shows what would have happened had Marty never traveled back in time and intervened (unhappily married parents). The other shows what happens after he does (happily married parents). Because we know what happens in each timeline, and the only difference between the timelines is Marty's intervention, we can attribute any difference between the counterfactual 1985s to Marty and the time machine and conclude that Marty's actions in 1955 caused his parents' happy marriage.

Now, back to our presidents. We need a control group with which we can compare Obama and his fellow leaders, and unlike in *Back to the Future* we don't have a time machine at our disposal. We can't see what would have happened to President George W. Bush if we went back in time and intervened in the Florida election to make Al Gore become president in 2000 (a counterfactual timeline that was very nearly factual).

One solution would be to compare presidents with a control group composed of runners-up. After all, presidential runners-up are (with exceptions) high-profile politicians too, ones who, on average, had similar past experiences as the actual presidents and who might be expected to have similar futures to those the presidents would have had, had they not been elected.

Scientific experiments favor randomization for a very good reason: randomized assignment to either an intervention or a control group helps ensure that no other variable is affecting the results. But elections are far from random; the U.S. Constitution is quite clear on this score: elections are to represent the will of the people, not the flip of a coin.

Today the vast majority of voters cast a ballot for president because they're a member of a certain party, because they like the policies their candidate is proposing, or maybe just because their preferred candidate feels like the right person for the job. Voters are not, we can safely say, making their choice because of one candidate's long-term risk of stroke, heart disease, or cancer. Candidate ages may—and certainly have—influenced elections. But to the extent that voters consider a candidate's age when casting their vote, they're probably not thinking about whether a fifty-year-old candidate's expected longevity or risk of disease exceeds that of other fifty-year-olds.

For our purposes, then, winning or losing an election operates as a chance occurrence. The outcome of the election itself isn't random; public sentiment and national politics decide elections. But we can say that it divides candidates randomly *in terms of their expected longevity compared with others their age.* We might say that which candidate gets exposed to the stresses of the presidency and which doesn't is "as good as random" with respect to their future health.

If we think about our presidential natural experiment in terms of *Back to the Future,* an election is a bit like the critical moment when Marty McFly's time machine touches down in 1955. An immediate splintering takes place on Election Day: one candidate becomes president, and all of us are sent down the timeline in which that candidate presides. With a time machine, we could go back, intervene to change the election results, start a new, counterfactual timeline in which the other candidate won, and then compare the two timelines to see how long the candidate lived in each case. But since we don't have a time machine, we work with what we have: the "runners-up."

The candidate who gets elected president is exposed to the office's rewards (power, fame, a nice house, a tricked-out Boeing 747) and its stresses ("a financial meltdown, two wars, and a massive oil spill"). The runner-up does what runners-up have always done, and what the president would likely have done in the same shoes—preserve their high profile, hold some other, less presidential role (after losing the 2000 presidential election to George W. Bush, Al Gore became America's most visible environmental activist—a job that, of course, carries its own stresses, but probably fewer than that of the presidency).

Election runners-up, therefore, make a pretty good counterfactual group to compare with election winners; what happens to them tells us what would have happened to presidents in the counterfactual world in which they never served as president.

Clearly there's a natural experiment here begging to be conducted. A group of us (Bapu, the Columbia economist Andrew Olenski, and the NYU orthopedic surgeon Matthew Abola) decided to take a closer look. We used data from seventeen countries around the world, studying the mortality of elected government leaders who held similar positions (presidents, premiers, prime ministers) and were elected in a way that, as in the United States, was as good as random with respect to their future health. We started all the way back in 1722 (the first election of a U.K. prime minister) and included elections until the time we did the study in 2015.

Our goal was to see how long candidates lived, on average, following an election, and to compare election winners with the group of runners-up. To do this, we had to account for several complicating factors, such as candidates who ran and lost, but later ran and won (for example, the early U.S. presidents John Adams and Thomas Jefferson, who both came in second place in prior elections, thus serving as vice president under the rules at the time, before later winning); differences in general life expectancy in different countries and in different centuries; and most important, differences in candidates' age or gender at the time of election.*

We accounted for age by first comparing the number of years a winning candidate lived beyond the year of the election (that is, the difference in age between when they died and when they were first elected) with the remaining life expectancy of individuals of the same sex and gender in the year of the election. This provided a difference between the *observed* and the *expected* number of years alive after election for winning candidates. We made this same comparison for runners-up: we calculated how many years they lived after the election they lost, then compared that number with their expected remaining years of life, based on their age and gender at the time of election. We then compared these two differences with each other, allowing us to account for the age and gender of winning candidates and runners-up and their differing remaining life expectancy at the time of election.

Our results vindicated the popular wisdom, not to mention our graying commanders in chief: after we adjusted for differences like age and sex, election winners lived an average of 2.7 years fewer than their runners-up. In other words, being elected head of government caused the leaders to age 2.7 years faster than they would have had they lost the election.

Does this result say exactly *why* election winners didn't live as long as runners-up? Not really. It provides evidence that "the presidency" or "the prime ministership," including the events after their term,

---

* This last factor was particularly important. If candidates who are older and/or men are more likely to win elections, we would incorrectly conclude that winning an election shortens life span, when it is simply that older candidates, in particular those who are men, may have lower remaining life expectancy than younger candidates, especially those who are women. When groups differ in certain factors, like age or gender, that are correlated with both the exposure of interest (in this case, whether a candidate won an election) *and* the outcome of interest (in this case, whether a candidate died earlier than would be expected), researchers worry about something called "confounding." We'll be talking about confounding and confounders in later chapters, but in general, when we say that we "adjusted for" or "accounted for" differences between groups, it's to avoid biased findings that stem from differences in group characteristics.

could reduce life expectancy. But from these data alone, we can't say exactly why that is. It could be that once elected, leaders start eating worse, sleeping less, smoking more, exercising less, or picking up any number of other unhealthy habits—some of which may persist after they leave office. It seems reasonable to lump any of these plausible explanations under "stress" and conclude that, indeed, the stress of being a head of government ages you faster. (It's worth noting that some elected leaders became targets of assassination, which obviously shortened their lives. But excluding assassinations from our analysis didn't affect our findings, likely because they're so rare.)

Importantly, these results don't tell us what would happen if *you* were to suddenly become president tomorrow. It only included people who were in an imminent position to become head of government. To borrow the terminology that scientists sometimes use, the findings of this study aren't "generalizable" to you. (That's assuming you are not, yourself, a president or world leader; otherwise, thank you, G20 summit attendees, for joining us!) We also can't say what happens to people elected to head of government outside the seventeen countries included in this study. Finally, we have to remember that this is an *average*—for some presidents, the effect could be lesser or greater. We have no way of knowing what it would be for any *given* elected leader.

Let's recap this natural experiment: We wanted to know whether heads of government age faster—that is, die earlier—than they otherwise would have had they not been head of a government, and we couldn't reasonably conduct a randomized controlled trial to find out. As far as the candidate's life expectancy is concerned, the result of an election is an as-good-as-random event, which meant candidates would be divided by chance into two balanced groups after the election: winners and runners-up. They are counterfactual to each other: what happened to the runners-up represents, on average, what would have happened to the winners had they not been elected, and vice versa. The difference in life expectancy between these two groups, 2.7 years, represents the average amount of accelerated aging attributable to serving as head of government.

Got it? Okay, now let's jump a little further down the rabbit hole.

—

The race for president isn't the only one in which winning and losing can be used as a randomizing event. Any casual viewer of the Olympics knows that the difference between a gold medal and a silver medal can be fractions of a second, or slight differences in judges' subjectively assigned points. While getting to the Olympics is of course not a random event—athletes work tirelessly for years to reach their level of performance—it's easy to imagine how chance occurrences could slow someone down a few hundredths of a second, turning a gold into a silver, or a silver into a bronze, or a bronze into obscurity.

The Utrecht University economist Adriaan Kalwij saw a natural experiment here. He wanted to see if winning or losing at the Olympics affected the life span of elite athletes. Of course, Olympians are in incredible shape, and on average they live longer than the rest of us. The question was whether competition results affected life expectancy *among their fellow medal winners*.

Specifically, Kalwij wanted to know this: What was the psychological effect of winning silver—coming so close to winning something you have worked your whole life to achieve and falling just short? Could it have long-term health effects? He cites the comedian Jerry Seinfeld, who sums up the hypothesis nicely in a bit from a 1998 comedy special: "If I was an Olympic athlete, I would rather come in last than win the silver, if you think about it. . . . You win the gold, you feel good. You win the bronze, you think, 'Well, at least I got something.' But if you win that silver, that's like, 'Congratulations, you almost won. Of all the losers, you came in first of that group. . . . You're the number one loser.'"

In his 2018 study, Kalwij parsed data from the 1904 through 1936 Olympics (giving him enough time to observe the life span of all but the two still-living medalists) to look for differences in longevity between gold, silver, and bronze medalists. On average, these athletes would presumably have had pretty similar life expectancies going into the Olympics, based on more or less similar degrees of physical fitness. As far as their life expectancy was concerned, who won gold, silver, and bronze was *as good as random*.

Sure enough, gold and bronze medalists had similar life expectancies: 74.8 years for bronze, 73.2 for gold—statistically, a nonsignificant difference. Silver medalists, however, didn't fare as well, with a life expectancy of only 70.8 years—significantly less than either gold or bronze. It seems Seinfeld was right: the psychological effect of falling *just* short of being crowned the "best in the world" can take years off your life.

———

Now, you may be skeptical of these results. You may not think it's fair to assume that what has happened to the Al Gores and Mitt Romneys of the world is what would have happened to the George W. Bushes and Barack Obamas, had their roles been reversed. Or maybe the assumption that Olympic gold medalists are basically the same as silver medalists, other than the metal in their medal, doesn't ring true to you. If so, that shows you are thinking critically of these experiments as we present them. Not only is that okay, but it's encouraged. We want you to listen to that part of your brain as you read this book.

When we study natural experiments, we try to come at them with as much skepticism as we can muster—which is why we deeply research and publish only a small fraction of the natural experiments we conceive, those that can stand up to rigorous scientific scrutiny. And even then, others who approach the same questions with different data and different methods may arrive at different findings. That, too, is okay.

As we look at more natural experiments in the pages ahead, our goal will not be to convince you that the studies and findings we present are the Absolute Truth, full stop. Research studies of all types have limitations. They are built on assumptions that are sometimes difficult to verify, making it impossible to be completely confident in any single study's finding. Rather, our goal is to show you how these experiments are built—on a foundation of chance—and let you arrive at your own conclusions (though we won't be shy about telling you our own).

Skeptical or not, you've had a few chances now to see how natural experiments can be designed to help resolve a question that would otherwise be impossible to answer. Let's try another one.

In 1987, members of the National Football League Players Association (the union representing professional football players in the NFL) went on strike as part of a contract dispute. Instead of canceling games due to lack of players, though, NFL teams hired replacement players to throw on their uniforms and play the scheduled games (the 2000 film *The Replacements* with Keanu Reeves is a fictionalized version of this event). These replacement players were skilled football players in their own right, with professional backgrounds similar to those of the NFL players. They simply hadn't made the cut to play at the highest level of the sport. Perhaps they would have stayed that way, but chance intervened, and the NFL players went on strike. The replacement players ended up playing just three games before the strike ended and the original players finished the season.

In the decades since the strike, the health of football players has been a topic of considerable interest, particularly the effects of chronic traumatic encephalopathy (CTE) from repeated head trauma, not to mention other potentially harmful exposures that accompany the life of a pro football player. While studies had shown that NFL players lived longer than the general population (not surprising given their physical fitness, higher incomes, and access to high-quality medical care), no studies had answered whether playing football in the NFL was causing players harm that would lead them, on average, to die sooner than they otherwise would.

Just like with the presidents, there is no experimental trial that could reasonably be done here. Even if you sometimes feel as though your long-suffering team must draft players by throwing darts at a dartboard, player selection is rarely left to chance. The 1987 players' strike offered us (Bapu, the cardiologist Maheer Gandhavadi, and the lead author of the study, the University of Pennsylvania economist and physician Atheendar Venkataramani) a nice natural experiment to try to quantify the effect on life spans of playing pro football.

The 1987 replacement players were no schlubs; these were mostly players who had played football at very high levels, either in college or in other professional leagues besides the NFL. The chief difference between the replacement players and the players on strike was that the former group fell just short in terms of talent and skill to play in the NFL. Perhaps if they had come up at a different time, in a different place, or played a different position, some of them could just as well have been playing in the NFL. And if not, while replacement players were not exactly NFL athletes themselves, they were likely closer to NFL athletes in physical health than to the general population.

Just like presidential runners-up, the replacement players offer us a counterfactual. They tell us something about what NFL players' lives *might* have looked like in other circumstances. As far as their long-term health is concerned, then, making it into the NFL could be considered as good as random. The replacement players, who played only three games in the NFL, are our control group; the NFL players who spent their entire career in the league are our experimental group.

We studied 879 replacement players and compared them with 2,933 NFL players who started their career in the five years surrounding the strike. Finding data on deaths was no easy feat. We collected death information on both groups of players from a variety of data sources, including death certificate data maintained on all Americans by the Centers for Disease Control and Prevention (CDC), online obituaries, and news articles. We considered not just *if* they died but *how* they died in the intervening thirty years.

What we found was that 4.7 percent of NFL players and 4.2 percent of replacement players had died. After accounting for several factors that could contribute to mortality differences between these groups (like players' year of birth, weight, height, and position they played), we found that in any given year NFL players were 38 percent more likely to die than replacement players. It's a meaningful number, but we should hasten to point out that it did not reach the conventionally used level of statistical significance, largely because relatively few deaths had occurred in the thirty years following the players' strike. So we couldn't definitively conclude that NFL players had lower life expectancies than their counterfactual counterparts, though our findings were suggestive of that possibility. As both groups of players get older, a clearer picture will emerge.

There's a bit more to this story, though. Both the NFL players and the replacement players tended to die as a result of those conditions common to men their age: heart disease, suicide, injuries, and cancer. But—and this is an important difference—there was a higher proportion of deaths from traffic accidents, unintentional harm (typically due to overdoses), and neurological diseases among the NFL players than there was for the replacement players. These are some of the causes of death that tend to be associated with CTE due to repeated head trauma.

When interpreting this study's findings, we should keep in mind that NFL players and replacement players likely had similar backgrounds *prior* to being drafted—the splintering moment that separates our experimental group from our control. Both would likely have played football since they were kids and through college. This is important because those are critical years in brain development, where repeated head trauma could put them at risk for CTE. Before they were even eligible to play in the NFL, they would have been under similar pressure to train extremely hard, with some turning to potentially unhealthy measures like anabolic steroids that could lead to increased risk of heart disease. Any long-term damage to players' bodies that occurred before joining the NFL could not be inferred from our analysis. Our study, then, was necessarily focused on what distinguished these two groups from each other, not which experiences they shared.

———

By now we've considered a few natural experiments in different milieus and have seen the types of questions that can be answered when we look closely at them. If the concepts are still a bit fuzzy, don't worry; we'll be visiting them again from different angles and in different situations. You're also probably holding on to at least a bit of skepticism. Again—we like that; it will serve you well in the chapters to come. It's time now to look at chance and the natural experiments it creates in the health-care system, where the stakes are high and the participants aren't presidents or Olympians or professional football players but, indeed, all the rest of us.

CHAPTER THREE

WHY ARE KIDS WITH SUMMER BIRTHDAYS MORE LIKELY TO GET THE FLU?

AS ANY PARENT can attest, having young children means going to the pediatrician—a lot. Current medical guidelines recommend that healthy children visit their pediatrician fourteen times by the time they turn three years old just for checkups, not to mention visits for when they get sick, which happens often. Needless to say, parents of young kids get to know their pediatrician's office pretty well—the discomfort of their waiting room chairs, the brightly hued wall art, the years-old magazines, the various staff personalities.

Parents also learn quickly how big a hassle it can be to go to the pediatrician. It's something the two of us know all too well; each of us has two young children. In households like ours, with two working parents, one parent inevitably has to take off at least half a day of work, strap the kid into the car or take public transit, sit in a waiting room, see the nurse and doctor, console the kid after any shots or tests, bring the kid back to day care or school or wherever they go, and *then* go back to work. For some parents, time spent going to the pediatrician is more than just a fleeting inconvenience; it can mean lost income. But parents want to make sure their kids are healthy and growing well, so they deal with the hassles the best they can.

A few years ago, I (Bapu) took my toddler-age son to the pediatrician for an annual checkup. He had been born in August, so, naturally, his appointment was scheduled for August of that year. At the end of the visit, the nurse told me to call the office in a few weeks to make an appointment for my son to get his flu shot; it wasn't available yet but would be in September. For kids and adults alike, the Centers for Disease Control and Prevention recommends an annual influenza* vaccination every fall, ideally by the end of October.

Though I wasn't looking forward to yet another trip to the pediatrician, I—trying to be a diligent father—called the clinic back in a few weeks for a shot appointment. But none were available on the days I could go. So I called my local CVS and Walgreens, but they didn't administer vaccines to toddlers. Eventually, I managed to get my son to the doctor for his shot, but the process was difficult and inconvenient. For my own part, I got a flu shot in five minutes at a vaccination event at work.

If a medical professional with flexibility in their work schedule had this much trouble getting their son a flu shot, other parents in a similar situation might not get their young kids back to the doctor at all. The ordeal got me thinking. If my son had been born in September rather than August, the flu shot would have been available at his annual checkup, around his birthday. He never would have had to come back for an extra visit.

You can see where this is heading. As I told this story to Chris—who also has a young son born in August—we agreed: it had all the early trappings of a great natural experiment, a problem way bigger than just one father and son. After all, influenza is a major public health problem in the United States, responsible for thousands of deaths, billions of dollars of medical expenses, and millions of days of economic productivity lost every year. While getting infected may not be much more than an annoyance for most young, healthy patients, they can easily spread it to adults and the elderly who may not fare so well.

This is how many of our ideas for research come about. Something happens in our lives, whether at home or at work in the hospital, that

* Colloquially, some may use the term "flu" to describe any illness that makes someone sick or have a fever, like the common cold. Medically speaking, "influenza," "flu," and "the flu" refer to the influenza virus and/or acute infection by the influenza virus. We will use the term "flu shot" to refer to the influenza vaccine to enhance readability, but otherwise will stick to the term "influenza."

makes us think, "Hmm, what if things had played out differently?" When you start taking in the world this way, you see these opportunities everywhere: "If the power hadn't gone out because of a storm, would this patient still have come to the emergency department?"; "If a different doctor had been on duty, would this rare diagnosis have been missed?"; "If an obstetrician's previous delivery hadn't gone wrong, would they still have chosen to perform a C-section this time, instead of the previously planned vaginal delivery?"

A few times a week, the two of us get together with our research colleagues and spitball ideas. As a group, we refine, think aloud, weigh the potential of a natural experiment. Could a serious (or sometimes not-so-serious*) research question be answered using these methods? And do we have the data to investigate it?

Most of the time, the answers to one of these two questions is no. A good number of pitches never make it past the "idea phase." But occasionally, there's an idea that holds water: it seems worthy of investigation *and* we have the ability to study it.

When we all sat down one day to talk about flu shots in kids with summer birthdays, the first thing we asked ourselves was whether there was a true natural experiment here: In other words, do kids with different birthdays get sent down different paths of care for flu shots *strictly by chance*? It was pretty clear to us that the answer could be yes. Young kids born in August—or June or March for that matter—likely did not get their flu shot at their annual physicals. Kids born in September, October, or November were much more likely to do so. (Any later than November and kids start to run the

---

* Some of our sillier studies have examined physician behavior outside the hospital. Stereotypically, doctors like to golf, but which specialties like to play most? Turns out, specialized surgeons like orthopedists, urologists, plastic surgeons, and otolaryngologists were the most represented doctors in the U.S. Golf Association database. Thoracic surgeons, vascular surgeons, and orthopedic surgeons were the most skilled golfers (they had the lowest handicaps). Another, using data from the Florida Highway Patrol, looked at physicians who received speeding tickets. Psychiatrists were the most likely to have been ticketed for extreme speeding—driving at least twenty miles per hour over the limit. Cardiologists who were caught speeding were the most likely to be zooming around in a luxury car. See Koplewitz et al., "Golf Habits Among Physicians and Surgeons"; and Zimerman et al., "Need for Speed."

risk of not having adequate immunity built up for the worst of flu season.) This meant that kids born in the fall could be said to be on an "easy flu shot" pathway, while kids born in other months were effectively on a "difficult flu shot" pathway.

But did this happen by chance? As far as flu shots were concerned, yes. There's no reason to think that someone born in April would, on average, have any biological or medical reason to get a flu shot that differs from someone born in October, nor is there evidence to suggest that spring babies are more susceptible to influenza than fall babies.

If we were to bring Marty McFly and his time machine back into the picture, we could imagine him going back in time and some-how changing the month in which kids were born (not sure how he would accomplish this, but let's suspend our disbelief for a moment). In this scenario, we wouldn't be fracturing events into two different timelines, as we did before with presidents versus runners-up, gold versus silver medalists, or NFL versus replacement players. Instead, we'd have to create twelve different timelines, one timeline for each month of the year in which a certain group of children could be born. We could then see the effect of birth month on those children in their rate of getting flu shots.

We don't need a time machine, of course. If birthdays are as good as random, the group of kids born in any given month should oper-ate as counterfactuals to kids born in any of the other eleven months (that is, what happens to kids born in September is what *would have happened* to kids born in August, had they been born in September, and vice versa).

This natural experiment seemed to have enough legs to merit fur-ther study. The next question was whether we had the data. We (Chris and Bapu, along with the Brown University economist Jae-min Woo) looked at a large database containing insurance claims for millions of Americans and their families covered by employer-sponsored health insurance. Why insurance claims? An insurance claim is generated anytime a patient uses their health insurance for health care. In this case, when a child goes to the pediatrician for an annual physical, an insurance claim is generated when the doctor asks the insurance company to pay the doctor for the visit. If a procedure is performed, such as a flu shot, an insurance claim is also generated.

While nobody likes dealing with insurance (patients and doctors alike, we can attest), insurance claims can be extremely helpful for research. These data, which do not include any identifying information on a patient like their name or address, tell us what happened to a given patient (whether a procedure was performed, test was ordered, prescription was filled), when it happened, and, because the claims also list patient diagnoses, *why* something happened to a patient. This level of information, captured for millions of patients over several years, provides us with invaluable data for these kinds of natural experiments.*

Armed with this database, we first set out to verify a core assumption: young kids generally go for their annual checkup near their birthday. If this assumption wasn't true, then the natural experiment would fall apart: What would be the point of comparing August-born kids with September-born kids if the timing of their checkups had nothing to do with their dates of birth? Of course, our hunch as parents and former children ourselves was that this was a pretty reasonable assumption; the American Academy of Pediatrics even recommends using a child's birthday as a reminder that they need their yearly checkup.

So we asked, What percentage of kids go for their annual checkup in the month of their birthday (plus or minus two weeks, since most kids probably won't go to the doctor on their exact birthday)? Using the database containing millions of children, we looked for insurance claims for annual checkups, noted the dates of those checkups, and noted when the kids' birthdays were. We didn't include kids under

---

* Technological advancements in computing have changed not just health care but the types of research we're able to do. We have electronic health records from doctors' offices and hospitals, administrative claims from insurers, and powerful computers that can process millions or billions of data points. Matched with tools from economics, statistics, and epidemiology, these advancements have dramatically increased possibilities for research over the past several decades.

the age of two because they go to the doctor so often, giving them ample chances to get the vaccine on a date not near their birthday; also, infants under six months aren't eligible for the flu shot. We broke the results down by age, in case there were any differences in young children compared with older teenagers. As it turns out, there were.

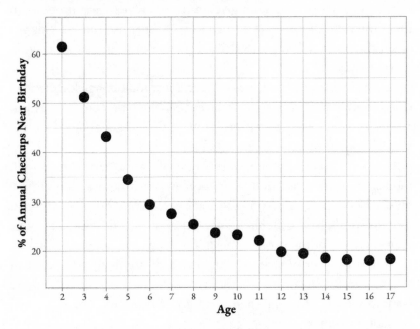

The data suggested that for young kids like ours it was indeed common for annual checkups to occur right around their birthday—a majority of two- and three-year-olds had their checkup in the month of their birthday or the two-week buffer before or after. What was interesting, however, was a clear pattern showing that as kids got older, they were less and less likely to have their checkup right around their birthday. About a third of five-year-olds went for a checkup near their birthday. By the time we got to teenagers, the percentage of kids going for a checkup near their birthday was no more than we would expect if the appointments were spread evenly throughout the year.

It made sense that young kids would go for their annual checkup closer to their birthdays than teenagers would. Toddlers need to check in with their pediatricians often to make sure they're developing appropriately, to screen for childhood illnesses, and to keep up with their routine (non-flu-shot) vaccinations. Teenagers don't have the same time-bound constraints; most of them just need a physical exam at some point in the year, for routine screenings, sports physicals, or vaccines that can be given during a wider time frame than those for young kids. It was, therefore, no surprise that as kids got older, their annual physicals drifted further and further away from their birthday.

So our first assumption was correct; most toddler-age kids tended to go to the doctor near their birthday. Now we could focus our analysis on kids aged two to five. (We didn't forget about the older kids, though—more on them in a bit.)

Let's sum up the foundations of this natural experiment. A kid's month of birth is as good as random when it comes to getting a flu shot because there's no plausible reason kids born in different months would have different biological need for a flu shot. Kids who happen to be born in one month are functionally similar to kids born in any other month. Toddler-age kids are likely to have their annual checkup near their birthday, which matters to us because we want to see what bearing their birthday has or doesn't have on their flu shot outcomes.

Based on our findings so far, we could, then, reasonably stipulate that kids with fall birthdays are more likely to go down the "easy flu shot" pathway.

With this squared away, we took the next step and asked this simple question: What percentage of kids born in each month get the flu shot?

To answer this question, we looked at a total of 1.12 million children aged two to five years over the course of two influenza seasons. The results speak for themselves:*

---

* To ensure our results were accurate, we also performed a regression analysis to be able to account for any possible imbalances in the characteristics of kids born in the various months that could lead to confounding in our results—for example, if more kids born in a certain month had a lung disease like asthma, and patients with asthma were more likely to get a flu shot. We also accounted for other chronic medi-

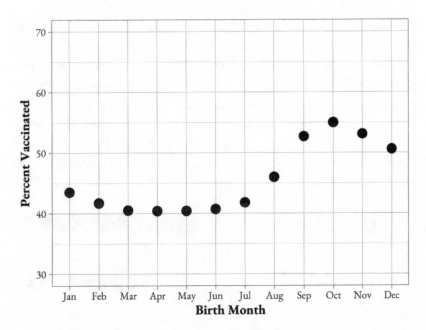

Kids born in fall months were vaccinated at markedly higher rates than kids born in other months. For example, kids born in October—when the flu shot is widely available at checkups—were vaccinated at a rate of 55 percent, while kids born in May were vaccinated at a rate of 40 percent. That's a really big difference. This means that if you were to take a hundred kids born in May, fifteen of the ones who don't get vaccinated *would have been vaccinated* had they been born in October. If we look on the national scale, this represents at least hundreds of thousands of kids not getting vaccinated simply because of when they happened to be born—some of whom will inevitably get sick.

Based on everything we've discussed so far, our hunch would be that this difference is due to kids born in October being on the "easy flu shot" pathway and kids born in July being on the "difficult flu shot" pathway. Is there any way to find out if we're right?

---

cal conditions, the overall age of the child, the average age of their parents, parents' chronic medical conditions, and differences between the two influenza seasons we studied. The results were essentially unchanged after these adjustments, which is what we would expect if birth month truly were as good as random.

Remember the older kids that we put aside earlier? As kids get older and their annual checkups become less closely aligned with their birthdays, we would expect to see the relationship between birth month and flu shots get progressively less pronounced. By the time we get to teenagers, who don't have their checkups systematically timed near their birthday, we would expect the effect to go away altogether. So we looked at vaccination rates by birth month across children of all ages—not just the two-to-five-year-olds—to see if this was the case.

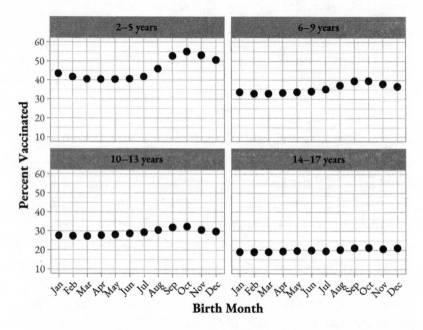

Lo and behold, as we moved into older age-groups, the link between birth month and flu shots started to gradually disappear too.* This was more evidence that for kids aged two to five, their as-good-as-random birth month was what decided whether they went down the easy or the difficult flu shot pathway.

---

* You also may have noticed that the percentage of children vaccinated was lower across all birth months as kids got older. Older children are less likely to be vaccinated against influenza in general. Additionally, older children may be vaccinated through programs that don't bill insurance, and such vaccinations wouldn't have appeared in our analysis.

What's at stake here was not simply a question of whether flu shots were administered. The flu shot is designed to ward off influenza, something it does with pretty remarkable efficacy, year in and year out. If birth months affect a child's likelihood of getting the flu shot, we would expect that kids with summer birthdays, who were less likely to get the flu shot, would be *more* likely to get influenza—right?

To answer this question, we revisited our group of toddler-age kids and again divided them up by their month of birth, but this time we looked not at flu shots but at what percentage of them were diagnosed with influenza by their doctor.

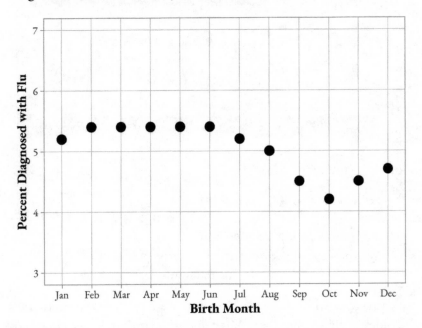

It's an inverse pattern from the flu shots we considered earlier: kids born in summer months—those who were *less* likely to be vaccinated—were *more* likely to be diagnosed with influenza than kids born in fall months.[*]

---

[*] After making regression adjustments similar to those we made for the flu shot analysis, these results were unchanged, which is what we would expect if month of birth is truly as good as random.

Bapu's hunch was confirmed: Kids like ours, born in summer months, are less likely to get flu shots than kids born in the fall. Moreover, they're more likely to get the flu.

Remember how the birth month pattern of vaccination went away as kids got older? If flu shots actually prevent influenza infection, we would expect to see similar birthday effects in which kids get influenza. For teenagers, therefore, there should be no real difference in infection rates across birth months. That's precisely what we found:

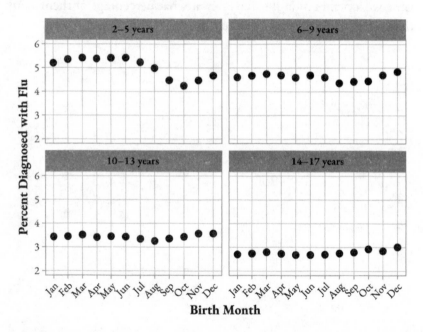

Teenagers, whose annual checkups weren't timed around their birthdays, didn't show any birth month patterns in vaccinations, and accordingly their rate of influenza infection didn't seem to be tied to their birthday, either.

For us, this was exciting stuff. These analyses provided us with convincing evidence that simply getting to the pediatrician's office was a substantial enough barrier that it prevented young kids from getting their annual flu shots at all, ultimately leading to greater influenza infection.

But as we all know, influenza is an infectious disease. This story doesn't end with sick kids.

——

A few years ago, Bapu had just moved into a new home in the Boston suburbs, and he got to talking with a teller at his new bank. The teller asked Bapu what he did for a living and, when he heard Bapu was a doctor, mentioned that his ninety-year-old father had been in the ICU with a severe case of influenza.

His story went like this: A couple of weeks prior, the teller's two-year-old son had had a friend over for a playdate. That friend had been coughing a bit and had a fever, but kids that age always seem to be sick, and the child's parents brought him over regardless. A few days later, the teller's father (grandfather of the two-year-old) woke up in the middle of the night unable to breathe. Shortly thereafter he went into cardiac arrest—his heart stopped beating. He had contracted the influenza virus, presumably by way of his grandson, which had led to pneumonia, cutting off oxygen to his heart. He was rushed to the emergency room, placed on a ventilator, and taken to the ICU.

As a pulmonologist, Chris knows this to be a familiar tale in the ICU. For many of his older patients, there are few if any greater sources of joy in their lives than their grandchildren. Grandparents want to see their grandkids often, and many do, particularly grandparents who help out busy parents by watching their toddler-age kids. Even before the COVID-19 pandemic, grandchildren served as motivators for grandparents to ignore their better instincts about infection control, especially during cold and influenza season.

But at risk of belaboring the point, young kids get sick *a lot*. Not for nothing are they sometimes disparaged as "snot-nosed kids." And as easy as it may be for grandparents to brush off "runny nose season" as a rite of passage, they might be surprised to hear that, according to a recent study, fully half of all cases of influenza among the elderly may be due to interactions with young children. Chris's patients are often unsurprised to learn they've caught influenza; it's likely been in their household. But they are surprised that they ended up in the ICU from it, with several describing it as feeling as if they've been "hit by a truck."

The bank teller's story, then, was no fluke. Fortunately, his father survived the ordeal—a lucky outcome for someone his age.

What's the best way to stop kids from catching, getting sick from, and spreading influenza to other kids, not to mention their own family members? Vaccination, of course. As with any vaccine, a flu shot exposes our bodies to nonfunctional particles of whatever influenza strains are expected to be circulating each year, allowing our immune systems to build a defense against the virus, should we encounter it.* We become less likely to contract influenza, less likely to be really sick if we do get infected, and less likely to spread the virus to others—which helps protect elderly and vulnerable members of our community.

The role that children play in the spread of influenza within communities can be summed up by a brief case study from Japan. Following a major influenza epidemic in 1957, the Japanese government made control of influenza a priority. Knowing that children were major spreaders, they began vaccinating school-age children against influenza in 1962; they made it mandatory in 1977. Then, in 1987, a new law allowed parents to opt their children out of influenza vaccination. By 1994, the Japanese government discontinued the program to vaccinate schoolchildren altogether.

In a research study of deaths in Japan over the latter half of the twentieth century, deaths from all causes and deaths from influenza and pneumonia during cold and influenza season fell during the 1960s, 1970s, and most of the 1980s. Then, in the late 1980s and the 1990s, as Japan saw a drop in child influenza vaccination

* One challenging aspect of influenza vaccination is that the influenza virus mutates regularly, leading to different strains of the virus circulating around the globe at any given time. The flu shots we should all get in the fall are designed to provide immunity against the strains of virus that are expected to circulate during flu season. Because epidemiologists can't predict which strains will circulate with 100 percent accuracy, flu shots may be more effective in preventing influenza in some years than in others. But even when the vaccine isn't a perfect match, it still offers protection.

rates, there was an increase both in overall deaths and in deaths due to influenza/pneumonia during cold and influenza season. This all occurred despite Japan otherwise prospering as a nation in the 1980s and 1990s, with advancements in medical technology, improved infrastructure and standard of living, and economic development that had continued from the prior decades. The study's authors concluded that the most likely explanation for the increased deaths during influenza season was the substantial drop in childhood flu shots after the 1987 repeal of the mandate and the 1994 discontinuation of the flu shot program for schoolchildren.

Since we knew kids are prone to spreading influenza to their close contacts—and that vaccinating them can stop the spread—we decided to take our analysis one step further. If toddler-age kids with spring or summer birthdays are less likely to get flu shots and thus more likely to get influenza, does that make them more likely to also spread it to their family? It would certainly seem that it should: Have you ever picked up a two-year-old, only to have them cough directly into your face and/or mouth? Or picked up a child's toy, only to find it mysteriously wet with what can only be toddler slobber? We have, more times than we can count.

So we went back to the insurance data. Because children in these data are linked to their parents, we could easily look at whether an adult family member in a household was diagnosed with influenza in a given influenza season. Now we would be dividing up those older family members not by their own birth months but by the birth month of the *child* in their home.

The differences were small—not surprising since only a few percent of kids are diagnosed with influenza to begin with—but they were measurable and statistically significant. We already knew that kids born in the fall were less likely to get influenza. Now we could show that older family members of kids born in fall months were also less likely to be diagnosed with influenza.[*]

---

[*] In this analysis, we adjusted for characteristics of the family, including the average age of older family members and whether they had chronic medical conditions.

It made sense when we first pitched the idea to our colleagues. Now we could confirm it: when it comes to getting the flu shot, birthdays matter.

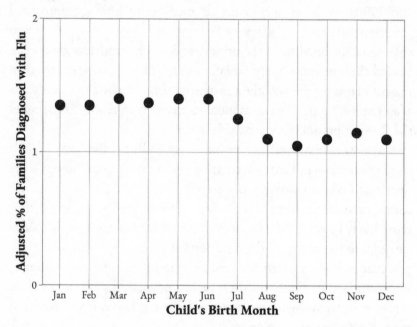

What does all this mean for the way our health-care system vaccinates kids? Think back to Bapu's frustrated phone calls to get his son vaccinated, compared with the ease with which he was vaccinated himself at work. Requiring kids to get the influenza vaccine in doctors' offices is no small impediment to care. Indeed, it's a huge barrier. Remember, influenza vaccination rates for toddlers with September birthdays are a whopping fifteen percentage points higher than for toddlers with August birthdays.

Of course, we're not the first people to think about barriers to vaccination; by now, you've probably spent some time thinking about why people do or do not get vaccinated against various diseases. (We'll be talking about aspects of COVID-19 in chapter 10.) Vaccine hesitancy has a long history, in the United States and around the globe.

The World Health Organization has proposed a framework for understanding why people don't get vaccinated based on three core factors. They call them the "3 Cs": complacency, meaning a low perceived risk of the disease and resultant de-prioritization of vaccines; confidence, meaning lack of trust in vaccines, health systems, and government bodies; and convenience, meaning availability, affordability, and physical access to the vaccine. With our toddlers, we had no reason to think that there would be any differences across birth months when it came to complacency or confidence. The parents of kids born in March shouldn't be different, on average, from parents of kids born in October when it comes to how they perceive the risk of influenza or the level of trust they place in vaccine manufacturers, doctors, or the government.

But when it comes to the third *C*—convenience—our study had a lot to say. Kids with birthdays before the fall—"difficult flu shot" months—are subject to a critical factor that makes getting vaccinated less convenient: these kids have to come back for an extra appointment after their annual checkup. For parents who lose money when they take off work, that inconvenience is quantifiable—even if the vaccine itself is free, which it often is—creating additional barriers for some.

So, what can we do to make flu shots more convenient for kids? Let's all agree that the solution is *not* to make sure that all children end up being born in September or October. We know that as kids get older, and for reasons that are, clinically speaking, somewhat arbitrary, they're able to get their flu shots at places other than their doctor's office. Older kids and adults can and do get their flu shots at local pharmacies, which are often much closer to home, have better hours, may not require an appointment, and are generally much more convenient. (Chris got his most recent flu shot in a few minutes at a CVS/Target while doing other shopping.)

As in nearly every area of life, the COVID-19 pandemic changed our vaccination patterns. With patients of all ages avoiding the doctor's office early in the pandemic, routine childhood vaccination against diseases like measles, polio, and chicken pox fell in 2020 to worrisomely low rates. Pediatricians and public health officials across the country raised alarm; yes, COVID-19 was concerning, but it didn't mean kids shouldn't be vaccinated against other, older diseases. With many people avoiding the doctor's office, pediatric providers were faced with a novel barrier to vaccination. They were forced to consider how they could make vaccinations easier for young kids.

Pediatric medicine rose to the challenge. In April 2020, in the earliest months of the pandemic, Arkansas Children's Hospital opened up a drive-through vaccine clinic for kids to get their scheduled vaccines without leaving their cars. Boston Medical Center partnered with an ambulance company to have nurses visit kids at their homes and vaccinate them in the back of idle ambulances. These temporary solutions not only helped patients but also helped prevent furloughs and layoffs of EMTs at a time when, despite COVID-19, overall demand for ambulances was substantially reduced.*

Seeing the potential for *another* public health crisis, if kids failed to be vaccinated for other diseases, the federal government eventually intervened. In August 2020, the U.S. Department of Health and Human Services allowed pharmacists in all states to administer routine vaccines to children as young as three years old—two years younger than the restriction previously in place in many states. If this intervention sticks around long term—and if pharmacists are given the resources they need to provide these services—parents of three- and four-year-olds will have a new option for their kids' flu shot, and the margin between our "easy shot" and our "difficult shot" groups might begin to narrow.

———

* A study of emergency medical services activations in the United States found that 911 calls for issues like injuries dropped substantially during lockdown phases of the COVID-19 pandemic—not surprising, since people would be engaging in fewer accident-prone activities. Interestingly, the percentage of 911 activations where the ambulance arrived and the patient died at the scene increased, suggesting that the reduction in demand for ambulance services was at least partially driven by people who were reluctant to call 911 for a medical problem in the first place, perhaps out of fear of COVID-19 infection, resulting in deadly delays in care.

You're probably well aware that inconvenience, logistical barriers, and financial barriers affect more than just flu shots for young kids; these barriers are omnipresent across our health-care system. We'll be exploring many of these areas in later chapters, but it's worth asking ourselves now, Why do logistics and convenience remain such prominent barriers to twenty-first-century care?

In many cases, the explanation is simple: human nature. When faced with an easy option and a hard one, we'll generally choose the easy one. Even when we know, if we really think about it, that the harder option may better serve us in the long run—that the inconvenience posed by the flu far outweighs the inconvenience of a single trip to the pediatrician—the path of least resistance often prevails.

Doctors aren't immune to those same forces. Despite all of our training, years of experience, and access to health information, we fall into the same patterns, both at work and at home. A study by Bapu, along with the Duke University economist and lawyer Michael Frakes and the MIT economist Jonathan Gruber, looked at how doctors behave when they are patients. Over a number of different factors, such as getting optimal treatment for diabetes or getting recommended vaccines, doctors were only minimally more likely to follow recommended care than their average patients. And unlike many of the patients, they couldn't plead ignorance.

As two doctors who struggle to maintain the diet and lifestyle choices we recommend to our patients, we weren't surprised by these results. Going to the doctor regularly, obtaining and taking medications, and making other changes to our daily lives are hard no matter who you are.

One way to change this is to reshape our "default" pathways. For kids born in October, the default pathway is to get their flu shot while they're already at the doctor; they would have to opt out of vaccination in order to avoid it. For kids born in April, the default pathway is not to get a flu shot; they can get one only if their parents devote additional effort to it.

The Nobel Prize–winning University of Chicago economist Richard Thaler, who spent his career studying individual decision making, and the Obama administration official and Harvard legal scholar Cass Sunstein have thought a lot about the way systems lead us to make certain decisions. They say the answer is not to urge people more forcefully toward hard things but simply to make the hard things easier.

They write of "nudges," which tend to push people toward better pathways, and "sludge" which tends to keep people on worse pathways. You've almost certainly encountered these. Have you ever eyed a tasty-looking pasta dish on a restaurant menu, only to note that it had thirteen hundred calories, steering you toward a salad instead? A government's motivation, in insisting on the display of calorie counts, is not just to inform you but to nudge you toward healthier choices. Or have you ever tried to cancel a subscription you no longer want, but found that the only way to do it was to call a phone number, wait on hold for ten minutes, and then have someone try to convince you otherwise? (We're looking at you, cable providers.) This is an example of sludge, intended to make it harder for you to opt out.

If a person really wants that pasta or really wants to cancel their subscription, nudges and sludge aren't going to stop them. But if all that's holding people back from making a desirable choice is convenience, then why not make that path easier than the alternative?

Researchers have looked at ways to make getting a flu shot the "default." In the 1996–1997 influenza season, a clinical trial in U.S. Navy day-care centers in San Diego vaccinated kids at day care, where kids would be going anyway. For kids in the trial, getting the flu shot became the default pathway. And not surprisingly, kids who were vaccinated were ultimately less likely to get influenza. Furthermore, their older household contacts were also less likely to get sick, missed fewer days of school or work, reported fewer earaches (sometimes associated with influenza), went to the doctor less, and needed fewer courses of antibiotics.

In another study, this time during the 2004–2005 influenza season, researchers offered in-school influenza vaccines at eleven U.S. schools to kids of varying ages, comparing them with seventeen nearby "control" schools, where no in-school flu shot was offered. Kids in the experimental group could get their shots where they would already be; the only additional effort on the part of their parents was to sign a consent form. Kids at the control schools could get flu shots however they normally would.

Given what we've seen so far, the results should be unsurprising. In households where kids got in-school flu shots, families were less likely to report influenza-like illnesses, less likely to use cold and influenza medications, and less likely to go to the doctor. All of these findings suggested that bringing the flu shots directly to kids could prevent the spread of influenza among children and within larger communities.

Similar trials have been run on adults. In the 2009–2010 influenza season, researchers at Rutgers University randomized adult staff members to one of two groups: one group had a flu shot appointment made for them; all they had to do was show up at the university at the appointed time. The other group was given information on where and how to sign up for an appointment. The first group was therefore part of an "opt out" program,* meaning they were presumed to want a flu shot unless they acted otherwise. The second group was in an "opt in" program; they could make an appointment for a shot if they so chose. As you might have guessed, patients in the "opt out" group were more likely to be vaccinated than patients in the "opt in" group. The difference was about twelve percentage points (a 45 percent vaccination rate in the opt-out group versus 33 percent in the opt-in group)—an effect similar to the one we observed in our study of toddlers and their birth months.

Today, many schools, workplaces, health centers, and other organizations are working hard to make flu shots more accessible, such

* "Opt out" programs have also been shown to help improve rates of organ donation. When consent for organ donation after death is presumed—and family members must actively opt out of donation on behalf of a loved one if they have religious or other objections—rates of organ donation are higher than when families must actively choose to let their deceased loved one serve as an organ donor. See Abadie and Gay, "Impact of Presumed Consent Legislation on Cadaveric Organ Donation."

as through special programs or after-hours vaccination clinics. Still, as a nation, we're falling short; in our best years, we vaccinate only about two-thirds of all children and half of all adults. Vaccine hesitancy is real, and it needs to be addressed in meaningful ways. But all this research shows us that if we want more people to get vaccinated, it's also important that we make it easy.

—

We've so far largely avoided the question of financial cost. As you probably well know, the U.S. health-care system is expensive. According to 2019 estimates, the United States as a nation spends about $3.8 trillion on health care each year, more per capita than other high-income countries. That's 17.7 percent of our gross domestic product, and it amounts to about $11,582 per person, on average. What do we get for all this money? A health-care system that is inefficient, inequitable, and poorly performing compared with other wealthy nations. Because we spend so much money on it and don't necessarily get what we should in return, health-care costs have been a major focus as we look for ways to improve our health-care system. And rightly so: high costs can be a barrier to ideal medical care. Patients and insurers have limited budgets, and patients have needs for medical care that must be met.

It's due to those financial burdens that insurers are constantly looking for ways to reduce care they deem "unnecessary," whether by making patients "qualify" for procedures or making doctors seek "prior authorization" before giving expensive medications to their patients. This is intentional "sludge"; friction built into the system to make sure money isn't spent on care unless it's "truly needed." (Perhaps you can tell by our liberal use of quotation marks that what is "necessary" is open to broad interpretation; we'll be exploring this idea in subsequent chapters.)

But there are financial costs to the care we receive that go either unmeasured or unnoticed, and they deserve our attention. Our flu shot study drew attention to one of them: For most people, there's no direct financial cost to getting the flu shot. That's to say nothing of the costs should a child or family member contract influenza. Such costs aren't easily measured; they don't affect insurers or patients in the same way as a $350 bill from a doctor or a $200 bill from a lab test. The cost of parents' time and missed work—estimated at one to two days with hundreds of dollars' worth of parents' lost productivity—not to mention the loss of prepaid child care, can add up and contribute to the billions of dollars of influenza costs the country faces each year.

The idea that difficult-to-measure, non-direct costs can get in the way of optimal care is not just theoretical; an interesting study of heart attack patients published in 2011 examined this very question. The Harvard physician Niteesh Choudhry and the health-care executive and physician William Shrank, and their colleagues, took more than fifty-eight hundred patients who were discharged from the hospital after a heart attack and randomized them into two groups: one group who had all of their essential heart attack medications provided to them for free, and another group who had to pay their usual co-pays. Patients *in both groups* had trouble taking their medications optimally, and patients who received completely free medications were only slightly more likely to take their medications: 44 percent of the time, on average, for those who got their medications for free, versus 39 percent for those who didn't.

This means that even though the free-medication group had a lighter financial burden—about $500 during the study period— there were other costs involved, ones that money couldn't address. To put it another way, people took their medications less than half the time, even when they were free, and this was for a serious medical condition! Why might this have been the case? Well, there's the time and energy involved in picking up medications every month, the disruption to daily routines involved in taking drugs each day, the potential side effects—all "costs" that would need to be addressed in order to overcome the default pathway of simply not taking a given medication. When we look at why we fail to live up to our health ideals, financial cost tells us only a very small part of the story.

Costs of convenience, meanwhile, can affect pretty much any

aspect of medical care. Patients living in rural areas are often farther away from large medical centers that provide the full spectrum of acute medical care. This is why for conditions like heart attacks, patients living in rural areas have been shown to be less likely to receive the most advanced heart attack care. Or consider long-acting birth control methods. While oral contraceptive pills need to be taken at the same time every day (a difficult and inconvenient way to take any medication), a single contraceptive shot works for several months, intrauterine devices work for years, and procedures like vasectomies or tubal ligations work indefinitely. Each one of these methods provides contraception with lower costs of convenience than a daily oral pill (while also being more effective), making the monetary cost of these more effective methods, we would argue, well worth the added financial expense.

Our flu shot study didn't tell us the most convenient way to get kids vaccinated; what it showed us is that inconvenience can have real public health consequences. Each community and each family operates with its own unique set of circumstances; there isn't a one-size-fits-all solution. If we want to maximize vaccination against influenza each year—and we truly do!—we have to make sure families have *many easy options* to get their kids vaccinated.

This holds true beyond flu shots, too. Nearly every type of medical care is encumbered with some sort of inconvenience, whether it's time spent sitting in a doctor's waiting room, time at the pharmacy waiting for prescriptions to be filled, time listening to "calming" music while on hold with your insurer.* The costs of these inconveniences may be obvious to anyone who's experienced them, but they go unnoticed by many of us whose lives—through either caring for patients, doing research, or making policy—are focused on improving patients' care.

---

* A 1994 study of genres of hold music on the Florida Protective Services System abuse hotline found that among five music styles (classical, country, jazz, popular, and relaxation) relaxation music was associated with the highest number of hang-ups, while jazz was associated with the fewest. See Ramos, "Effects of On-Hold Telephone Music on the Number of Premature Disconnections to a Statewide Protective Services Abuse Hot Line."

Everyone knows that health care is expensive. But research has shown us, time and time again, that it's often the *non*monetary costs—those harder to measure but easy to appreciate variables— that make it challenging for us to do the right thing: to do what our doctors recommend, to do what's in the best interest of ourselves, our families, and our communities.

CHAPTER FOUR

TOM BRADY, ADHD, AND A REALLY BAD HEADACHE

O F THE MANY stereotypes about Bostonians that a person is likely to hear—whether about the accent, the driving, or the preoccupation with Dunkin' Donuts—the one that rings truest, at least to these two non-native Bostonians, is our obsession with our professional sports teams. Particularly the New England Patriots. In case you haven't heard of them, the Patriots are a wildly successful football team that spent twenty seasons being led by—and this title may be up for debate—the Greatest Quarterback of All Time, Tom Brady.

While we spent our formative years as physicians making rounds in Boston hospitals, Tom Brady and the Patriots were busy dominating the NFL and winning numerous Super Bowls (some of which we watched from our patients' bedsides). The terms "legend" and "hero" don't even begin to explain how many Bostonians feel about Brady, who remains a constant topic of conversation and news coverage, even after having left New England in 2020 to play for the Tampa Bay Buccaneers.

Though today Brady has undoubtedly reached the quarterback pantheon, few would have guessed at his place in football history when he started his college career in 1995. A top high school player, Brady had been recruited by the University of Michigan. But he was hardly a star when he arrived; he served as the team's seventh-string quarterback. Eager to start, Brady focused on improving himself as an athlete. He was redshirted—the process by which college athletes delay the official beginning of their four-year collegiate-sports careers to their sophomore year, allowing them to spend their freshman year developing athletically and academically, even as they practice with the team. As a redshirt* freshman, Brady worked tirelessly on his game, including sessions with a sports psychologist. He would make starting quarterback his junior year and was later selected to play for the Patriots.

This 199th overall draft pick, the Patriots' soon-to-be fourth-string quarterback, would become a legend of both his sport and his city.

The story begs a question: How much did that redshirt year at the University of Michigan affect Brady's career? In a counterfactual world in which he *hadn't* taken that extra year for self-improvement, would he still have been drafted into the NFL and become who he is today? It's impossible to know for certain, barring a Marty McFly–type intervention. But at elite levels of professional sports, where *all* the players are exceptional, an extra year of development could be the edge that differentiates a pro career from obscurity.

How could we find out if an additional year of training is, on average, beneficial for young athletes who might find themselves in the situation Tom Brady did back in 1995? We can't just look at red-shirted freshmen and see if they're more likely to play in the NFL, since there are so many factors that may influence outcomes—who were the other players on their collegiate team, what academic, social, or physical pressures (such as injuries) might have contributed to an athlete's decision to redshirt. And we can't reasonably run a randomized trial; no coach is going to let us flip a coin to determine a team's starting lineup, fun as that might be for us.

As you might have guessed, natural experiments have been able to shed light on the value of extra experience in professional sports. Studies from the 1980s of professional hockey players (popularized by Malcolm Gladwell in his book *Outliers*) took advantage of a birthday effect not unlike the kind we saw in our discussion of flu shots.

---

* The term "redshirt" comes from the color of the jersey that the players may wear during practice to differentiate them from the main team.

It happened that youth hockey players were divided into groups by the year of their birth. That means children born in January of a given year would play with a group of kids almost all of whom are younger than they are. January-born children will be, on average, five or six months older than other kids in their group, and almost a year older than those born in December of that year. When children are young, a few months of age can make a big difference in both physical and psychological development. For ice hockey players, it allows for that many more months of experience on skates (not to mention a growth spurt or two).

The downstream consequences of what has been called the "relative age effect" are that kids who excel in hockey at a young age (because they're older and more developed than their peers) are the ones who gain access to more competitive leagues, not to mention other opportunities to develop their skills as hockey players—making them even better players still, giving them yet more opportunities to improve and excel. This, researchers hypothesized, is why players at the professional level were disproportionately born closer to the start of the year. In the 1982–1983 season (the season researchers studied), 62.8 percent of the players in the National Hockey League were born in January–June, versus 38.2 percent in July–December.

Researchers have found evidence of similar phenomena in Major League Baseball and professional club soccer in Europe. A study of German tennis players found that as they advanced into progressively higher levels of competition, the relative age effect appeared only more pronounced. In the study, 29.6 percent of all ranked players were born in January, February, or March; that number rose to 38.1 percent when looking at the best players in a region, and 42.1 percent of the best players in the country.

In other words, when it comes to competitive sports, some players enjoyed an advantage simply from having been born at the right time of year. But what impact could the relative age effect have outside the world of sports?

—

Anywhere in which age cutoffs arbitrarily divide kids into different groups a situation will be generated in which some are older than others—sometimes significantly. The most obvious example of this is in school. When a state dictates that a kindergarten entrant be "five years old before September 1," that kindergarten class is going to be composed of kids whose ages span as much as a year. A child born on August 31 will be 364 days younger than one born on September 1, even though both will belong in the same class.

At that early age, one additional year of life is no small thing. The oldest kids in the kindergarten class could have as much as 20 percent more experience here on planet Earth, not to mention the accompanying physical growth, than the youngest kids in the same class. Teachers and school systems, however, apply the same set of expectations for all kids in that class, regardless of the month of their birth. They're taught the same lessons, evaluated by the same metrics, and expected to behave the same way. It may not make sense that we expect the same behavior and scholastic performance from kids with 20 percent differences in age, but to some extent we must, and we certainly do.

A few of us (Bapu, along with Harvard colleagues Timothy Layton, Michael Barnett, and Tanner Hicks) wanted to know what impact the relative age effect might have in the classroom when it comes to children's health. In particular, we wanted to see if it affected diagnosis rates of attention deficit hyperactivity disorder, or ADHD. A condition marked by inattention, hyperactivity, and impulsivity, ADHD has been increasingly diagnosed in school-age children over the past several decades; the CDC estimated in 2016 that some 9.4 percent of children aged two to eighteen (12.9 percent of boys and 5.6 percent of girls) have received a diagnosis of ADHD.

Our hypothesis was that when kids who were up to a year apart in age sat in the same class, with the same expectations placed upon them by teachers and parents, the younger kids would have more trouble meeting those expectations. They would have a harder time sitting at a desk all day, paying attention, and suppressing impulsive behavior, simply because they were younger. In turn, teachers would be more likely to raise concerns about ADHD for these younger kids, concerns that could make their way to parents and, ultimately, that could find kids in the doctor's office. Doctors, who are by now primed to think about ADHD when they hear that a child is having behavioral trouble compared with their peers, may be more likely to diagnose ADHD and even to prescribe medications.

We weren't the first to consider the role of relative age in ADHD diagnosis. Previous research had provided some evidence in support of our hypothesis. But it either relied on data from surveys (less reliable than actual diagnoses), didn't include large enough numbers of kids at school entry, wasn't conducted in the United States, or examined older data that may not reflect current medical practice. Still, the earlier findings were persuasive enough to urge us onward.

Digging into the same massive insurance claims database that informed the flu shot study in the last chapter, we examined data on more than 400,000 American children who entered kindergarten from 2012 to 2014. Because we knew the states in which the children lived, we could see when their birthdays fell relative to the state's cutoff date for kindergarten entry. So, for example, at the time the data was collected, eighteen states used September 1 as their cutoff, which meant that kids born in August would have just turned five when they started kindergarten, whereas kids born in September would be just shy of six.

As with influenza, there should be no obvious biological differences in the risk of ADHD based simply on a child's birthday. So we could group kids by their birth month and assume that they were counterfactual to each other; that is, what happened to the group of kids born in August is what would have happened to the kids born in September had they been born in August, and vice versa. If we saw differences in ADHD rates between kids born in one month versus the other, we could deduce that they were the result of external factors, and not some biologically inherent feature.

Building on this intuition, we compared the rate of ADHD diagnosis for kids born in August with that of kids born in September. We hypothesized that for kids going to school in states with September 1 cutoffs, kids with August birthdays—the youngest in their class—would be more likely to be diagnosed with ADHD than those with September birthdays, the oldest in the same class.

Here's what we found: in states with a September 1 cutoff, kids born in August had a 34 percent higher rate of ADHD diagnosis and treatment than those in the same class born in September of the previous year.

Were our findings due to the relative age effect? It seemed likely, but we wanted to see if we could find further support. There were two ways to go about it. One was that we could compare kids born in July versus August and September versus October in those states with a September 1 cutoff, to make sure that any observed differences in ADHD rates between August and September kids weren't mirrored elsewhere. After all, if our hypothesis was correct, we wouldn't expect to see big differences in the July/August or September/October groups, kids who sat in the same classrooms and whose ages might differ by only a few weeks.

Alternatively, we could compare kids born in August and September in states that *didn't* have a September 1 cutoff—where the cutoff for kindergarten was August 1 or October 1, say. In these states, the August and September classmates should only, on average, be a month apart in age, so we shouldn't see a marked difference in ADHD diagnosis. If we *did* see a significant difference between those August and September kids, it would suggest to us that some other factor was at play, and not just the school entry cutoff (for example, in line with flu shots, August kids might be more likely to have had an extra annual doctor's visit, which leads to a greater likelihood of an ADHD diagnosis).

What did these analyses show? In states with a September 1 cutoff, there was no significant difference in ADHD diagnosis rates between kids in the same class born in July versus August or September versus October. And in states *without* a September 1 cutoff, there wasn't a significant difference between August- and September-born kids.

Taken together, it bolstered our initial hypothesis: the relative age effect in ADHD diagnosis of young kids was real.

We could take things a step further still. While it made sense that ADHD diagnoses would be influenced by a child's age relative to peers, it wouldn't make sense for a child's relative age to affect the diagnosis of diseases like asthma and diabetes. Unlike ADHD, whose diagnosis depends on comparing children's behavior with that of their peers, these diseases are more objectively diagnosed (with pulmonary function tests for asthma, blood tests for diabetes). If we *did* observe a difference in rates of asthma or diabetes in August- and September-born children, that would raise a red flag for us. There must then be some other underlying biological difference between August- and September-born children.

We therefore repeated our analysis, only this time looking at diagnosis rates for asthma, diabetes, and several other conditions. Not surprisingly, there was no significant difference between August-born and September-born kids for these "falsification" conditions.

As for ADHD, we didn't just stop at diagnosis. Where there's a diagnosis, a treatment follows. We were interested in medication use among kids said to have ADHD. Stimulant drugs such as Ritalin and Adderall are commonly prescribed, and when used appropriately, they can be beneficial in terms of calming hyperactivity and enhancing focus. But they carry with them the risk of appetite suppression, not to mention psychiatric and sleep disturbance.

Our question: Were younger kids more likely to be prescribed these treatments than their older classmates? It turns out they were, and not by a little. Kids diagnosed with ADHD and born in August received an average of *120* more days of medication than kids born in September.

In other words, younger kids with ADHD were being treated more intensely, even though, as our previous study suggested, there was no apparent biological reason to do so. Moreover, doctors didn't seem to be revising their diagnoses on the basis of a child's relative age.

We have to admit that, as clinicians, we can well imagine why that's the case. As a younger child gets older, their behavior might seem to "improve," which doctors and parents could quite reasonably attribute to the effects of medication—leading to refill after refill of the drug. However, the actual reason the child's behavior is changing could simply be that they're maturing, the relative age gap between them and their peers starting to close. It becomes only truer as they get older still: the relative difference between a five- and a six-year-old is a lot greater than the relative difference between a nine- and a ten-year-old.

We blew by an important statistic earlier: ADHD is more than twice as common in boys as it is in girls. There are different types of ADHD—the hyperactive and inattentive types. When it comes to the hyperactive type, the difference between the genders is only more pronounced, four times as prevalent in boys as in girls.

To see how relative age might manifest itself differently in boys and girls, we ran our original analyses again, only this time looking at the genders separately. The relative age effect seemed to be stronger in boys than in girls, a finding that shouldn't be surprising considering that boys make up a larger share of ADHD diagnoses in general. (For girls, the size of the effect was so small that it didn't rise to the level of statistical significance.)

What's going on here? It's hard to say for sure. It could be that developmental differences are more pronounced among young boys, such that a year of age for kindergarten boys is a bigger developmental gap—or at least is perceived that way—than it is for girls.* Because ADHD is more commonly diagnosed in boys, it may also be that teachers, parents, and doctors are more likely to raise a concern for ADHD in a kindergarten-age boy, withholding judgment on a kindergarten-age girl to see how she progresses throughout the year, when she may potentially "catch up" with her peers.

———

Long before this study was published in 2018, debate was already swirling around the best practices for diagnosing and treating ADHD. If 9.4 percent of kids were diagnosed, was it being diagnosed too often? Were our expectations for how young kids should behave in school unrealistic? What constituted "normal" behavior

---

* While research suggests that many of the previously believed differences between boys and girls are not based in biology and represent social constructs, there also appear to be true biological differences between sexes in early childhood development.

anyway? Did we need to rethink our overall approach to teaching young children?

The birthday study added an alarming fact to the ongoing debate: arbitrary factors like age cutoffs for school entry could be driving overdiagnosis and overtreatment for ADHD.

There are other ways the relative age effect can manifest itself in our health. A study from the U.K. showed that the youngest kids in a school class year were not only more likely to be diagnosed with ADHD and intellectual disability but also more likely to be diagnosed with depression. A review of data in Alberta, Canada, from 1979 to 1992 showed that among individuals under twenty who committed suicide, a disproportionate share (55.3 percent) were in the younger half of their school class. A study in Norway, meanwhile, found that being young for your grade was associated with increased probability of teenage pregnancy.

The relative age effect has been shown to affect classroom outcomes beyond a child's health. In a study of children in England with a school entry cutoff of September 1, researchers found that standardized test scores were consistently lower for boys and girls born in August compared with their older, September-born peers. The size of the effect, which they called the "August birth penalty," was most pronounced in the youngest kids they studied, the five-year-olds, though it was present as old as age eighteen. After accounting for other potential factors (such as when other kids in a given class were born, when in the school year kids entered their class, or whether kids switched schools), the researchers came to the conclusion that "the major reason why August-born children perform significantly worse than September-born children in the Key Stage tests is simply that they are almost a year younger when they sit [for] them."

A study by economists of children in Florida showed similar findings: August-born kids had lower standardized test scores than September-born kids. Additional analyses shed light on how this effect could ripple throughout a child's educational career. Compared with September-born kids, the August-born kids were also more likely to be diagnosed with behavioral, cognitive, or physical disabilities, and more likely to be in remedial reading or math courses. August-born kids were less likely to be enrolled in programs for gifted students, less likely to be enrolled in advanced reading or math courses, less likely to be enrolled in Advanced Placement courses, and less likely to graduate from high school on the standard schedule. By and large, the effects remained even after controlling for gender, race, and maternal level of education.

So, what do we make of all this? Let's go back to Tom Brady. By redshirting, Brady got an extra year to focus on self-improvement before officially starting his college football career. It's impossible to know for certain the effect of that one year. But even if the effect was small, it's not hard to imagine it might have made the difference between being picked 199th in the NFL draft that year (out of 254 drafted players) and not being selected at all. Perhaps without his redshirt year, Tom Brady wouldn't be the household name he is today.

You don't have to be a football fan to wonder what an extra year of preparation might do for a kid with an August birthday. The Brown University economist Emily Oster, in her book *The Family Firm,* raises a provocative question: Should parents of kids with summer birthdays "redshirt" their kindergartners—hold them back for a year before starting school? On the one hand, it would help children avoid the adverse consequences of the relative age effect. On the other, parents would have to consider whether whatever their child would be doing for that extra year would actually be better for them than starting school and accept with it any risks of the relative age effect. The jury on that question is still out.

———

The relative age effect, at its core, highlights two important concepts when it comes to health. We've discussed the first one already— that a child's age relative to their peers can affect long-term health and educational outcomes. The second one may be less obvious. It centers on the critical role that diagnosis plays in medicine and the problems that can occur when diagnoses involve some degree of subjectivity. While for pro hockey players the relative age effect is a piece of interesting trivia, it's a lot more serious when it shows up in kindergarten classrooms and stimulant prescriptions for five-year-olds. And while one could interpret our study's findings to suggest that the relative age effect was resulting in kids born in September being *underdiagnosed* with ADHD, research suggests it's more likely that it's the August-born kids who were being overdiagnosed and overtreated.

Overdiagnosing patients with conditions they don't truly have is a problem that can extend well beyond a line in their medical chart or an unnecessary prescription or two. It can send patients down long paths, with cascading events that can shape their care for many years. Diagnosis and treatment for any medical condition—even if the diagnosis is made on shaky grounds—can persist indefinitely.

Let's be clear: there are plenty of kids born in August who are *accurately* diagnosed with ADHD and who greatly benefit from treatment. But the relative age effect seen in our study suggests that some fraction of kids born in August and diagnosed with ADHD would not have been similarly diagnosed had they been born in September. Some kids "grow out" of that diagnosis; others do not.

The fact is that once patients are started down certain paths of care, it can be hard to divert them—even if they should never have been on that path in the first place. One study by Bapu, Michael Barnett, and Andrew Olenski showed that patients who were treated by emergency doctors who tend to prescribe more opioids than their peers were more likely not only to receive an opioid prescription but to *maintain* ongoing opioid prescriptions long after their emergency visit. Surely some of those patients would have improved with the passing of time. In other words, some patients ended up on long-term opioid therapy to treat their pain simply because they happened to be seen by one doctor rather than another—not because their pain was truly worse or its underlying cause more severe.

In a similar study by the Harvard Medical School student Zhuo Shi, the Harvard physician and researcher Ateev Mehrotra, Bapu, and others, patients with upper respiratory infections who were, again by chance, treated by urgent care doctors who tend to prescribe more antibiotics (even though antibiotics don't help with the majority of infections, which are viral) were more likely to be prescribed an antibiotic by them. No surprise there. But what was surprising is that those patients were more likely to receive antibiotics for infections in the *future* too, by different doctors. These patients, given antibiotics in the past that "worked," were presumably more likely to seek out antibiotics and receive them in the future.

Just like with opioids, some patients (perhaps even most) would have gotten better without antibiotics. And again, there were downstream consequences: had patients seen an urgent care doctor with a different set of tendencies, they might take fewer antibiotics across a lifetime.

—

We noted earlier that part of the challenge when it comes to diagnosing ADHD lies in its subjectivity.* ADHD is based on the presence of hyperactivity, impulsivity, and inattentiveness. If you look at a full list of the associated symptoms, it's not hard to see how subjectivity can factor into a diagnosis: fidgetiness, difficulty remaining seated, inappropriate running around or climbing, difficulty playing quietly, always being "on the go," excessive talking, difficulty waiting turns, blurting out answers too quickly, interrupting others, inattention to detail, making careless mistakes, difficulty maintaining attention, seeming not to listen, difficulty organizing, failing to follow through on tasks, losing objects, being easily distracted by irrelevant stimuli, or being forgetful in routine activities.

Putting aside the question of whether these symptoms are even all that abnormal for a five-year-old (or for that matter, for fidgety adults such as ourselves), we can all agree that in general kindergartners and first graders struggle to remain seated for long periods of time, will make noise and run around when they play, and will occa-

* There is some degree of subjectivity involved in the process of deciding things like cutoff values for "objective" diagnostic tests (for example, a hemoglobin A1C test above 6.5 percent indicates diabetes, while a systolic blood pressure above 130 or diastolic pressure above 80 indicates hypertension). But when it comes to making diagnoses, there is certainly less subjectivity in diagnosing diabetes or hypertension than there is diagnosing ADHD.

sionally ignore adults. Absent the kinds of objective criteria upon which most medical conditions are diagnosed, such as laboratory, imaging, or physiological measurements, it's only natural that we'd compare kids with their peers, making way for relative age effects in the way teachers, doctors, and parents assess them.[*]

We're sympathetic to our pediatrician colleagues. They're trying their best with the information they have, and making an ADHD diagnosis is often challenging. Even gathering accurate information on a child can be difficult, coming secondhand from a parent or a caregiver as it often does. Or a doctor might have plenty of data, but then have to extract the pertinent data points. It's an unenviable task.

Diagnosis might seem easier to achieve in areas where objective measures exist—hard-and-fast numbers such as blood pressure and cell counts. If only it were so. Even with all the right information in hand, the number of diseases that could explain a given set of symptoms or laboratory values can be enormous. The same disease may also not present the same way in each patient. For one patient, a heart attack may present as crushing, sub-sternal chest pain accompanied by sweating and shortness of breath. For another patient, the symptoms may feel like heartburn or indigestion, neck pain, or arm pain (these are less common, but they do happen). In the end, we as doctors have to pull together whatever data we have and arrive at an answer. We do so using a combination of conscious reasoning and subconscious pattern recognition. It's a human process, in other words, and one that is susceptible to all the biases and mental shortcuts that routinely lead us humans down the wrong path.

The relative age effect in ADHD is an example of a bias known in behavioral science as the "representativeness heuristic." It's easier to compare all kindergartners with one set of so-called normal behaviors than it is to figure out where each individual kid may be along the typical developmental timeline. Our mind uses a heuristic, a mental shortcut, to apply expectations to things that appear to

---

[*] ADHD diagnoses aren't necessarily based on established diagnostic criteria, either, making even more room for biases.

belong to the same category. The representativeness heuristic tells us "this is how kindergartners should act," glossing over the reality that kindergartners who are nearly a year apart in age could reasonably be expected to behave very differently from one another. Heuristics can be helpful in our daily lives; we can safely assume that a given grocery store will sell eggs and milk, even if we haven't been to the store before, because that's what grocery stores generally do. But it can lead to problematic biases, in ADHD and beyond (such as in the operating room, as we'll see in chapter 8).

"Availability bias" is another example of the way that diagnoses can routinely be skewed. It happens when we pull from our most recent experiences in making an assessment. A classic study from the renowned behavioral scientists Amos Tversky and Daniel Kahneman asked subjects to imagine a typical text in the English language, and to consider the letter *r*. They then asked if *r* was more likely to appear as the first letter in a word or as the third letter in a word. They did the same for the letters *k, l, n,* and *v.* The researchers' choice of letters wasn't arbitrary: each appears more often in the third position in English words than in the first position.

For each letter, however, a majority of study subjects said the opposite—that the letters appeared in the first position more often. The culprit was the availability bias. It's simply much easier to think of words that start with *r* than it is to think of words with *r* in the third position. Words with an initial *r* are more "available" in our minds.*

A study by the UCLA physician-economist Dan Ly showed how the availability heuristic can affect a doctor's diagnostic reasoning. Looking at records of more than seventy-three hundred physicians, the study examined the way pulmonary embolism is diagnosed—a blood clot in the lung that can cause shortness of breath. At baseline, doctors used either a blood test or a CT scan in about 9 percent of patients who showed up at a Veterans Affairs hospital emergency room complaining of shortness of breath. However, after diagnos-

---

* In case you were wondering, this paragraph contains only three words beginning with *r* (all of them the letter *r* itself) and eight words with *r* in the third position.

ing one patient with a pulmonary embolism, doctors started testing for them more often in subsequent patients. In the ten days after a pulmonary embolism diagnosis, doctors tested an additional 1.4 percent of patients, before eventually returning to their baseline. While this is not a huge effect percentage-wise, with an estimated 130 million emergency department visits in the United States annually, this effect would translate to thousands of additional scans every year.

We can reasonably assume that the subsequent patients' symptoms were unrelated to those of the original patient: the first case wasn't a patient zero in a sudden outbreak of embolisms (which, to be clear, are not infectious). Doctors started testing for pulmonary embolisms more often *simply because they had recently diagnosed one.* Pulmonary embolism was more "available" in their minds.

(We'll be talking a lot about cognitive biases and how they affect physician behavior in the following chapters. Suffice it to say for now that even with all the training it requires to become a doctor, we are far from immune to the failures caused by these mental shortcuts.)

Gurpreet Dhaliwal writes and speaks powerfully about how doctors make diagnoses and the role that biases often play. Practicing and teaching at the University of California, San Francisco, Dhaliwal is a physician whom fellow doctors might refer to as a "master clinician," someone who has carefully honed the art and craft of making diagnoses. "Without ever giving it any thought," he writes in *The Journal of the American Medical Association,* "most students and physicians come to reason adequately using the same inborn neural circuitry we use to reason through life's myriad situations that require us to diagnose and act." It's this inborn neural circuitry that causes us to take mental shortcuts—and that can add up to cognitive biases. The answer, Dhaliwal says, is for doctors to focus on the diagnostic reasoning process itself, to "view it as a procedure worthy of improvement and mastery." Only then can we begin to overcome the tendencies that may be coloring our decisions.

In other words, you can't prevent having your last patient influence the way you search for a diagnosis on the next one unless you're aware of the bias. You can't diagnose a young patient's behavioral issues at school most accurately without acknowledging the role that their relative age might be playing on people's judgments.

As parents ourselves, we know how easy it is to look at our child's behavior and ask, for example, "Is this normal for a three-year-old?" We forget that besides there being a wide range of "normal" behavior, there is also a wide range of ages within the class of "three-year-olds" (or "kindergartners" or "first graders").

We are by no means implying that teachers, pediatricians, and parents don't already do these things—many do. But the data suggest that somewhere along the teacher-parent-doctor pathway, the relative age effect (coupled with the representativeness heuristic) takes hold. And since, when it comes to diagnosis and treatment, the buck stops with the doctor, it could be beneficial to introduce tools to remind doctors of relative age.

It lends itself to some low-hanging potential fixes. Here's one: electronic health records could flag patients who are young for their class so that when a pediatrician hears about behavior that is potentially abnormal, they interpret it in the right context.

—

Overdiagnosis—diagnosing someone with a medical condition that they do not have or that is unlikely to lead to health problems—is one example of a more broadly known issue in medicine: diagnostic error. It's related to underdiagnosis, where we dismiss a real problem as normal (assuming a patient is "just a snorer" when they actually have obstructive sleep apnea that should be treated), and misdiagnosis (a patient with a torn aorta is said to be having a heart attack, two very different conditions that require very different treatments but that can manifest themselves with similar symptoms). Any of these diagnostic errors can lead to patients receiving unnecessary care or missing out on necessary care, either of which can lead to serious problems and even death.

In 2015, the National Academy of Medicine released a major report, written by a group of doctors and researchers, about improving diagnosis in health care (full disclosure: Bapu was one of them).

After examining decades' worth of research, the group concluded that diagnostic errors have been—and remain—a common flaw in health care. About 5 percent of U.S. adults who seek outpatient care will experience a diagnostic error; diagnostic errors could contribute to as much as 10 percent of deaths, and up to 17 percent of adverse events that occur in the hospital can be attributed to diagnostic errors. These figures suggest that at some point in their lives most people will experience a diagnostic error, potentially one with life-or-death consequences.

We have both been doctors long enough to say with confidence that despite our best efforts we have made diagnostic errors in the clinic or the hospital, some with serious consequences. Our smarter, more knowledgeable, and more capable colleagues have, too. Making errors as a doctor, when it's our job *not* to make errors, is humbling in the best of circumstances, crushing in the worst. And with millions of patients moving through the health-care system each day, there is all too much potential for diagnostic errors to occur.

Diagnostic errors are common enough that I (Chris) have seen them outside work, too.

Shortly after my wife, Emily, and I came home from the hospital after our second son was born, she developed the worst headache of her life. It was so severe she could barely think straight; this was unlike any other headache she had experienced before. Knowing that women who have recently given birth are at increased risk for bleeding in the brain—which can manifest itself as a severe "thunderclap" headache—I drove Emily to the closest emergency room.

Hearing that Emily was postpartum and had a severe headache, the emergency department quickly sent her for a CT scan to see if there was bleeding in her brain. Because the condition (formally known as an intracerebral hemorrhage) can require rapid treatment, the radiologist who interprets CT scans did a "wet read"—an immediate look at the scan to check for any time-sensitive, life-threatening findings like bleeding. The wet read on Emily's CT said that there was no bleeding and that her brain looked normal. Phew!

The problem was that Emily still had a severe headache. She needed a proper diagnosis. "It's probably a migraine," she was told, and she was given pain medication. After about half an hour, her headache got slightly better—enough so that all Emily wanted to do was lie down until it went away. I brought her home, and we were instructed—as most patients are—to follow up with her regular doctor.

The headache minimally improved, but it didn't go away. Emily was still quite uncomfortable. Moreover, she didn't have a history of migraines, which made her suspicious of her diagnosis. So, she pulled up her records from the emergency department on the online patient portal and looked at the report from her CT scan. By now, the radiologist had had time to go back to her scan and give it a thorough look, beyond the initial "wet read." There was a clear culprit: The sinuses on one side of Emily's head appeared to be blocked. The blockage prevented drainage, creating a painful pressure buildup. It explained her headache much better than the migraine diagnosis.

Feeling the problem needed to be addressed further, the next day she made an appointment with an otolaryngologist who saw the scan and immediately prescribed medications to treat a sinus infection and help with drainage; she would later need surgery to remove the blockage, which ended up being caused by a tumor, fortunately benign.

Emily is fine now, and she hasn't had any more severe headaches. Mercifully, the misdiagnosis didn't cause her any long-term harm. She also had the advantage of knowing a lot about medicine herself (she's a pharmacist) and being married to someone who can help make sense of CT scans (though my skills are mostly limited to the lungs).

But it's easy to imagine a scenario that went another way, one in which she never went back and looked at that CT scan report. She would have thought she'd had a fluke migraine. She probably would have gotten better with time as the infection receded, as infections often do. The final results of the CT scan could have sat in her medical record until someone happened to look at them, if they did at all. We could have gone for months, years, even a lifetime thinking she had migraine headaches—even though it was actually pain triggered by episodically blocked sinuses.

—

The National Academy of Medicine report on diagnostic errors notes there are many sources of error, including "inadequate collaboration and communication among clinicians, patients, and their families; a health care work system that is not well designed to support the diagnostic process; limited feedback to clinicians about diagnostic performance; and a culture that discourages transparency and disclosure of diagnostic errors—impeding attempts to learn from these events and improve diagnosis."

Emily's story hits on a few of these factors. We should note that in it everybody did their basic jobs as they should: The emergency doctor considered and ultimately ruled out a life-threatening emergency. The radiologist's wet read correctly diagnosed the absence of a hemorrhage, and the later report called attention to her sinuses (this even though the radiologist was tasked only with checking Emily's brain).

The problem was one of communication. The report on the CT scan wasn't conveyed to the emergency department in time for it to affect Emily's immediate care, nor was it communicated back to Emily. While the report might have made it back to one of her doctors in a few days, if she wasn't reporting an ongoing or worsening problem, it might not have been acted upon.

Moreover, it's unlikely the overworked emergency doctor would ever know that there had been a missed diagnosis, making it difficult to learn from Emily's case and adjust their practice in the future. It is not an exaggeration to say that a story like this could play out exactly the same way even had the best emergency doctor and best radiologist in the world been under similar circumstances.

It's a distressingly common occurrence: a doctor who makes a misdiagnosis never finds out because the system is simply not set up to give doctors feedback on their diagnostic performance. For doctors like us who practice in hospitals, we often only find out we made a wrong diagnosis when it becomes apparent immediately. Once a patient leaves the hospital, we can only hope we got it right.

One study estimated that each year thousands of Medicare patients die within a week of being sent home from the emergency department; while clearly some new problem could arise within a week, a missed diagnosis is likely responsible for many of these deaths. We're confident the doctors who saw those patients would want to know which patients died after being sent home so that they could avoid errors in the future, but it's unlikely they would ever find out.

When doctors *do* get feedback, they can change their practice. Opioid pain medications, including drugs dispensed from a doctor's prescriptions, lead to thousands of tragic overdose deaths each year. With some notable exceptions, doctors prescribe these drugs with good intentions—because they want to treat the pain their patients are presenting. But they also know they can be dangerous to their patients. Knowing exactly how much to give a patient can be hard, even when there are safe-prescribing guidelines.

In a study designed to look at how doctors respond to feedback, the USC psychologist and behavioral scientist Jason Doctor and his colleagues randomized 861 prescribers in San Diego into two groups: one that was informed, by a letter from the San Diego County medical examiner, when a real patient recently prescribed opioids by that doctor died of an overdose, and a control group that received no such letter. Over the next three months, the group that received the letter decreased the amount of opioids they prescribed by 9.7 percent, while control prescribers had no significant change. The group that received the letter was also less likely than the control group to start their patients on a new course of opioid medications.

While the study is an example of "availability bias" at work (the letter might have raised temporary awareness of the harms of opioid prescribing, which could revert to the baseline over time), it's also a stark demonstration of how receiving feedback on our practice habits can influence the way we treat patients. It provided doctors with an instance in which their assessment of the risk and benefit of opioids proved wrong. While it might be overwhelming to receive such feedback for every diagnosis or treatment we provide, the ability to learn more about what happens to our patients after we intervene in their lives could make us much better at our craft.

—

We are both doctors whose primary specialty is internal medicine, a field that deals in preventing, detecting, and treating diseases of the internal organs (though Chris is also subspecialized in pulmonary and critical care medicine). Internists pride themselves on their diagnoses; while he was in training, one of Chris's supervising chief residents quipped that the MD after our names actually stood for "Make Diagnoses." Many of us get a particular thrill out of solving diagnostic mysteries and making particularly complex or elusive diagnoses. Diagnostic errors of any kind harm our patients, and learning how they happen might just make us better at avoiding them in the future.

Some diagnoses, however, are easier to make than others.

You need only minimal training to know that a patient who collapses in the grocery store and has no pulse is in cardiac arrest. We all realize this patient needs help—and *fast*. What's not as easy is accomplishing that goal. The challenges here are not just in diagnosis but in logistics. Treatment for cardiac arrest may start in a grocery store, in an office, or on the sidewalk. It may involve dozens of people, and it can take place over miles, as emergency medical services (EMS) teams care for patients in an ambulance while transporting them to the hospital for definitive care.

In the next chapter, we'll hop a ride to the hospital—lights and sirens on—and take a look at a natural experiment that shows us how every critical minute counts.

CHAPTER FIVE

ARE MARATHONS HAZARDOUS TO YOUR HEALTH?

L EGEND HAS IT that in 490 BCE a Greek messenger named Pheidippides ran about forty kilometers from the city of Marathon to Athens to report the news that Athenians had defeated the invading Persian forces. Upon sharing the news, he collapsed and promptly died of exhaustion, as depicted in a famous 1869 work by the French painter Luc-Olivier Merson.

The modern marathon's checkered origin story apparently isn't enough to dissuade roughly one million people worldwide from competing in such runs, now defined as 42.195 kilometers in length, or about 26.2 miles, and which take even the fastest runners in the world more than two hours to complete. Of course, the veracity of this two-thousand-year-old legend and even the identity of the messenger are subjects of debate. There are details of the story that often get left out, too: Pheidippides was said to have run about 150 miles to seek help from the Spartans shortly *before* his fatal run from Marathon to Athens, which certainly would have contributed to his exhaustion. Ancient origins aside, it's safe to say that marathons have carried known health risks ever since competitive marathoning was introduced in 1896, when the race was run from Marathon to Athens in the first modern Olympic Games.

Nowadays in the United States, marathons can range from modest events with a few hundred competitors to massive events that take over entire cities. Featuring more than 50,000 runners, 12,000 volunteers, and 2.5 million spectators each year, the New York City Marathon is the world's largest, but other marathons in American cities host thousands of runners and spectators as well.

The demands don't fall on runners alone: These events can present massive disruptions and logistical challenges for host cities, which have to make advance plans for road closures and introduce public safety measures for runners and spectators alike. Medical care is an important part of those plans. As the story of Pheidippides might suggest, marathons can present health hazards for even the fittest athletes as they push themselves to their physical limits. With thousands of participants running, medical teams have to prepare for a host of potential issues. Musculoskeletal injuries are common (for instance, ankle sprains), and though they're rarely life threatening, afflicted runners will still need assistance and treatment. But these types of injuries aren't what worry marathon medical teams the most.

The 1986 Pittsburgh Marathon was run on an eighty-seven-degree day with 60 percent humidity. Knowing that higher temperatures and humidity would put athletes at greater risk for dehydration and overheating (exertional heatstroke, technically speaking), medical teams warned runners to drink plenty of water and not to attempt their best times given the weather conditions. Water and aid stations were set up at roughly every mile marker, with medical field stations located toward the end of the course. They were staffed by a collective 100 doctors, 40 podiatrists, 125 nurses, 150 medical students, 80 emergency medical personnel, and dozens of physical therapists and other personnel, with 24 ambulances at the ready, all to attend to the roughly 2,900 runners. But these preparations were no match for the weather, which led many racers to start walking early in the course or drop out altogether. The journalist Ellen Perlmutter reported for *The Physician and Sportsmedicine:*

> The Pittsburgh Marathon was supposed to be a contest among runners. Instead, it became a battle for survival, a race that some runners and physicians contended should not have been run at all . . . by the end, more than half of the 2,897 runners had been treated for heat related injuries.

The average human body wasn't designed with this kind of sweltering marathon in mind (*our* human bodies certainly weren't). Admittedly, humans weren't built to eat dozens of processed franks in a sitting either, and yet every Fourth of July the eyes of the nation fall on Coney Island to watch Nathan's Hot Dog Eating Contest, where we fully expect to see competitors fall ill as they push their stomachs to their natural limits.* Flirting with the impossible is simply what human beings do.

And just as buckets are on hand at Nathan's, marathon medical teams assume many runners will require assistance, and they prepare accordingly. Heat-related injuries, which can be life threatening and demand immediate attention, are treated through rehydration and in some cases with cold-water baths. Runners in cold and rainy climates may need to be rewarmed using the Mylar blankets commonly seen at the finish line. Medical teams have to worry about

---

* Except, of course, the reigning record holders, Joey Chestnut and Miki Sudo, who have eaten 76 and 48.5 hot dogs in ten minutes in the men's and women's contests, respectively.

over-hydration, when runners drink more water than they're losing in sweat.* They also worry about runners who collapse—a common sight at finish lines, where medical tents are generally positioned. This often occurs when runners suddenly *stop* running, blood pooling in their lower extremities, temporarily preventing circulation around the body. Collapse is often treated easily, but it can sometimes be a sign of a more serious threat, such as a heart attack or even cardiac arrest.

Marathon medical tents are equipped with all kinds of equipment and supplies to handle critically ill patients. In addition to common first aid supplies, current guidelines recommend that defibrillators, breathing tube kits, supplemental oxygen, IV hydration fluids, IV medications, inhalers, vital sign monitors, blood analyzers, and water submersion tubs all be made available to staff.

Then there are the threats a medical team can't foresee. When terrorists bombed the finish line of the Boston Marathon in 2013, medical personnel caring for runners at the finish line responded immediately to treat victims. Sushrut Jangi, a physician working in the tent that day, wrote of his experience in *The New England Journal of Medicine:* "One nurse told me she remembered EMTs running out to the site of the explosion the moment the bombs burst. 'They were off before I could blink,' she said. Many physicians followed. 'After I saw a guy in a wheelchair coming into the tent with a head wound,' [the physician Pierre Rouzier] said, 'I decided to go to the scene.' He texted his wife a goodbye message: *There's a bomb at the finish line and we have to help.* 'I didn't want to die,' he said, 'but there were people out there.'"

Medical personnel were prepared for injuries, even critical ones, but they were expecting them to be running related, not trauma

---

* Under normal circumstances, drinking dangerous amounts of water is pretty uncommon. But during a marathon, it can be hard for runners to gauge how much water their bodies truly need when they are losing a lot of fluid through sweat. Excessive water intake can throw off the body's electrolyte balance, which can be deadly. For this reason, marathon planners space out water stations along the course to help runners avoid accidentally drinking too much water, and runners are advised accordingly.

from improvised explosive devices. Still, they applied tourniquets to patients who were bleeding out and helped get them rapidly to nearby hospitals for definitive care.* Hospital emergency departments had also prepared for a sudden influx of patients; again, they were expecting athletic complications, not bombing victims, but they had the capacity to treat the incoming patients.

The bombs at the Boston Marathon ultimately killed 3 people and injured 264. While it's impossible to quantify, it seems likely that more victims would have succumbed to their injuries had marathon medical teams not been at the ready and adequately supplied.

Preparations for the Boston Marathon start about six months prior to the race, which is traditionally run on Patriots' Day (the third Monday in April, a local holiday in Massachusetts). Organized by the Massachusetts Emergency Management Agency and managed from their underground bunker, race-day interventions include the deployment of thousands of personnel and the supplies and equipment they will need to ensure public safety for runners and spectators. The state police, National Guard, FBI, Department of Homeland Security, bomb squads, hazardous materials teams, the Department of Public Health, and the Red Cross, as well as local police, fire, and emergency medical services agencies from along the marathon route, all help in various ways to ensure the race runs smoothly and safely.

Suffice it to say, then, that marathon day is a big deal in Boston. But so far we've talked only about what marathons mean for the health of the runners and the crews that serve them. Boston has a population of more than half a million people. *What about everyone else?*

———

* Boston has a reputation for being a "medical city," with several major teaching hospitals, which might have contributed to the city's ability to handle the marathon's numerous injuries. Massachusetts General Hospital and Brigham and Women's treated thirty-one patients each, Boston Medical Center treated twenty-three, Beth Israel Deaconess treated twenty-one, Tufts Medical Center and St. Elizabeth's Medical Center treated eighteen each, and Boston Children's Hospital treated ten children. See Gawande, "Why Boston's Hospitals Were Ready."

A few years back, I (Bapu) was driving into downtown Boston to watch my wife, Neena, run in a 5K charity race. It wasn't the Boston Marathon, but it was Neena's first organized run, and I wanted to cheer her on. I planned to park near Mass General Hospital, the big teaching hospital where I work, since the race route went right by the area. But as I got close to the hospital, I found I had a problem: the road to where I usually parked was closed due to the race. I circled the area looking for another spot near the hospital but couldn't find one (this is Boston, after all, a parking nightmare in the best of circumstances). In the end I missed the race, cursing my decision to drive instead of taking the subway.

Feeling terrible about missing her race, I explained to Neena what happened when she got home a few hours later. Neena was disappointed but she understood, being no stranger to Boston parking herself. She then paused for a moment and said offhandedly, "I wonder what happened to all the *other* people who needed to get to Mass General today?"

That comment got me thinking, "What *did* happen to all the other people who needed to get to the hospital?" While I was hoping to use my connection to Mass General to score a good parking space, there were, we can safely assume, people driving to Mass General with more pressing concerns—patients with real, life-threatening problems. Neena's 5K was a relatively short race, passing through Beacon Hill, where Mass General is located, into Cambridge and then back. A bigger race like the Boston Marathon could cause even bigger disruptions, affecting access to many of the major hospitals in the city, and for a much longer time. Several thousand runners might be at risk for injuries, dehydration, and overheating, while millions of other people in the Greater Boston area would be at risk for life's routine threats—heart attacks, infections, strokes, you name it.

There were the makings of a fascinating natural experiment here. Could we measure the effect of marathons on *all* patients, the runners and non-runners alike?

—

Just as we've seen in previous chapters, for a natural experiment to take place, there must be a situation in which patients get assigned to one group or another simply by chance. Marathons don't happen by chance; they're planned well in advance, by the city and by participants. In the event that an otherwise healthy twenty-five-year-old runner has a heart attack on the course, that timing is anything but random: it happened precisely because it was marathon day. But for those of us who aren't running, having a heart attack on a marathon day—rather than, say, the day before or the day after—can be said to be the product of chance.

When it comes to heart attacks, a few minutes of delayed care can be the difference between life and death. Your heart provides a 24/7 service pumping blood—and the oxygen and nutrients it contains—to your entire body, including to the heart itself. A heart attack happens when the heart suddenly isn't receiving enough blood to support its regular activity—for instance, from a blockage of the coronary arteries. Most of the time, the heart will keep beating in these conditions, but it will alert its owner that it's in trouble through symptoms that can include chest pain, palpitations (the physical sensation of your heart beating), shortness of breath, neck or jaw pain, arm or shoulder pain, and nausea or vomiting, among others. Cardiac arrest occurs if the heart has so little oxygen that it can't pump blood at all, or if there's an electrical abnormality in the heart preventing it from pumping effectively. When the heart isn't pumping blood, the brain loses its supply of oxygen, causing loss of consciousness, and that can ultimately lead to death if the heart's beating isn't restored. Interventions like CPR, electrical shocks from a defibrillator, coronary artery stenting, or emergency surgery can help restore the heart's ability to pump blood—but only if performed quickly.

With all this in mind, let's think for a moment about a hypothetical patient, whom we'll call John.

John is an eighty-two-year-old former smoker living in Watertown, Massachusetts, a suburb of Boston that's a short way across the Charles River from several major Boston hospitals where heart attacks are treated. John has arthritis in his knees and hips and can walk around his block, but he will decidedly not be running in the Boston Marathon. If he happens to develop crushing chest pain from a heart attack and calls 911 the day *before* the Boston Marathon, an ambulance team should be able to get him to the hospital in a few minutes—lights and sirens can do a lot to relieve Boston traffic. But if that heart attack happens to come about the day *of* the Boston Marathon, it's going to take John significantly longer to get to the hospital. An ambulance will have to either take an alternate, longer route to the hospital or endure delays as it works its way through the marathon and its crowds. (The difference would be more extreme if John opts to have his neighbor drive him to the hospital instead.)

As we've noted, the timing of the marathon isn't random. But the time is as good as random when it comes to heart attacks *among people who aren't running in the marathon.* The natural experiment is set. We have our two groups: those who have heart attacks on marathon day and those who have heart attacks in the days immediately before and after.

We do, however, start running into problems if we look only at a single marathon. The 2018 Boston Marathon, for example, was run on a cold, windy, rainy day, and the days surrounding it were likewise cold. If we were to only study this one marathon, we might misestimate the effect of marathons on heart attacks, since lower air temperatures have been associated with higher rates of heart attacks. That would give us an estimate of the effect of the 2018 Boston Marathon, in particular, but it wouldn't necessarily tell us anything about the effect of the Boston Marathon in general.

Better would be to consider the generalized effect of the Boston Marathon by looking at a bunch of Boston Marathons and averaging the outcomes in the days before or after each marathon and comparing them with the averaged marathon days. Better still, if we wanted to look at the effect of major marathons in general, we could average the days before and after *all* major marathons, in many cities over many years, and compare them with all the different marathon days in question. By averaging more and more marathons into a single analysis—called an "event study"—we minimize the individual circumstances surrounding any single marathon, like the weather.

In a study published in *The New England Journal of Medicine,* we (Bapu, along with the University of Utah professor Clay Mann, the Weill Cornell physician Leia Wedlund, and Andrew Olenski) examined eleven different major U.S. marathons[*] over the course of a decade and asked, What happened on marathon days to people who weren't running the marathon but who happened to live close by? How did those who had heart attacks or cardiac arrests fare on marathon days compared with the days surrounding them?

To ensure we were capturing patients who weren't running in the marathon, we used Medicare data containing insurance claims for patients over age sixty-five who were hospitalized for a heart attack or cardiac arrest. We didn't mean to imply by this that athletes over age sixty-five can't run in marathons; they can and do. But it's rare enough in that age-group—and patients who have heart attacks and cardiac arrests are likely enough to have other chronic medical conditions that would hinder marathon participation— that we could evaluate the sixty-five-and-over group without concern that marathon-induced heart attacks were skewing the data.[†] Using zip code data on hospital locations and marathon routes, we then identified patients who were treated at a hospital impacted by the marathon ("marathon-affected hospitals") either on the day of a marathon or in the few weeks surrounding the marathon date. In total, we found 1,145 hospitalizations for heart attacks or cardiac arrests in these marathon-affected hospitals on marathon dates, and

---

[*] Boston, Chicago, Honolulu, Houston, Los Angeles, Minneapolis, New York City, Orlando, Philadelphia, Seattle, and Washington, D.C.

[†] The average age of patients in the study was about seventy-seven. Serious chronic medical conditions were very common, with congestive heart failure, hypertension (high blood pressure), hypercholesterolemia (high cholesterol), and diabetes found in more than 50 percent of patients in the study. Alzheimer's disease, atrial fibrillation, kidney disease, lung disease, cancer, and prior strokes were also common. It's fair to say, then, that this group of people was highly unlikely to be running in the marathon.

11,074 hospitalizations in those same hospitals *on the same day of the week as the marathon* in the five weeks before and the five weeks after the marathon.

One immediate finding: similar numbers of patients per day were hospitalized for heart attacks or cardiac arrests on marathon days compared with non-marathon days. This suggested two things: first, the marathons didn't lead to an influx of elderly patients with acute heart problems; and second, the marathons, despite their disruption and hassle, didn't cause patients to forgo care for these conditions altogether—an outcome that shouldn't be surprising considering these acute heart problems are among the most severe medical emergencies one can suffer from.

We also saw that patients who were hospitalized with these cardiac conditions on marathon days were similar to the patients who were hospitalized on pre- and post-marathon days when it came to factors like age, sex, race, and preexisting medical conditions. The patients who came in on pre- or post-marathon days, therefore, would serve as a good control group to the patients who came to hospitals on marathon days. Any difference in outcomes could safely be attributed to changes in care brought about by the marathon.

So what did we find?

For patients hospitalized for heart attacks or cardiac arrests on marathon days, 28.2 percent died within thirty days of being hospitalized (a standard measure of treatment outcomes) compared with 24.9 percent of patients hospitalized on the surrounding non-marathon days. In other words, marathon days led to an absolute increase of 3.3 percentage points in thirty-day mortality.* To put the figure another way: for every thirty patients who have a heart attack or cardiac arrest on the day of a major marathon, there is one patient who will die within thirty days who would have lived had they fallen ill on a different day.

Before considering what that meant, we wanted to be confident

---

* After we accounted for potential differences between days of the week, cities, patient populations, and hospitals across all eleven marathons in an adjusted statistical model, this difference remained fairly consistent.

that it was the marathons—and the disruptions they cause—that led to the difference. So we ran a few additional analyses. First, we looked at a set of similar patients admitted with heart attacks or cardiac arrests to other nearby hospitals—facilities just outside the area of the marathon. These patients would be subject to many of the same regional factors (like the weather on a given day), but they wouldn't be affected by delays from road closures, since a marathon wasn't snarling traffic in their area in the same way. We wouldn't expect there to be much of a difference between marathon days and non-marathon days at these hospitals—which is exactly what we found.

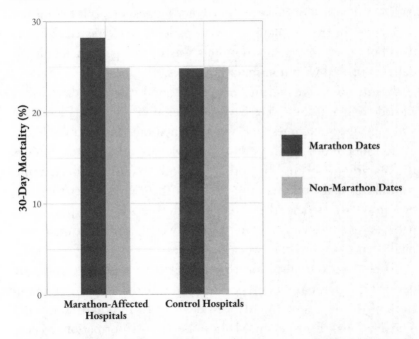

Next, we wanted to make sure there was no difference in the care provided on marathon days that might explain the difference in mortality. What if, for example, the doctors who usually treat heart attacks are volunteering at the marathon finish line and not available to provide their usual care to heart attack patients? To do this, we checked how often various lifesaving heart procedures were performed for these patients, such as percutaneous coronary intervention (stenting), coronary artery bypass surgery, or mechanically assisted blood pumping procedures. Again, we found that there was no difference between marathon dates and non-marathon dates in the use of these procedures.

What if patients sought care at different locations on marathon dates in response to the marathon's disruptions to roads? For example, could ambulances have been more likely to take patients to the nearby "control" hospitals, unaffected by road closures, on those days? If the care at these hospitals (often smaller community hospitals with fewer resources) was worse than the care at the hospitals affected by the marathon (often larger urban academic medical centers), we might expect to see an increase in mortality on marathon days, not because of delays in emergency transport, but because of differences in the hospitals at which patients were treated. But the distribution of care across hospitals was unchanged on marathon dates compared with non-marathon dates.

By this point, we had made a pretty good case that disruptions caused by marathons were having material effects on patient care and mortality outcomes, and we had ruled out the variables likeliest to muddle our findings. No, there weren't other factors besides the marathon causing disruptions in both marathon-affected and control hospitals; no, marathon runners themselves weren't keeling over in the streets;* no, there were no differences in the types of care patients were receiving; and no, patients weren't shifting care to hospitals that tended to have worse outcomes.

To confirm our suspicion that transit time was the culprit, we decided to look at ambulances. The Medicare database doesn't keep track of the details of ambulance rides, but EMS organizations do. The National Emergency Medical Services Information System (NEMSIS) is a national repository of data collected from ambulance activations from all over the country, and it includes detailed information on ambulance response locations, travel times, and travel

---

* To be extra confident, we repeated the analysis only in patients who had five or more chronic medical conditions who would be *exceedingly* unlikely to be running a marathon; we found similar results. We even went so far as to check the internet for any news reports of *runner* fatalities in the marathons. We didn't find any evidence to challenge these assumptions.

distances, in addition to details of patient care. Using the NEMSIS data, we could compare what actually happened in ambulances on marathon dates with other dates, and in marathon-affected areas compared with non-affected areas.

Here's what we found: In the mornings of marathon days, when nearby roads would be closed, ambulance transport times (from the scene to the hospital) were an average of 18.1 minutes, compared with 13.7 minutes on non-marathon dates, a difference of 4.4 minutes. Notably, there was no difference in the number of miles ambulances drove, suggesting that they were delayed, rather than diverted to other hospitals or forced to take physically longer routes. Meanwhile, in nearby zip codes not affected by marathon road closures, there was, as expected, no difference in transport times on marathon dates compared with non-marathon dates. Also, marathons are run in the mornings; when we looked at ambulance transport times in the evenings of marathon days—when the roads were open again—the effect went away.

The ambulance data also allowed us to investigate another potential explanation of our findings. Maybe people delayed calling 911 on marathon days, knowing that getting to the hospital would be a hassle. If so, perhaps they'd be willing to wait a bit longer to see if any symptoms, like chest pain or chest discomfort, might resolve. If people took longer to call 911, it's possible that mortality rates could be higher on marathon days simply because people sought care later, their heart becoming more injured all the while. But we found no differences in these times, which suggested that patient delays weren't the culprit.

It seems that marathon-related road closures really were delaying ambulances, and older patients with heart attacks and cardiac arrests were dying as a result. Three people died in the bombing of the Boston Marathon in 2013, a horrific event that changed the way the region thinks about and prepares for Marathon Monday each year. Our study suggested that marathon-related disruptions may lead to many more deaths across the United States each year, especially among older patients living in an area who may need to get to the hospital quickly. Moreover, it showed that even short delays in care—on the order of a few minutes—can be the difference between life and death when it comes to heart attacks or cardiac arrests.

It seems Bapu's wife, Neena, had been onto something after all.

———

If they're such a risk to runners and local communities, should we just cancel all the marathons? Of course not. We didn't suggest that parents should time their children's birth for the fall, for ADHD and flu shot purposes, and we're not suggesting that we do away with major marathons. In all likelihood, the benefit of marathons to public health—all the people inspired by them to take up running, or to step up their pace—outweighs the harm. Still, we have quantifiable evidence suggesting that events like these pose direct health risks to participants and indirect risks to patients living in the surrounding communities. The question now is, What do we do about it?

We've observed that time is of the essence when it comes to heart attacks and cardiac arrests. As they say in emergency medicine, time is tissue: the longer we wait for definitive treatment, the more cells die off and weaken the heart. When a bystander quickly performs CPR and/or applies an automated defibrillator,* when ambulances get to hospitals faster, and when hospitals provide definitive treatments promptly, the injury to patients' hearts can be mitigated. But the question of "How fast is fast enough?" is not so easy to answer—for cardiac emergencies and other medical problems alike. To get a sense of some of the challenges, let's take a look at the very beginning of the treatment process for cardiac arrest: CPR.

---

* We recommend everyone receive training in cardiopulmonary resuscitation (CPR) and the use of automated external defibrillators (AEDs), the devices you see hanging on walls below a sign with a heart and lightning bolt. Patients who suffer from cardiac arrest outside the hospital are more likely to survive if bystanders call 911, immediately perform CPR, and apply an AED while waiting for an ambulance to arrive, since every second really does count. Classes from organizations like the American Red Cross are available, many of them online, that could mean the difference between life and death for a loved one or even a stranger.

In 2004, the CDC partnered with Emory University to establish the Cardiac Arrest Registry to Enhance Survival, or CARES, a database that has collected data on hundreds of thousands of cases of out-of-hospital cardiac arrest across the United States. In one of their early studies looking at about twenty-eight thousand cases of cardiac arrest in which CPR was performed immediately by someone nearby while waiting for EMS teams to arrive (known as "bystander CPR"), it was associated with a significant increase in the chance of survival: 11.2 percent survived, compared with 7.0 percent when no bystander CPR was performed. In a study using an analogous registry in Sweden, survival was 10.5 percent for patients who received CPR while waiting for EMS teams, compared with 4.0 percent for patients who didn't get CPR. Other studies showing similar findings in various settings have made it clear that early CPR from bystanders is associated with better survival after cardiac arrest.

What these studies don't tell us is to what extent earlier CPR is *causing* improved survival. We have to imagine that taking early action to restore the pumping of blood throughout the body improves patient survival. The problem we run into is in trying to figure out exactly *how much* early CPR can be credited for this finding. Early CPR may be associated with factors that improve survival regardless of whether it's performed. If patients living in higher-income neighborhoods are both more likely to receive early CPR than patients in low-income neighborhoods and more likely to survive in general, it can make early CPR appear more beneficial than it truly is. When distinguishing factors such as income—or age, sex, race, educational level, geography—are associated with both the intervention of interest (in this case, early CPR) and the outcome of interest (in this case, survival), it makes it more challenging to tease out how much of an association can be attributed to your intervention.

This is what economists, statisticians, and epidemiologists refer to as confounding. By now you'll be familiar with the concept, if not the term, but for a clearer picture of what we mean, consider this example. A researcher decides to examine whether prep courses for high school students lead to better scores on the SAT college admissions test than self-directed study using a prep book. So the researcher finds a hundred kids who took a prep course and another hundred kids who used a prep book and compares their scores. On average kids who took a prep course did seventy-five points better than kids who self-studied with a book. Can we conclude, then, that prep courses cause students to increase their test scores by seventy-five points compared with a book? Well, no.

While it *might* be the case that courses are better than books, we have to think about the other factors that contribute to higher SAT scores and are associated with a greater likelihood of a student taking a prep course. One of these factors is wealth; students from wealthier families tend to perform better on the SAT for a variety of reasons that add up over the course of their childhood. An SAT prep course can cost hundreds of dollars or more; meanwhile, a prep book costs about $20. It's safe to assume, then, that wealthy students, on average, are going to be more likely to take a prep course because they can afford it. But because they come from wealthier families, they were going to score higher on the SAT, on average, all along, regardless of whether they took a course or used a book.

So we don't know whether the seventy-five-point difference tells us that a course really is better, or that higher-scoring wealthy kids were overrepresented among course takers—or, most likely, some combination of the two.

In this case, we say that wealth *confounds* the relationship between prep courses and test scores (alternatively, we simply say that wealth is a "confounder").

There are two ways we can avoid such confounders in research. First, if we can readily measure these factors—*every single one of them*—we can statistically adjust for them in our analyses. After this adjustment, what remains is the effect we're trying to quantify. We do this by measuring the relationship between the confounders and the outcome we care about (so for instance, wealth and SAT score) and summing them together. If we have accounted for *every single* confounding factor, we can estimate to what extent the exposure of interest *caused* a change in an outcome. In our example, if we know how much wealth alone leads to better SAT scores, we can separate that effect out from the specific effect, if any, of the prep course.

But if we can't quantify the effect of every possible confounder, we can't adjust for them. The only way we can account for unmeasured confounding factors is through the second option: randomization. When patients are randomly assigned to either an intervention or a control group, as in the randomized trials that determine the effectiveness of most of the medications we use, it breaks apart any existing relationships between the intervention and its potential confounders. This includes factors we can easily measure, like age, and ones we can't measure or may not even know about—factors like a patient's education, income, or family support, all of which may be correlated with both medication use and outcomes.

Returning to our SAT example, even if we were able to account for parental wealth, what about parental education, parental occupation, or quality of local schools, to name just three? All of these likely influence SAT scores too. Confounders like these are like pests: When there's one, there are often many. So many, in fact, that when one conducts an analysis, it can be impossible to get rid of them.

So, if we really want to know the effect of a prep course on SAT scores, randomization is the way to go. As long as kids are assigned to groups randomly and we have enough of them, we should end up with similar numbers of wealthy kids (and kids born to parents with different levels of education, and who attend different schools) in each group. When groups are balanced through randomization, it means that any effect of wealth—or of *any* factor, known or unknown—will also be balanced between the two groups. At the end of the experiment, we can thus attribute any differences between the two groups to the factor we purposefully wanted to be different (in this case, prep course versus prep book).

In other words, randomization allows us to establish causation.

In 2012, researchers in Stockholm, Sweden, wanted to understand the effect of early bystander CPR, so they conducted a randomized trial. After recruiting several thousand CPR-trained volunteers, they used a mobile phone positioning system that could determine if their volunteers were within five hundred meters of a patient with cardiac arrest. If so, a volunteer could be summoned to the scene. In the experiment, when an emergency call for a cardiac arrest came in, patients were randomly assigned to a group. Either a nearby volunteer would be notified to help them until EMS arrived (the intervention group), or the emergency would run its usual course without the assistance of a volunteer (the control group).

A total of 667 cardiac arrests were recorded. Of those, 306 were randomly assigned a volunteer to assist them. The remaining 361 received the usual care of waiting for an ambulance to arrive. Not surprisingly, bystander CPR was more likely to take place when a volunteer was dispatched than when one was not (62 percent in the intervention group versus 48 percent in the control group), highlighting the ability of mobile technology to enhance rates of bystander CPR. In the final telling, survival was higher in the group with dispatched volunteers than in the controls (11.2 percent versus 8.6 percent), though not enough to rise to the level of statistical significance. It's certainly an encouraging finding in support of the idea that early CPR can improve mortality rates, however, and a larger study would be required to establish it more firmly.

The power of a study like this one and the marathon study is not to simply confirm what we already know, that timing is critical when it comes to cardiac emergencies. Anyone who has spent a day in the emergency department can tell you that. Their power is in the ability to *quantify* these effects. They put real numbers on the value of acting quickly, spelled out in minutes and seconds, in life and death. It is only with figures such as these that legislators, city planners, and hospital administrators can most effectively decide how best to allocate those other numbers around which lives too often depend: dollars and cents.

—

First responders are often thrown into hectic situations where the best path forward isn't clear. Part of the heroism of their work is their ability to stay focused and get the job done amid chaos, confusion, and uncertainty. They are forced to make rapid decisions on the fly—many with potentially grave consequences—that are often far more complex than which detour they should take.

We've so far treated EMS teams as though they were all the same.

In fact, the ambulances that respond to the majority of 911 calls tend to fall within two categories: basic life support (BLS) and advanced life support (ALS).* Generally speaking, BLS ambulances are composed of emergency medical technicians, who are able to provide certain basic, noninvasive treatments as well as performing CPR if needed. ALS ambulances, meanwhile, tend to be staffed with EMTs and a paramedic. Because a paramedic has received advanced training, ALS ambulances are able to give IV medications; perform ECGs[†] and cardiac monitoring; and insert breathing tubes. ALS teams have more options to treat patients on the scene. BLS teams, meanwhile, have no choice but to bring patients to emergency departments for more advanced care. If a call comes in to a 911 dispatcher for a cardiac arrest, their usual preference is to send an ALS team to the scene when available. But that's not always possible, and any ambulance is obviously better than none.

You can by now anticipate our question: Do ALS ambulances in fact lead to better outcomes than BLS ones? And if so, by how much?

In a study led by the University of Chicago health policy researcher Prachi Sanghavi, we (Bapu, along with the Harvard economist Joseph Newhouse, and the Harvard statistician Alan Zaslavsky) tried to get a sense of how BLS and ALS ambulances might differ when it comes to cardiac arrest patients. We began by diving into the Medicare data and identifying about thirty-three thousand cases of 911 calls for cardiac arrests. Of those, 5 percent were treated with BLS ambulances and 95 percent with ALS ambulances.

At first glance, the raw data contradicted our intuition. BLS transport was associated with a 13.1 percent survival, while ALS transport was associated with 9.6 percent survival—a difference of

---

* There are other types of specialized EMS teams that get involved in certain situations, but they are much less common than typical BLS and ALS teams.

† An ECG, or electrocardiogram (you may be more familiar with the abbreviation EKG, a nod to the German physicians who developed the *Elektrokardiogramm*), is a measurement of the electrical activity of the heart, which is altered during most severe cardiac emergencies. A trained eye can detect life-threatening heart problems on an ECG.

3.5 percentage points *in favor of basic teams*. What were we to make of these numbers? Why would patients treated by more advanced practitioners be more likely to die?

First, we needed to rule out the confounders. Was it possible that patients treated by BLS were more likely to survive to begin with? Perhaps they were less extreme cases, and that's why a BLS team was assigned to them. We performed an adjusted analysis by matching ALS cases and BLS cases who we estimated would have been equally likely to be treated by an ALS ambulance.* Even after this adjustment, the results were similar: survival with BLS was estimated to be 3.9 percentage points higher than patients with ALS teams.

There were other factors that might be confounding the results. It's possible that ALS ambulances were more likely to respond to calls for the sickest patients, people who were less likely to survive to begin with. This is always a possibility when we lack a randomizing event (such as a marathon), and we couldn't discount it.

But was it possible that ALS teams were doing something inadvertently harmful, something that BLS teams either couldn't or weren't?

When ALS teams arrive on the scene of a cardiac arrest, they have a choice to make: stay and work to restart the patient's heart using their advanced treatments before loading them into the ambulance and heading to the hospital, *or* load them up immediately and continue resuscitation in the ambulance. This choice—slangily referred to as "stay and play" versus "scoop and run"—isn't always easy. On the one hand, treating patients prior to transport allows EMS teams to provide high-quality CPR early, when chances of restarting a

---

* This method, known as "propensity score matching," uses a prediction model to try to create counterfactual groups who we think, at the outset, are equally likely to receive a treatment but then, by chance, either receive it or don't. Among individuals who had a similar predicted likelihood of receiving an intervention—say, ALS services—we then look at the differences in outcomes between those who received the intervention (ALS patients) and those who did not (BLS patients). Unfortunately, this technique doesn't make for perfect natural experiments, since our matching is only as good as the model we create, and there's no natural randomization available to help us account for influencing factors we don't know or don't measure.

heart are highest. And as we've seen, getting started earlier seems to confer an advantage on patients. But if the underlying reason for the cardiac arrest is, say, a massive heart attack, loading them up immediately to get to the hospital soonest, where a major intervention could be staged, might be the sounder option.

In a separate study of about 44,000 patients with cardiac arrests across North America, a research team based at the University of British Columbia looked at differences in the survival of patients who were treated at the scene ("stay and play") versus those transported while still in cardiac arrest ("scoop and run"). Of the forty-four thousand, about 74 percent were resuscitated at the scene, with the remaining 26 percent brought to the hospital in cardiac arrest. They drilled down into each group and found that of those resuscitated on the scene, 12.6 percent would go on to survive their hospitalization. Only 3.8 percent of those transported during their cardiac arrest survived—a significant difference in survival rates, seemingly suggesting that "stay and play" might be the more effective course.

As in the last study, however, researchers had to account for the possibility that those who were successfully resuscitated at the scene were more likely to survive all along, compared with those who could not be and were therefore transported to the hospital while in cardiac arrest. So they also matched patients who they estimated were equally likely to be treated on the scene versus immediately brought into the hospital and compared their outcomes. After this adjustment, they estimated that those treated on the scene had survival rates 4.6 percentage points higher than those transported during their cardiac arrest. The results of this study suggested that the "stay and play" approach—an approach really only available to ALS teams—was better than the "scoop and run" approach.

It's hard to reconcile these two studies, one that seemed to favor "scoop and run" and the other that seemed to favor "stay and play." Both studies are subject to the same limitation: they lack a true randomizing event that would let us account for the confounding factors that might be skewing our results. Given these murky research findings, it's hard to conclude that EMS teams who choose to sometimes "stay and play" and sometimes "scoop and run," based on their training, their experience, and their evaluation of the patient in front of them, aren't making good decisions.

The ambiguity only underscores the importance of natural experiments. When we take advantage of naturally occurring randomness, we can worry less about what our predictive models might be missing and be more confident in the conclusions our studies lead us to.* The challenge, as ever, is uncovering those randomizing events in the wild—which is why our antennas are ever tuned toward finding them.

———

So far we've looked at the way that minutes matter when it comes to cardiac events. But heart attacks and cardiac arrests are unlike many other medical conditions in the way that they tend to appear as sudden discrete events that require immediate care. But figuring out how quickly we need to act when it comes to *other* medical issues isn't always straightforward. Getting the timing of care just right is, in fact, a big part of the "art" of medicine. When we care for patients in the hospital who have multiple ongoing problems, we frequently choose which tests and treatments to prioritize and which to delay, since only so many things can be done at once. In electing to pursue one treatment first, we necessarily delay the other.

Take a primary care doctor seeing a patient who reports one week of fatigue. There are many, many conditions that lead to fatigue. A doctor can narrow down the possibilities quite a bit by inquiring about the patient's health, circumstances, or recent exposures to potential infections, but they'll still be faced with the question of what testing to do and, significantly, when to do it. Does that test-

---

* This being said, in a follow-up study looking at a number of conditions, including heart attacks, we took advantage of regional variation in the availability of ALS ambulances, hypothesizing their greater availability in a region would increase the likelihood that a given patient would receive an ALS ambulance compared with an otherwise-similar patient who lived in a region where ALS was less available. We found higher mortality with ALS for trauma, stroke, and heart attacks than with BLS and no differences for severe breathing problems. See Sanghavi et al., "Outcomes of Basic Versus Advanced Life Support for Out-of-Hospital Medical Emergencies."

ing need to happen immediately or can it wait a few days, to see if the fatigue resolves on its own? Does any rigorous evidence exist to guide that decision, or must a doctor rely on intuition and experience alone?

Watchful waiting—offering a "tincture of time," as some doctors call it—is often the right course; many conditions get better on their own. Waiting can not only reduce the risks of unnecessary care for patients who don't need it (more on this in the chapters to come) but also provide useful diagnostic information, since observing whether a patient gets better or worse over time can help us figure out what might be going on in their bodies. Of course, delaying care for too long comes with its own risks, and they can be severe. Fatigue is associated with cancers, infections, and depression, to name just a few major ailments. Balancing the risks of rapid care with the risks of delays is a core component of medical decision making.

In the ICU, for instance, we know that if a patient has a bacterial infection that's so severe it's causing sepsis, it's best to give them antibiotics within minutes. But if their case is less severe and they don't have sepsis—perhaps they are feeling well enough to be sent home—how long can a doctor wait before administering antibiotics? A few minutes? A few hours? A day or two? Does the patient need antibiotics at all? Each type of infection is different, and the research informing our decisions in any given situation is often lacking, so generally we opt for sooner rather than later.

The same uncertainty exists for cancer. Most cancers would ideally be treated sooner rather than later, but only some are considered medical emergencies that need treatment immediately (during the weekend even, if that's when a diagnosis is made). For other cancers, how long exactly can we wait to provide treatment before harmful effects set in? A day or two? A week? Two weeks?

Or what about a patient who falls and fractures their hip? They may need it surgically repaired, but often these surgeries don't need to be performed immediately. If the surgery schedule is busy, patients may have to wait to have their hip repaired. But how long is too long? A few hours or a few days?

In most cases, the answer to such questions is frustratingly opaque.

But now that you're a budding expert in thinking about how chance phenomena can guide us toward better health care, you have a sense of the situations that might offer us clarity. So, let's put those skills to work. Let's brainstorm how natural experiments could be helpful in determining the timing with which medical care needs to occur, an issue all of us will face at one time or another.

Let's start with pneumonia, which is often treated with antibiotics and can have grave consequences if left untreated. A question we might pose: Should someone with mild pneumonia receive antibiotics at all? And should they be admitted to the hospital immediately, or can we wait and see for a day or two? In the absence of a randomized trial, which is ethically problematic for reasons you by now can imagine, how could we find an answer? Are there naturally occurring events that might hasten or delay *some* pneumonia sufferers in seeking treatment?

One idea would be to rely on the human tendency not to seek medical care on holidays, days in which most people would rather be at home with friends and families, even if they aren't feeling too well. For patients with milder cases of pneumonia, a three-day weekend (like Memorial Day or Labor Day) might delay their care until the Tuesday after. Could we compare patients who come in with pneumonia on a Tuesday following a holiday weekend with those who come in on other Tuesdays, assuming that some number of the patients who come in on "holiday Tuesday" will have delayed their care one to two days? If a one-to-two-day delay in care for pneumonia actually affects outcomes, we should see that patients who come in with pneumonia on Tuesdays after a holiday should be in quantifiably worse shape (maybe they're more likely to be admitted to an ICU) than pneumonia patients who come in on a typical Tuesday.

How about cancer? Some cancers grow slowly over many years, so when they're found, it's often not an emergency to treat them (unlike acute leukemias, which require more immediate treatment once diagnosed). An oncologist or surgeon may determine that treatment can wait. But without a randomized trial, how can we know for sure if a delay—a day, a week, a month—puts the patient at risk for worse outcomes? Here, again, natural experiments could come to our rescue. For patients with cancer, arbitrary factors may ultimately determine how long a patient has to wait before getting treatments—delays such as when an appointment is available at a cancer center. Could we compare two groups of patients with the same type of cancer, one group who got treated while a cancer center was undergoing repairs, forcing longer wait times, another who got care at regular times?

Or here's another idea. Several times a year, new cancer drugs are approved, suddenly becoming available to oncologists and patients. Let's say a new drug came out that's a game changer, offering an add-on treatment for a cancer that's otherwise difficult to manage. Many oncologists will want to give it to their patients as soon as it's available. Patients who were diagnosed with this cancer *after* the drug was approved will have gotten the drug right away, since it was available when their treatment began. But patients who were diagnosed a month *before* the approval date won't get it until they're one month into their preexisting course of treatments; patients diagnosed two months before the approval date will have to wait two months to get the new drug. Since the timing of the approval and availability of the drug is unrelated to the timing of these patients' cancer diagnoses, a natural experiment is created wherein patients are "assigned" a delay of zero, one, or two months. By comparing the outcomes of these groups, we can estimate the effect of delaying treatment with this powerful new drug.

And finally, hip fractures. When a patient falls and breaks their hip, it can, in severe enough cases, require surgical repair. However, most of these surgeries don't need to be performed on the spot. Existing clinical trials suggest they should be done within forty-eight hours. If we wanted to see the effect of a shorter delay—say, twelve hours—we could compare the outcomes of patients who break their hip while one of the hospital's orthopedic surgeons is out of town on vacation—increasing the overall wait times for surgery—with those who break their hip while no surgeons are on vacation.

These are just ideas, and none of them is perfect. Patients who can wait until Tuesday for pneumonia care may be delaying their care because they're simply less sick. It could be that the cancer center repairs delayed care by only a single day—not long enough to lead to any measurable differences. An orthopedic surgeon going on vacation might not have the effect on scheduling that we expected. Regardless, these examples help demonstrate the way that we've come to think as researchers steeped in the world of natural experiments. Because as we've seen, finding the answer we're looking for often starts with learning how to ask the right question.

—

In the next chapter, we're going to visit the next phase of care for cardiac emergencies: hospital care by cardiologists. This time, we won't be focusing on the timing of care but instead make good on one of our ideas above by asking the question, What *does* happen when the doctor you really need is out of town?

CHAPTER SIX

WHAT HAPPENS WHEN ALL THE CARDIOLOGISTS LEAVE TOWN?

WHILE IN MEDICAL school, doctors in training are expected to absorb a daunting amount of information, encompassing all that's known about the human body, its normal function, and its disease states. The process was often likened by our instructors to drinking water from a fire hose, and having been on the business end of the spray, we can say the analogy rings true.

One way we doctors make it easier to remember critical information is through storytelling. Facts and figures are easier to recall when they're attached to a specific (often hypothetical) patient in a specific situation with specific details and a specific treatment plan. These "clinical vignettes" serve as anchoring points as we learn new topics, whether they're recognizing the signs and symptoms of lupus or treating type 2 diabetes.

In that time-honored spirit, then, let's start this chapter with a vignette. Its subject is fictional but based on real patients we've cared for over the years. Let's call her Roberta.

Roberta is a seventy-seven-year-old woman who lives in a small two-bedroom house in the suburbs. For her age, she's in reasonably good health. She smoked for about ten years but quit when her first child was born; she has high blood pressure, for which she takes medication; and she's about fifteen pounds overweight.

One Sunday morning in autumn, she decides it's finally time to rake the leaves in her front yard and heads outside. But after about twenty minutes, she's breathless and takes a break. Five minutes of rest and then Roberta gets back to raking, but soon she becomes breathless yet again. She opts to power through—until she suddenly feels a squeezing sensation in her chest and becomes very nauseated. She sits down on the ground, pulls out her phone, and calls 911. While she waits for paramedics to arrive, Roberta remains seated, the crushing sensation in her chest persistent.

An ambulance, sirens wailing and lights flashing, pulls up to her home. A paramedic and an EMT quickly load her into the ambulance. Her heart is beating rapidly, but her blood pressure is normal. They ask her about her allergies and medical history— just high blood pressure, she says—before sticking electrodes to her chest to perform an ECG, an electrocardiogram, to analyze her heart's electrical activity.

"Ma'am, it looks like you might be having a heart attack," the paramedic tells Roberta after reading a printout from the ECG. "We're going to take you to the nearest major hospital as fast as possible where they can treat this. In the meantime, I need you to chew and swallow this aspirin," he says, handing Roberta a small tablet. Worried she might die, Roberta chews the pill and squeezes the paramedic's hand.

The ambulance radios ahead to a nearby university-affiliated teaching hospital, which treats most heart attacks in the region. Roberta's symptoms aren't any better by the time they arrive, when, in a frenzy of activity, she is whisked out of the ambulance and into the emergency department. There, doctors and nurses are at the ready. The paramedics relay the events to the cardiologist, a young doctor in a bright, freshly starched white coat.

"We're going to take good care of you," she says, "I promise." The cardiologist then explains to Roberta that she might need to undergo an invasive procedure for her heart, which right now appears to have reduced blood flow due to a partial blockage, caus- ing her heart attack.

"Are you sure?" Roberta asks, nervous at the prospect.

"We're going to run some additional tests. Depending on the results, you might not need it."

Roberta nods in anxious understanding.
"My colleague who usually does the procedure is actually out
of town at a research conference," the cardiologist adds in passing.
"But if you need the procedure, rest assured, we can get it done."
"Okay," Roberta replies hesitantly. "Do what you have to do."

—

According to the Events Industry Council, a trade group focusing on special events, more than one billion people worldwide take part in conventions, conferences, major meetings, or business events each year, contributing to a multitrillion-dollar industry. Maybe you've been to one of these yourself: as one of a few dozen small businesses at a local trade show; as one of a few hundred engaged couples looking for a photographer at a regional wedding expo; or as one of tens of thousands of comic enthusiasts at the annual Comic-Con convention in San Diego.

At their best, such conventions can offer an informative and exciting window into a world of people, products, and services—so much so that it can be easy for attendees to forget about what might be going on back at home. At their worst, with their labyrinthine rows and fluorescent lighting, conferences allow you to imagine how mice in laboratory studies must feel.

Tens of thousands of doctors attend professional conferences each year, usually put on annually by large organizations in their specialty. These can be a lot of fun: catching up with old friends and colleagues, attending lectures from leading experts, presenting research, even participating in hands-on workshops with cutting-edge medical devices. (We grant that these might not fit a universally accepted definition of "fun.") They also offer a great excuse for busy physicians to visit popular tourist destinations and do some sightseeing, often in the company of their families.

Two large cardiology societies, the American Heart Association and the American College of Cardiology, put on conventions each year. As many as twenty thousand health professionals, many of them practicing cardiologists, attend these meetings. The same could be observed for other medical specialties, which together host hundreds of major meetings worldwide, routinely attracting thousands of doctors.

What that means for those of us back at home is a certain familiar experience: You're trying to get in touch with a fellow doctor, one whose patient requires care, only to find that they're out of town—in Las Vegas or New Orleans or Chicago—attending that year's event. Usually, those doctors have a colleague "covering" patients in their absence. This could be a more seasoned physician, one who for whatever reason opted not to attend, or it could be a more junior doctor who isn't going because they don't have research to present or lectures to give. Regardless of who stays and who goes, the result is fewer doctors left at home.

But patients don't stop having heart attacks just because there's a national cardiology meeting on the calendar. As you've seen, if a patient has a sudden heart attack and calls 911, EMS teams will do what they always do—rush the patient to the nearest hospital equipped to treat them. In many metropolitan areas, the hospitals with these specialized capabilities are large, academic medical centers.

Academic medical centers—like the one where we work—are "academic" because they are affiliated with medical schools. These large "teaching hospitals," as they're sometimes called, are generally where research-focused doctors practice medicine, and they tend to be where the latest treatments are made available first. Our own research may not involve developing the latest surgical techniques or novel cancer therapies, but we, like many others who work at academic centers, enjoy the atmosphere of discovery they foster, knowing that the next great breakthrough could be happening behind any door.

In cardiology, academic medical centers are where advanced treatments for heart problems are provided and improved upon. For patients with heart attacks, for example, these hospitals have a "cath lab," a specialized operating room where cardiologists with advanced training rapidly perform percutaneous coronary intervention, which involves stenting open coronary arteries to relieve the blockages that cause heart attacks. Some academic medical centers are considered "centers of excellence" for cardiac care, providing not only specialized procedures but also doctors with expertise in managing complex heart problems like inadequate pump function (heart failure) or disruptions in the heart's electrical activity (arrhythmias).

Just like any workplace, when colleagues are away—whether at a conference, on parental leave, on jury duty, or out sick—miscommunications, mistakes, and oversights are sure to follow. And since we're talking about medicine, the implications may be more serious than a flubbed deadline.

Common sense might suggest that, in general, having fewer doctors around is a bad thing. We know, for example, that on weekends, when hospital staffing is low, outcomes are worse for patients with medical emergencies, including heart attacks. But is having fewer doctors around *always* a bad thing? And what can cardiology conferences reveal to us about the answer?

Let's start our examination by rewinding the clock forty years. In 1983, doctors in Jerusalem embarked on one of the largest physician strikes in history. For about four months, doctors stopped providing everything but critical hospital services as they bargained with the government over their wages. Elective procedures were delayed, and only outpatient care was provided in several impromptu aid stations set up around the city.

There were, all at once, far fewer doctors around Jerusalem's hospitals. And because the timing of the strike couldn't reasonably be associated with the health of their patients—they didn't go on strike due to a sudden change in the health of the population—the conditions for a natural experiment arose. Patients who happened to get sick just before or just after the strike were a control group, treated at a time when the normal amount of care was offered. Those who happened to get sick during the strike were an intervention group. Did fewer doctors mean worse care for this latter group?

In a study that examined death records, a team of researchers from Hebrew University of Jerusalem found that, surprisingly, there was no great change in the number of deaths during the strike compared with just before or just after, or for that matter compared with the same time period the year before. The absence of doctors other than for critical services didn't lead to any marked increase in mortality (though patients might have suffered in other ways and delays in care could have had effects that weren't immediately apparent).

Surprising though they are, these findings aren't unique; in the time between that 1983 Israeli strike and today, studies of other physician strikes around the world have also found that mortality either stays the same or even *goes down* during strikes,* leading many to conclude that, in general, more doctors doesn't mean better health (provided essential services remain available).

What does this all mean for our fictional patient Roberta, whose heart attack brought her to the hospital during the few days in which a national cardiology meeting was being held? Is her anxiety about the absent cardiologist well founded? Or should she be . . . relieved?

—

Cardiology conferences appeared to present us with a great opportunity to learn what effect the presence of fewer doctors has on patient outcomes. But before starting, we (Bapu, along with the UCSF oncologist and health policy researcher Vinay Prasad and the USC economists Dana Goldman and John Romley) had to ask the essential question: Were the conditions met here for a natural experiment?

In the last chapter, our natural experiment depended on the assumption that patients with cardiac arrests or heart attacks were getting sick *regardless of whether there was a marathon that day.* In the study of the Israeli physician strike, we assumed that patients who got sick would have done so *whether or not there was a strike.* Only if those conditions were met could deviations from the norm be attributed to the marathon or the strike.

Here, our natural experiment depended on a similar assumption: that patients who had a heart attack during the dates of these conferences would have had heart attacks *whether or not their cardiologist*

---

* It's hard to say exactly why mortality might go *down* during a strike, but it could be due to a stoppage of things like elective or semi-elective procedures—which carry small, but real, risks of death—or delays in other types of care that carry risk.

was out of town at a meeting. Is this a safe assumption? We certainly thought so. Is there any reason to think a patient who had a heart attack while raking the leaves would not have had the heart attack (or not raked the leaves) if they'd known their would-be cardiologist—a doctor they had likely never met—was out of town? It seems highly doubtful. There's every reason to believe that the timing of cardiology meetings is completely unrelated to the odds of patients back at home having heart attacks—conditions that occur suddenly and are notoriously difficult to anticipate.

We were ready to dive into the numbers. We looked at ten years of data. In that time, twenty major cardiology conferences had been held, one each year for the American Heart Association and the American College of Cardiology. To look at what happens to patients with acute cardiac problems, we again turned to Medicare recipients. We examined hospitalizations for heart attacks, cardiac arrests, or heart failure from around the country from 2002 to 2011. For each hospitalization, we noted the date when the patient arrived at the hospital, whether they had a specialized heart procedure (like cardiac stenting or bypass graft surgery), and whether the patient died within thirty days of being hospitalized.

We then looked at when these hospitalizations occurred in relation to the American Heart Association and American College of Cardiology's annual meetings. Those treated during the meetings would be our treatment group, those treated before or after would be our control. To try to make our control group as similar as possible to our treatment group, we considered just those patients hospitalized with heart problems in the three weeks immediately before and immediately after each meeting. Overall, we analyzed more than 200,000 patients.

Our first order of business was to ensure that the patients who were hospitalized during meeting and nonmeeting dates were otherwise similar, and it turns out they were basically indistinguishable: both groups were about evenly split between males and females; their average age was seventy-nine; their racial breakdown was comparable; and they had similar rates of preexisting conditions such as heart disease, diabetes, kidney disease, high blood pressure, and high cholesterol—all conditions that put them at risk for acute heart problems.

We anticipated that there might be differences in mortality depending on how high risk the patient was (meaning how likely they were to die from their cardiac problem). Higher-risk patients—generally patients with more preexisting conditions—would be more likely to need a complex intervention, and thus could be more affected by cardiologists going out of town. So, based on the patients' preexisting conditions, we also divided patients into "low risk" and "high risk" groups.

The preliminary analysis supported our assumption that patients in the two groups were at equal risk of having an acute heart problem, regardless of whether a cardiology meeting was taking place. In other words, the preconditions for a natural experiment had been met. We could now reasonably infer that any difference in death rates between the two groups could be attributed to differences in the care they received.

What did we find?

Let's start with the "high risk" patients.

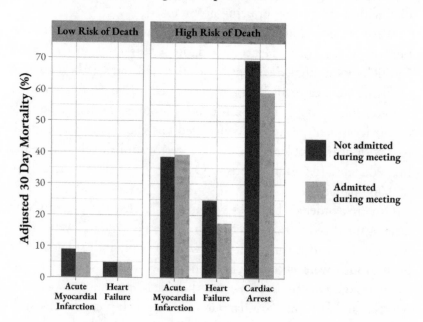

For the six thousand or so patients in this high-risk group with either heart failure or cardiac arrest, mortality was significantly *lower* when patients were hospitalized during the dates of national cardiology meetings compared with the nonmeeting dates. This bears restating: high-risk patients who were seen at a time when fewer doctors were in town were *more* likely to survive their treatment than the same patients seen when the regular roster of doctors was working. The difference was meaningful, too. High-risk heart failure patients had a thirty-day mortality rate of about 25 percent on nonmeeting dates. It dropped to 17 percent on meeting dates. Put differently, the findings suggest that for every hundred high-risk heart failure patients who came into the hospital on a meeting date, about eight survived who would have died had they come in on a nonmeeting date. We found similarly meaningful effects in patients with cardiac arrest. High-risk patients with cardiac arrest who came in on nonmeeting dates had a mortality rate of 69 percent compared with 59 percent for patients who came in on meeting dates. Mortality for heart attacks, meanwhile, appeared to remain more or less constant.

The next question: Did the care that patients receive differ? It turns out it did. We found that the use of cardiac stenting (an invasive procedure to improve blood flow to the heart for heart attack patients) fell from 28.2 percent of high-risk patients on nonmeeting dates to 20.8 percent of patients on meeting dates.

As we noted earlier, these findings represented treatment that took place at academic medical centers only. For the approximately fifty thousand high-risk patients not treated at academic medical centers—who were cared for at community hospitals—we found no difference in mortality rates between the meeting and the nonmeeting groups. We assumed from the start that cardiologists at teaching hospitals were those most likely to attend conventions; they're the doctors striving to be at the forefront of their field, the ones at whom conventions are aimed. The difference in results between teaching and community hospitals lends credence to the idea that *something* about the cardiology care at teaching hospitals was changing during meetings. The difference in staff seemed to us the most likely culprit.

To summarize the results so far: In the academic centers where many researchers are located, higher-risk patients seemed to do better while those cardiologists were away. This was an interesting initial result. But to be more confident in these conclusions, we had more work to do.

To prove that our findings were indeed due to cardiology conferences, we ran the analyses under different scenarios. First, we checked whether the outcomes for cardiac patients were a consequence of cardiology meetings specifically, and not doctor meetings in general. As expected, there was no change in death rates from heart problems when orthopedists, cancer doctors, and gastroenterologists were out of town. Cardiology meetings were the instigator of these changes.

Second, we wanted to see whether our findings were reflective of hospital-wide changes in outcomes—broader changes in mortality that just happened to occur, year after year, during cardiology meetings. While cardiologists are essential for a functional hospital, they aren't involved in the care of the majority of patients in a hospital; it seemed unlikely to us that cardiology meetings could disrupt care of patients treated by other types of doctors. But better safe than sorry. We ran another analysis, this time using the original cardiology meeting dates but looking at death rates from *non-heart* conditions—hip fractures, stomach bleeding, and so on—to see if there were any differences in outcomes for these conditions during cardiology meetings. Again, unsurprisingly, there were not. Cardiology meetings were affecting cardiac patients alone.

The biggest question remained: Why? Why did high-risk cardiac patients at academic medical centers have lower mortality during the dates of national cardiology meetings, at a time when cardiologists were *more* likely to be out of town and when *fewer* specialized procedures were performed?

We were feeling more and more certain the answer resided within the doctors themselves. To find out more, we would need to drill down into the cardiologists and their practice habits.

—

For a new analysis, we (Bapu, Andrew Olenski, Dana Goldman, John Romley, and the Harvard cardiologists and health policy researchers Daniel Blumenthal and Robert Yeh) again looked at Medicare patients, but this time we narrowed our group down to just patients who showed up with heart attacks at academic medical centers. We wanted to look at a specific type of cardiologist as well, called interventional cardiologists. These are the ones most often called upon to perform specialized interventions on the heart, such as coronary artery stenting, in patients with heart attacks. (General cardiologists don't typically perform these procedures.) We wanted to understand what happened to patients hospitalized with heart attacks during the dates not of national cardiology conferences but of interventional cardiology meetings. We hoped the focus would allow us to pinpoint exactly how care was changing when these doctors were away.

So we looked at two different types of heart attacks: major heart attacks that almost always need special procedures (called ST-elevation myocardial infarctions, or STEMIs), and less severe ones that only sometimes need special procedures (non-STEMIs). Now to be clear, these "less severe," non-STEMI heart attacks are still a big deal. Just like STEMIs, they're life-threatening medical emergencies that require prompt treatment, that are properly frightening to patients, and that represent serious underlying heart disease. The reason cardiologists distinguish between the two is that the blockages that occur in non-STEMIs tend to be less complete than those in STEMIs and undertaking a risky procedure for an incomplete blockage may not be the best answer.

Our findings: patients who had non-STEMIs—where the decision about whether to perform a procedure is more subjective—were less likely to receive cardiac stenting *and* had lower mortality rates during interventional cardiology meetings.

So when an older patient came to an academic medical center with a non-STEMI heart attack during the dates of a national cardiology meeting—a patient very much like our Roberta, in other words—they were less likely to undergo a procedure and more likely to be alive thirty days later.

This is probably not what Roberta thought when she was approached by the cardiologist in the suspiciously unblemished lab coat.

How profound are the effects we're describing? On their face, it would be easy to dismiss them. Patients who had these less severe heart attacks had a mortality rate of 13.9 percent on meeting dates compared with 15.9 percent on nonmeeting dates—a 2-percentage-point reduction. Interestingly, this improvement in mortality was driven solely by patients who did *not* undergo procedures; their mortality dropped from 19.5 percent to 16.9 percent during cardiology meetings. (Outcomes for patients who underwent procedures remained unchanged.)

The problem, in other words, was that certain patients were being given procedures when they'd have been better off with none.

What does a two-percentage-point improvement in death rates mean? For every fifty Medicare patients coming to a teaching hospital with a non-STEMI heart attack, one of them will survive if they happen to come in on a meeting date but will die if they come in on a nonmeeting date. If that isn't persuasive, consider this: a two-percentage-point reduction in mortality is similar in magnitude to some of *the best treatments we have available for heart attacks.* For example, clinical trials of patients of all ages hospitalized with severe heart attacks (STEMIs) show that, compared with intravenous medications that improve blood flow to the heart (called thrombolytics), cardiac stenting decreases the death rate by an average of, yes, two percentage points. These invasive procedures, performed at considerable cost and risk, improve mortality at a level on par with change that takes place automatically during conferences.

We wanted to take one last step, in an attempt to learn more about the cardiologists in our study—the ones who left and the ones who stayed. There were some surface similarities. The interventional cardiologists were almost all men (95.4 percent of the doctors who attended meetings and 96.0 percent of those who stayed behind). Also, physicians in both groups had an average age of fifty-one, and they had been practicing medicine for similar amounts of time.

But there were major differences too: meeting attendees were more likely than "stayers" to have attended a highly ranked medical school (23 percent versus 15 percent), more likely to have led a clinical research trial (10.3 percent versus 3.9 percent), more likely to have gotten a research grant from the National Institutes of Health (5.3 percent versus 0.4 percent), and more likely to have published in medical journals (an average of nineteen publications versus six).

The other major difference between the interventional cardiologists who attended meetings and those who stayed behind was in the number of heart attack procedures they performed annually. The stayers not only performed fewer cardiac procedures during those meetings; they performed fewer cardiac stenting procedures year-round: on average 39 percent fewer in Medicare patients annually, compared with cardiologists who attended meetings.

Consider whom you would choose to have treat you for a heart attack: the doctor with the top-ranked med school degree, the long list of publications, and the greater procedural experience? Or one of their seemingly less distinguished peers? Before this study, we might've been swayed by the impressive credentials. Now we can only conclude that for some patients the doctor who favors more invasive cardiac care not only may be providing unnecessary care but may be harming patients.

———

These studies were, in a word, controversial. Many cardiologists found the results implausible, and they weren't shy about saying so. Some thought the findings made for good cocktail party conversation but that they weren't actionable. *What would they have us do, have cardiology conferences year-round?* Not long after the initial study was released, the president of the American Heart Association expressed his own skepticism: "Bottom line for us at the American Heart Association: there's nothing in this study that we see that would lead us to recommend a change in clinical practice."

Critics aside, though, the findings had something to tell us. They convincingly showed that some forms of invasive cardiac care may be overused, in large part because cardiologists lack the precise guidelines to judge which patients will benefit from care and which won't. In an editorial that accompanied the study, the University of California, San Francisco cardiologist Dr. Rita Redberg wrote, "How should we interpret these findings? One possibility is that more interventions in high-risk patients with heart failure and cardiac arrest lead to higher mortality. Indeed, some high-risk interventions, such as balloon pumps or ventricular assist devices, are being used in populations in which they are not shown to improve outcomes."

—

All medical care, especially invasive procedures like cardiac stenting, entails both risks and benefits. Randomized controlled trials can help inform doctors about the types of patients for whom the benefits of a medical procedure will, on average, outweigh the risks. But what is true on average may not be true for the patient sitting in the exam room before you. Which is why doctors exercise their clinical judgment when deciding what treatments to offer.

Some clinical decisions are black and white: For a middle-aged adult without significant medical problems who has a particular type of severe heart attack, cardiac stenting will almost always be the right thing to do. But other decisions fall into gray areas: For an elderly woman with multiple medical problems who has the exact same type of heart attack, the risks of cardiac stenting *might* outweigh the benefits. And if some doctors tend to err on the side of stenting in such patients, it may well be that these patients are, on average, harmed by the procedure. For these patients, less may be more.

It's among the paramount questions in the practice of medicine, one we ask ourselves all the time: Do the benefits of this procedure, drug, or test outweigh the potential risk to the patient? Because each patient is unique, this can be a tough question to evaluate at the bedside, and two physicians might arrive at completely different answers (even when high-quality randomized trials are available, which often they are not). This too is part of the "art" of medicine.

Let's take a step back now. Suppose a cardiologist is presented, all at once, with two hundred heart attack patients and told they're allowed to perform cardiac stenting procedures on just fifty of them. While the decision of whom to prioritize might vary across doctors, a cardiologist could quite easily choose fifty patients out of the two hundred for whom the benefit of cardiac stenting would likely exceed the risks.

But of course, patients don't present themselves in this way and, crucially for our purposes, cardiologists don't face such constraints. The desire to help patients using the tools one has learned steers cardiologists—consciously and subconsciously—toward more, not less, care.

Doctors who err on the side of "doing more" will eventually perform procedures in patients for whom the benefit is *less* than the risk. When this happens, some patients may have worse outcomes than if no procedure had been offered at all. On the flip side, cardiologists who err on the side of "doing less" will eventually fail to perform procedures on patients who would have benefited from them.

As a doctor, you can be haunted by the counterfactual. Would a patient have been better off if I'd acted? If I hadn't?

———

What we're talking about here is a tendency toward *action* over *inaction*. The urge for doctors to give more care is generally stronger than the urge to give less. But it's not just doctors who are guilty of this thinking. In fact, if there's a problem that needs to be addressed, it's species-wide.

To take an example from a completely different professional sphere, consider the goalkeeper. In soccer, when a player is given a penalty kick, that player has the chance to kick the ball into the goal from just eleven meters away, without any opposition other than the goalkeeper. Once the ball is kicked, the goalkeeper's job is to block it from entering the goal. Reductively speaking, as a goalkeeper you have three choices: jump to one side, jump to the other side, or stay more or less put and defend the middle of the goal. Because penalty kicks are generally fired at the goal at impressive speeds and kickers are careful not to betray their true target through body language, a goalkeeper doesn't really have time to see which way the ball is going before taking action; a jump to either side is just a guess of where the opposing player might kick it.

In a study of 286 penalty kicks in top professional leagues, researchers found that the best strategy for preventing the most goals was for the goalkeeper to stay put, right in the middle. Despite this, goalkeepers jumped to one side or the other fully 94 percent of the time. When researchers surveyed goalkeepers, it was clear that one of the reasons they jumped is that it was their job to do *something* to try to block the ball.

Drs. Deborah Grady and Rita Redberg of the University of California, San Francisco have explored this tendency in doctors. "There are many reasons why clinicians in the United States may provide more care than is needed," they wrote in 2010 in *Archives of Internal Medicine.* "These include payment systems that reward procedures disproportionately compared with talking to patients, expectations of patients who equate testing and interventions with better care, the glamor of technology, that it may be quicker to order a test or write a prescription than explain to a patient why they are not being treated, and of course, defensive medicine. Another reason is 'technology creep.' After a device is approved for use with a high-risk population in which there is a proven benefit, its use often expands to lower-risk groups in which the benefit does not outweigh the risk."

This brings us back again to Roberta and cardiology meetings. Could it be that the cardiologists who attend these meetings are more likely to perform specialized medical procedures in situations where the procedures are more harmful than beneficial? Were these physicians falling victim to the bias characterized by the adage "when all you have is a hammer, everything looks like a nail," resulting in the unintentional overuse of care for some patients? And could the cardiologists who remain at home during meetings be less prone to those tendencies?

The data doesn't answer any of these questions definitively. Nor is it fair to lay the entirety of the blame at the meeting-attending doctors' feet. After all, it's possible that the reductions in cardiologist staffing and coverage that may occur during meeting dates contribute to fewer of certain specialized procedures being performed. What our studies allowed us to see, the way no randomized trial could, was a tendency toward a specific type of over-care that was silently in our midst.

—

Dr. Ashish Jha, dean of the Brown University School of Public Health and President Joe Biden's COVID-19 response coordinator, remembers when he first learned about the problems that can arise from excessive care. "My interest in healthcare quality was sparked when, as a medical student [in the 1990s], I started caring for patients on the hospital ward," he recalls. "It became clear to me very quickly that despite heroic efforts of terrific physicians and nurses, patients often failed to get the right care and too often, were injured by the care that was designed to help them."

The idea that less care can be better is not a new one, but it goes against our human intuition. If a heart attack is due to blockages in the arteries to the heart, how could it be a bad thing to open them up? If mammograms help find breast cancer and pap smears help find cervical cancer, how could it be possible to get them too often? In medicine, however, sometimes we can achieve better results with fewer tests, fewer procedures, or less information. But this can be an unpalatable notion for patients and doctors alike.

Metastatic lung cancer, for example, is severe lung cancer that has spread to other parts of the body. Sadly, patients with this advanced cancer have a very limited life expectancy after diagnosis since once the cancer has spread, it is difficult to cure and treatment options are limited. Many patients seek treatment to extend their lives (and new treatments have recently been developed that have improved life expectancy), but living with metastatic lung cancer can be difficult, painful, and uncomfortable.

Palliative care is a field of medicine focused on providing relief of uncomfortable symptoms. For patients with metastatic lung cancer, palliative care would involve treating symptoms such as shortness of breath, pain, anxiety, and others that contribute to lower *quality* of life while living with cancer; meanwhile, chemotherapy and other cancer-targeting treatments are often used for their ability to extend the *duration* of patients' lives.

In a widely discussed clinical trial published in 2010, the Harvard oncologist and palliative care researcher Jennifer Temel and her colleagues took a group of 151 patients who had just been diagnosed with metastatic lung cancer to see if incorporating palliative care services might help extend their lives. Shortly after their diagnosis, the patients were randomized to receive either (a) standard cancer care, with the option to receive palliative care at some point if desired, or (b) the same cancer care, but they would be connected with palliative care services right away so that these services would be available throughout their entire treatment course for cancer— not just later at the end of their lives.

After following these patients throughout the course of their cancer care, the study found that patients in the early palliative care group lived an average of 2.7 months longer than the patients who didn't get early palliative care (11.6 months versus 8.9 months). The early palliative care group also had improvements in their quality of life and mood. The kicker of this study—and why we bring it up now—was that the patients in the early palliative care group lived 2.7 months longer while also receiving *less aggressive cancer care* at the end of their lives, focused instead on simpler, symptom-based care. By having their symptoms alleviated through palliative care, patients were more comfortable *and* lived longer, with less unpleasant, risky, and costly chemotherapy.

Recognizing the difficulty of choosing less care, the American Board of Internal Medicine and Consumer Reports launched the Choosing Wisely campaign in 2012 to provide both doctors and patients with easy information about medical care that could be unnecessary or harmful. Their mission was to "promote conversations between clinicians and patients by helping patients choose care that is supported by evidence, not duplicative of other tests or procedures already received, free from harm, and truly necessary." To accomplish this, Choosing Wisely has published dozens of "top 5" lists of situations in many different areas of medicine in which "less is more." For example, they say, "Don't perform CT screening for lung cancer among patients at low risk for lung cancer." These screening scans—when done on the wrong patients—tend to cause more problems than they solve through false positive results or detecting real problems that may not *need* treatment but get treated anyway. Interestingly, the tendency applies just as well to disadvantaged patients, who may suffer from too much care in some areas and too little in others (such as preventive or mental health care).

If pressed, most physicians will admit that they err on the side of more medical care. We ourselves are not immune to it. We've given antibiotics when we were pretty sure an infection was viral and didn't require them; we've tested for all kinds of rare and exotic diseases, even when we knew the chances of the patient having the disease were extremely low (what some refer to as the "shotgun" approach to diagnosis); we've ordered CT scans of every part of the body without expecting to find anything, "just in case." Most of the time, this care ends up being unnecessary. But every once in a while, what is "unnecessary" yields a finding that saves a life, and the tendency toward more care is reinforced.

How do we solve this conundrum? As the Harvard cardiologist, writer, and national correspondent for *The New England Journal of Medicine* Dr. Lisa Rosenbaum has written, "Perhaps the most accurate conclusion is that sometimes less is more, sometimes more is more, and often we just don't know." It's a frustrating view of the situation, but as practicing doctors we can't deny its truth. All we can do is, through continued study and research, try to illuminate the gray areas, in hopes that in time they can be made more black and white.

In the meantime, we're reminded of a piece of med school advice from a seasoned trauma surgeon evaluating a clinically unstable patient—a quotation originally attributed to a 1940s theater producer frustrated with an overacting cast member: "Don't just do something; stand there!" Most doctors would have to acknowledge that this is sage advice, if hard advice to accept. Because when you're standing at the foot of a bed, looking at a patient facing life or death, and you're asked, "Doctor, what should we do?" often the hardest answer to give is, "Nothing. Let's just keep watching for now."

CHAPTER SEVEN

BIG DOCTOR IS WATCHING

I N 1924, THE Western Electric Company, in connection with the National Research Council of the National Academy of Sciences, launched a program to study factors that might contribute to plant worker productivity. Their initial experiments were focused on lighting in the company's factory, where researchers attempted to find the level of illumination that would result in the highest worker productivity. They started by comparing a handful of workers under constant illumination with an experimental group who had to work with the lights being progressively dimmed on different days. According to the research report, both groups' productivity increased over the course of the experiment—at least until the experimental group was no longer able to see what they were doing. At that point, unsurprisingly, their productivity fell, and they began to complain that they couldn't reasonably work under such conditions.

Other than discovering that, indeed, it's hard to work in the dark, researchers were somewhat perplexed by their results. They were able to conclude that lighting levels weren't a meaningful driver of worker productivity. But more interesting was that both groups *increased* their productivity levels over the course of many days. It suggested that there was some factor (or factors) common to both groups that was driving increased performance, but they weren't sure what it might be.

The researchers went on to test a number of factors, like varying break times and work hours, but none of them seemed to explain the increases in productivity, compared with baseline, that they saw over the course of their experiments. They posited that perhaps there was some aspect of the experiment itself that boosted productivity. Had workers and managers developed better working relationships as they participated in the research studies?

It was a different set of interpersonal relationships, though, that soon caught researchers' attention: the workers' rapport with the experimenters themselves. At first, they had seemed understandably wary of their observers—these scientists who had turned their factory into a lab, the workers into lab rats. But over time the workers became more comfortable with the research staff, just as their productivity improved.

It raised the question: Could the mere presence of observers have influenced study participants? Did they become more productive simply because they were being observed?

"Insomuch as the interviewer and the observer were a part of the situation they were studying," reads the report of the research done at the Hawthorne Works, "their relations with the operators and supervisors must also be considered. Of the two, the observer was much more closely associated with the operators and therefore was more likely to influence their behavior."

In the decades since the experiments were conducted, concerns have arisen surrounding the scientific validity of the Hawthorne studies, as well as their specific conclusions. Nevertheless, the idea that a research participant's awareness that they're being observed could cause them to behave in a way they otherwise wouldn't—a phenomenon that's become known as the Hawthorne effect—remains a consideration in research involving human subjects, and it's been amply demonstrated in other settings. While the size and the significance of the effect can vary from situation to situation, anyone who has quickly closed the celebrity gossip website when their boss walked by or decided to suddenly start flossing the day of their dental exam can attest to the idea's plausibility.

But what does the Hawthorne effect have to do with medicine?

—

To state the obvious, doctors aren't perfect. We know this, your doctor knows this, and if patients don't know it, they find out quickly enough. It doesn't take long for any health-care professional to realize it will be nearly impossible to get through a career in medicine without making some sort of error of consequence in the course of caring for patients. That doesn't stop us from trying to get as many things right as much of the time as possible, but because we are just as human as the patients we treat, perfection is a goal that is simply out of reach.

Errors come in different flavors. We've already talked about diagnostic errors, which can happen even when doctors have access to plenty of information but nonetheless arrive, for any number of reasons, at the incorrect conclusion. We may also err in our choice of treatment. A doctor might choose to treat a patient with a urinary tract infection using a standard antibiotic, only to find out from the lab two days later that the bacteria causing the infection was resistant to that antibiotic, rendering it ineffective against the infection. These are the types of errors that a doctor might look back upon and say, "Knowing what I knew at the time, I wouldn't have done anything differently."

Then there are errors that should theoretically always be avoidable, regardless of the complexity or uncertainty of a situation. For example, accidentally leaving a surgical instrument inside a patient during surgery, operating on the wrong body part, or transfusing the wrong blood type. But in a system composed of inherently error-prone human beings with millions upon millions of treatments given and tests performed every year, even these preventable errors occur with unfortunate frequency. Some may be of little to no consequence, while others can contribute to substantial harm to patients, even death.

This is not to say that we don't take great care to try to avoid such unforced errors. Layers of protection are in place to minimize the chance that one person's mistake will harm a patient. We use computerized systems and automated processes when beneficial. When we can't automate and risks are high, we have multiple people perform checks. For example, when we prescribe a medication in the hospital, the order is reviewed by both a pharmacist and a nurse before being given to a patient. With multiple layers of protection, a mistake getting through a hole in one layer should hopefully be caught by the next layer, something referred to as the Swiss cheese model of error prevention. Only when vulnerabilities in each layer are aligned does a mistake slip through every hole.

When patients are harmed despite all these efforts, the doctors, nurses, and other clinicians responsible often struggle with the psychological blow of having accidentally hurt someone they took an oath to help. Major errors generally have multiple contributing factors, but it can be hard for the individuals involved not to place responsibility squarely on their own shoulders.

In an incident at our hospital that was written up in *The New England Journal of Medicine*, "distractions that interfered with the surgeon's performance of routine tasks," alongside other factors, led to "deviation from rule-based behavior," ultimately causing a patient to receive the wrong surgery on her wrist. Though the correct surgery was performed shortly thereafter and the patient recovered well, she understandably lost trust in both the hospital and her surgeon, who described the incident as "devastating" to both his patient and himself. "I hope that none of you ever have to go through what my patient and I went through," he said in a conference with other physicians.

Suffice it to say that despite each individual health-care worker's efforts to avoid mistakes, the hospital remains a dangerous place. How could it not be? It's an institution run by humans, for humans. Hospitals know that the potential for error is lurking around every corner, making patient safety (both as a concept and as a discipline of professional practice) a progressively higher priority over the past several decades, as medical care has become more technologically advanced and complex.

In a pivotal work published in 1991, known as the Harvard Medical Practice Study, researchers reviewed the records of about thirty thousand randomly selected hospitalizations occurring in the state of New York during the year 1984. Their sample included all kinds of different patients, drawing from fifty-one randomly selected non-psychiatric hospitals across the state. Their goal was to estimate just how dangerous hospitals might be (or at least how dangerous they were back in 1984). At the time, rates of preventable adverse events weren't routinely measured—a particular problem when it came to medical malpractice lawsuits, since it was difficult for the legal system to determine whether adverse events were due to an individual's negligence or simply reflected broader failings of the health-care system.

Researchers scoured thousands of records. They were looking for unintentional injuries that were a direct result of medical care—specifically those that resulted in patients being discharged from the hospital with some level of disability.* Examples included collapsed lungs (pneumothorax) due to improper insertion of large IV catheters in the neck, falls from a hospital bed, or initial failure to diagnose an ectopic pregnancy.

What they found was sobering. Adverse events like these occurred in 3.7 percent of hospitalizations—which amounted to an estimated 98,600 adverse events in hospitals across the state of New York in

---

* Because the study was meant to inform litigation surrounding medical malpractice, they did not include incidents of medical errors that did not result in harm to patients. However, today's patient safety scholars pay close attention to these "near misses," since they tend to reveal an underlying unsafe process that, if left unaddressed, would likely eventually lead to actual harm to a patient.

1984. Of those, 13.6 percent contributed to a patient's death, while 2.6 percent contributed to permanently disabling injuries.

This landmark study, along with similar research, would ultimately help characterize the nature of preventable errors in the provision of hospital care. While definitions of the adverse events and the estimates of their frequencies would vary across studies, one thing was becoming unmistakably clear: preventable errors in the hospital were a pervasive, costly problem that was killing patients.

At the turn of the millennium, the National Academy of Medicine released two famous reports, titled *To Err Is Human: Building a Safer Health System* and *Crossing the Quality Chasm: A New Health System for the 21st Century,* that put together the results of research like the Harvard Medical Practice Study and many others. The reports challenged the status quo of hospital care and catalyzed the modern safety movement. *To Err Is Human* estimated that preventable medical errors lead to the death of somewhere between 44,000 and 98,000 patients every year in the United States, making preventable medical error a leading cause of death.

In addition to the harm done to patients, preventable errors were estimated to contribute to billions of dollars of additional healthcare spending annually. The reports called on the medical community to approach preventable errors and patient safety as a systemic problem, rather than a collection of isolated incidents. While identifying preventable errors is challenging enough, estimating the number of deaths they truly cause (as opposed to errors that occurred in a patient who died but were not the cause of death), and finding ways to prevent them, has also proven quite difficult. More recent estimates still suggest that at least tens of thousands of patient deaths are indeed caused by preventable medical errors each year.

If hospitals are supposed to be places of help and healing, why can they be such dangerous places for patients?

An honest rendering of the question first needs to acknowledge that hospital patients generally have an acute problem that sends them there, putting them at higher risk for harms from *any* care they may receive, good or bad. It also puts them at higher risk for the natural complications of their disease. On top of that, almost everything we do for hospitalized patients carries some sort of risk, even things that might seem harmless. Monitoring patients and doing blood tests carry risks of overdiagnosis, as we've discussed previously; observed abnormalities on a test might have us treating "problems" that aren't actual problems. Then, of course, there are the known risks and side effects of the care patients receive in the hospital, such as medication and surgery, that can include significant harm. When doctors proceed with these treatments, it's because they believe the potential benefits outweigh the potential risks—risks that can range from mild discomfort to severe disability or death.

The risks of medical errors are layered on top of these inherent risks. Fortunately, most errors don't have major consequences: most mistaken prescriptions don't end up doing harm, most falls don't lead to broken hips or head injuries, most surgical errors can be corrected. But as the saying goes, "Every system is perfectly designed to get the results it gets."* With humans at the helm, a certain amount of fallibility is unavoidable. Patient safety, therefore, has to focus on eliminating risks whenever possible and minimizing risk everywhere else.

———

The primary organization overseeing and regulating patient safety practices in U.S. hospitals is the Joint Commission,† which enforces a common set of standards designed to help minimize the risk of events that might harm patients. Hospitals earn an accreditation

---

* This quotation is often attributed to the renowned engineer and statistician W. Edwards Deming, and it is highly consistent with his teachings. However, this quotation most likely originated with the inventor Arthur Jones and was later adapted to the health-care system by the physician and health-care-quality scholar Paul Batalden, who cites Deming as a major influence. See IHI Multimedia Team, "Like Magic?"

† Formerly called the Joint Commission on Accreditation of Healthcare Organizations, or JCAHO (pronounced "jay-coh"), the Joint Commission is a nongovernmental organization that has historically been used by U.S. government programs like Medicare and Medicaid to ensure compliance with their patient safety standards before paying for patient care services rendered at a given hospital. As such, Joint Commission standards guide many patient safety practices at U.S. hospitals.

from the Joint Commission by way of unannounced visits by inspectors, who are given full access to the hospital for a week to assess its facilities and equipment, observe how patients are cared for, review operating procedures and protocols, and interview staff members about how they go about their work. Inspectors perform "tracers," following an individual patient around the hospital as they receive care, observing what happens to the patient throughout, and interviewing any staff member they want to about the daily processes in the hospital. For example, inspectors will check if operating room teams are following a standard protocol to ensure they're doing the right surgery on the right patient by performing a "time-out": a pause to say—out loud—the patient's identity, the surgery they're planning to do, and where on the body the procedure is to take place with the undivided attention of the entire OR team.

Unannounced Joint Commission inspections can be a stressful time for hospitals, particularly the administrators who oversee patient care operations and executives responsible for business operations. If the inspection goes poorly, the hospital can be cited for violations, or in the worst case, lose its accreditation, conferring on it considerable reputational and financial damage. Hospitals and their administrators are therefore incentivized to make sure staff are putting their best foot forward when inspectors show up for their weeklong inspections.

On their website, the American Nursing Association paints a picture that would sound familiar to anyone who has worked in a hospital when Joint Commission inspectors show up:

> All of a sudden, you hear "Code J" announced over the PA system—and the nightmare begins . . . "Peter, clear the hallways and hide the Christmas decorations in the storage room. Julie, make sure our I.V. sites and irrigation sets are dated. Cathy, check the charts . . ."

Having experienced Joint Commission inspections at numerous hospitals throughout our careers, we can attest that this account is by no means exaggerated. Obscure rules and regulations—like where we can and cannot leave our personal water bottles—suddenly become urgent. Protocols that may normally be followed "in spirit" are now followed to a T in case a clipboard-holding inspector strolls your way. Answers to potential questions an inspector might ask— like "Where do you keep chemical safety information?" or "What does it mean if a 'code pink'* is called?"—may be emailed out to staff as a reminder.

In sum, when staff find out that the Joint Commission has shown up to inspect them for the next five days, they know their behavior will be under a microscope. Having learned about the Hawthorne effect, you may sense where this is going.

—

How would hospital staff answer if we asked them, "Do you perform your job *differently* when inspectors are around?" We imagine most, if they were being honest, would say yes, they're aware that things often go a bit more "by the book" when inspectors are around. But if we followed up with a second question, "Do you perform your job *better* when inspectors are around?" we imagine most would say no; they'd reason that the quality of the care they provide isn't influenced by inspectors, and any changes they make are just little things designed to please them. So, if we really wanted to find out whether the Hawthorne effect was present and measurable in medicine, we'd need more than a survey. We'd need an experiment.

In a 2006 study, researchers in Germany decided to look into whether the Hawthorne effect influenced the behavior of doctors, nurses, and other hospital staff in the intensive care unit. Specifically, they wanted to see if staff working in five different ICUs were more likely to clean their hands with alcohol rub before and after contacting patients, as they're instructed to do, if they knew they were being watched. They started by sending in an "undercover" observer—a person whose normal job was to come to the unit and review medi-

---

* In many hospitals, "code pink" means that there is concern that a baby or child might have been abducted—fortunately a rare event—triggering a lockdown of the hospital and maternity ward until the child is located.

cal records and whose presence on the unit would not have been out of the ordinary. This covert observer watched ICU staff for a total of twenty hours, finding that they washed their hands 29 percent of the times they were supposed to (an unfortunately typical percentage for this type of study).

Months later, the observer returned, but this time ICU staff were informed that someone would be on the unit observing their "hygienic performance." During this announced period, the observer watched staff for another twenty hours and found that they washed their hands 45 percent of the times they were supposed to—a 55 percent relative increase.*

Based on this study alone, it would be hard to say whether an increase in hand hygiene might have resulted in better outcomes for the patients in these ICUs at these times, such as lower infection rates from bacterial spread, or even lower mortality rates. But what if the experiment conducted to study the Hawthorne effect wasn't done in just a handful of ICUs, and wasn't confined to hand sanitizing. What if, instead, *entire* staffs at hospitals across the country suddenly knew they were being watched? Would that lead to better focus and attention? Would they more closely adhere to safety protocols across the board, in every unit and operating room? And importantly, would it lead to better outcomes for hospitalized patients?

To answer these questions, we (Bapu, along with Michael Barnett and Andrew Olenski) turned to the data. Because Joint Commission inspectors make their visits unannounced—a way that is as good as random as far as patients are concerned—a natural experiment occurs at these times. And since we wanted to study what was happening to patients during their hospitalizations, we could turn to our trusty Medicare data, especially since older Americans make up a large share of hospitalized patients.

After their inspection is complete, the Joint Commission makes

---

* The increase was still present after statistical adjustment for potentially confounding factors like whether a staff member was a doctor or a nurse, or which of the five ICUs the event took place in.

public the dates of their accreditation inspections for every hospital they visited. This allowed us to isolate the weeks in which inspectors were present in a given hospital. The weeks before and after inspection offered a good counterfactual: they tell us *what would have happened* during the week of the inspection *had inspectors not been present.* We could therefore attribute any differences in what happened to patients during inspection weeks compared with non-inspection weeks to the effect of the inspection itself—the Hawthorne effect to a T.

Combining Joint Commission inspection dates with Medicare data, we were able to identify a total of 3,417 inspections in 1,984 different general medical-surgical hospitals from 2008 to 2012. This led us to a sample of about 250,000 hospital admissions during inspection weeks, occurring throughout the year, and about 1.5 million hospital admissions in the three weeks before and three weeks following the inspections.

Our main hypothesis was that because the entire hospital is aware that they are under inspection for the week that the Joint Commission is present, the behavior of hospital staff would change enough that there would be fewer adverse events like bedsores, infected intravenous catheters, or surgical complications, not to mention preventable deaths—things that Joint Commission regulations are designed to prevent. We also wanted to see if there were any differences between major academic/teaching hospitals—whose reputations as centers of excellence are on the line during inspections—and other hospitals.

One of our first steps was to see if the patients admitted to the hospital during the two periods were similar, to confirm that they could reasonably serve as counterfactuals to each other. Indeed, we found no meaningful differences in age, sex, race, rates of chronic conditions (such as diabetes or atrial fibrillation), or rates of acute problems (such as stroke or heart attack) for patients admitted during inspection weeks compared with the surrounding weeks. That makes intuitive sense. Most patients have probably never heard of the Joint Commission, and they wouldn't know when an inspection was occurring. It seems highly unlikely they would base their decision to seek medical care at a given hospital on a given day based on whether an inspection was occurring.

Next, we looked at thirty-day mortality rates[*] for patients admitted to the hospital during each of the seven weeks we wanted to study—the three weeks before the inspection, the week of the inspection, and the three weeks after.

For patients admitted to the hospital during the non-inspection weeks, the average mortality rate was 7.21 percent; for patients admitted during the week of the inspection, the mortality rate was significantly lower at 7.03 percent, or an absolute difference of 0.18 percentage points (after adjusting for small differences in the patient characteristics we measured, the difference was slightly smaller at 0.12 percentage points). From the week-to-week patterns, it was clear that there was something unique about the inspection week; after it's over, the mortality rate goes back up to where it was before the inspection.

We then looked specifically at major academic/teaching hospitals, since these hospitals often have reputations to protect and may therefore take Joint Commission visits especially seriously. These larger hospitals have infrastructure—in particular, large, coordinated teams—that mobilizes when inspection visits occur. These factors led us to hypothesize that any effects of inspections might therefore be larger in these kinds of hospitals. When we looked just at the major academic/teaching hospitals, the difference *was* in fact larger: mortality was, on average, 6.41 percent during non-inspection weeks compared with 5.93 percent during inspection weeks, an absolute difference of 0.49 percentage points (or 0.38 percentage points after adjustment).

In other words, patients admitted during an inspection week were, as we'd suspected, less likely to die within the next thirty days than patients admitted in the weeks surrounding the inspec-

---

[*] As a reminder, the thirty-day mortality rate is the percentage of patients who died within thirty days of being admitted to the hospital.

tion. Inspections—and the changes in health-care worker behavior brought about by them—led to better care for patients.

As you've likely noticed, these percentages are small. But it's important to remember just how many patients a fraction of a percent can represent. In the entire five-year time period of the study, there were about 900,000 hospital admissions to major teaching hospitals like the ones we analyzed. If the mortality reduction brought about by the inspection was hypothetically present for every week of the year, there would have been 3,600 fewer deaths among Medicare patients. It's unrealistic to think that this effect could be sustained across a year, even if hospitals were under constant inspection. But the numbers can be useful in thinking about what a 0.38 percentage point absolute difference in mortality might represent on a larger scale.

We still had to make sure these results weren't due to other factors, so we ran a few additional analyses. Joint Commission inspections were less likely to occur on major holidays, which meant those holidays would be more likely to be included in the surrounding weeks of an inspection (that is, in the control group). If patients admitted on major holidays were more likely to die (because care is worse or only the sickest patients show up at the hospital on a major holiday), this would bias our results. So, we repeated our analysis after removing admissions on Thanksgiving Day, Christmas Day, New Year's Day, and July 4. The results were unchanged.

We also thought that doctors might be incentivized to try to keep high-risk patients out of the hospital during inspection weeks (which could reduce strain on hospital staff), perhaps by avoiding admitting more medically complicated patients or rescheduling surgeries. But we found that hospitals essentially performed the same number and types of surgical procedures during inspection weeks compared with surrounding weeks. We also found that doctors were no less likely to admit patients to the hospital. So neither of these factors explained our findings.

Finally, we created some computerized simulations where we redid the analysis while pretending that the inspection happened on a random date instead of the date it actually occurred. Since we wouldn't expect there to be any effect of a pretend inspection, if we *did* see any effects in a computer simulation, it would suggest that our original results could have been due to random chance and not the effect of a real inspection. We ran such simulations over and over—a thousand times, to be precise—and we found no differences in mortality during pretend inspections, making it highly unlikely that the original results were a chance finding.

At this point, the data was pointing to the Joint Commission inspections causing reductions in mortality. The Hawthorne effect for hospital staff was real.

Now, all of this might seem obvious to anyone with a basic understanding of human psychology. We all perform our jobs a little more dutifully when someone is looking over our shoulder, and doctors and nurses are no exception. It should be little wonder, then, that outcomes would improve slightly during inspections. The riddle, as it turned out, was not so much in the presence of the effect as in its mechanics.

If the whole point of these inspections is to make sure safety protocols are followed to avoid preventable errors, we ought to see evidence of *that* in the data, too. If nurses pay closer attention to their patients while inspectors are in the hospital, we might expect there to be fewer injuries from patients falling down and fewer blood clots from inactivity. Or if surgical teams are paying closer attention to safety protocols in the operating room, we might see fewer cases of surgical accidents, postoperative wound complications, or deaths from surgical complications in general. If medical doctors are paying closer attention, they might make the right diagnosis faster and more often, potentially averting infections or deaths from cardiac arrest.

But when we looked at the rates of these errors and ones like them,[*] there were no significant differences between the inspection

---

[*] Specifically, patient safety indicators, a collection of specific preventable errors that government programs like Medicare and Medicaid use to evaluate hospital quality and safety.

weeks and the surrounding, non-inspection weeks. For example, rates of *Clostridium difficile* infection—a potentially deadly gastro-intestinal infection that can be acquired in the hospital—were 1.47 cases per 100 admissions during inspection weeks compared with 1.48 during the surrounding weeks. Similarly, we saw no differences in quality and safety scores that measure problems like bedsores, postoperative complications, or in-hospital hip fractures.

In sum, we saw a meaningful decrease in mortality for patients admitted during the inspection, but it wasn't explained by anything we could measure. It pointed to a vexing question: If preventable errors weren't the source of the improvement, what was?*

Perhaps our idea of preventable errors—like hospital-acquired infections, surgical mistakes, or falls—was too limited in its scope. Maybe other kinds of errors were at work that weren't easily mea-sured. Could it have been the presence of fewer distractions (other than the hovering inspectors, that is)? Could greater attention to patient care, as opposed to the many things that could distract doctors and nurses in the hospital—such as constant pages, other clinical obligations, or breaking news—have led to better and more accurate diagnoses, surgeries performed more carefully, complica-tions detected sooner, records more accurately kept, more personal-ized and lower-risk treatments offered, better bedside support?

For all their power, natural experiments have their limits. To get to the bottom of such questions, other types of more focused research may be required. Rigorous in-depth interviews with differ-ent types of health-care workers would need to be conducted, to see what they do differently during inspection weeks. Detailed reviews of electronic health record data—for example, studying the clinical notes of doctors, nurses, and therapists—could yield insights.

Ultimately, though our study of the Hawthorne effect in hospitals

---

* It's worth noting that many safety measures that might be more tightly followed during inspections haven't actually been proven to reduce mortality—even com-monsense interventions like wearing a special gown around patients colonized with antibiotic-resistant bacteria to prevent spread. It is possible, however, that if many of these measures were more strictly followed at the same time, we might be able to see an aggregate effect.

suggested its unmistakable presence, it might have raised more questions than it answered.

———

Inspection effects aside, the potential for medical error haunts medical professionals. I (Chris) will never forget the first one I made—or at least the first one I'm aware of.

I was an intern physician at the time, having only recently graduated from medical school, and I was working on a general medical ward in one of my residency's teaching hospitals. Intern year is often the most strenuous, demanding, busy, and stressful year of training a doctor will endure. We are asked to take everything we learned in medical school and apply it to real patients who need our help. Although life for interns is far from glamorous—leaving the hospital mainly just to shower and sleep, referring to graham cracker and peanut butter sandwiches as "lunch"—I loved that year. Taking responsibility for a life, having a sick stranger place their trust in you, is an awesome experience in the literal sense, and it's what I had been preparing for for many years. It was a thrill and a privilege. Although there were days when I never saw daylight except through my patients' hospital windows, it seemed that each day of that intern year was as exciting as the day before it.

But the thrill was accompanied by no small dose of terror: What if I screwed up? Of course, interns have heavy supervision from senior residents and attending physicians, and they get a lot of help from nurses, pharmacists, therapists, and other clinicians along the way. But there were many things we had responsibility for, since an intern is generally the central physician on a team caring for up to ten or more patients at a time on the hospital ward. We had to respond to pages from nurses when there was a problem, write orders for tests and medications, communicate with the specialists who consulted on our patients, and keep family members up to date. Even with help and backup, it's still possible to drop the ball, no matter how careful you are.

A few months into my intern year I was admitting two new patients to the hospital, both of whom had come in overnight with shortness of breath. Both patients were elderly men, both wearing the same hospital-issued patient gowns, both using supplemental oxygen through tubes in their noses. And because the hospital was nearly full, both were in the same room. One of them was short of breath because he had chronic obstructive pulmonary disease (COPD) from many years of smoking. He was in the midst of an exacerbation of the disease due to a common cold, coughing heavily and wheezing. The other patient was short of breath due to heart failure. His heart wasn't pumping blood efficiently, leading to excess fluid buildup in his legs and lungs. This patient *also* had COPD, but he was hospitalized for heart failure, not an exacerbation of that illness.

A mainstay of treatment for an exacerbation of COPD is an anti-inflammatory steroid such as prednisone, which helps calm down the patient's immune system in their lungs, opening up their airways and making it easier to breathe. For patients with heart failure and fluid backing up into their lungs, the mainstay of treatment is a diuretic, a medication that helps the patient remove excess fluid through their urine.

Both diagnoses were straightforward, and I had already treated a handful of patients with COPD and with heart failure at this point in my short career. It was a busy day for me otherwise, since a few of my other eight patients were being discharged, and I had to make sure they would be able to go home with all the additional care and medications they needed. After discussing my other patients with my senior resident and attending physician on rounds, I told them my plans for these two new patients with shortness of breath. They agreed with those plans. So after answering a few pages from nurses and consultants, reviewing an ECG that had set off an alarm on another patient (it was nothing serious), and talking to the daughter of yet another patient, upset her father hadn't been discharged yet, I went into the electronic chart on the computer and ordered prednisone for the patient with the COPD exacerbation and a diuretic for the patient with heart failure.

About an hour later, the nurse taking care of the patient with heart failure came to the resident workroom—and by "workroom"

I mean a closet with four computers and two phones, housing two interns, a senior resident, and a med student—and politely updated me as I filled out discharge paperwork. "Chris, I gave the patient the prednisone you ordered, but were you planning on ordering a diuretic, too, like we discussed on rounds?"

"That patient doesn't need any diuretic; he just has a COPD exacerbation," I replied over the sounds of my co-intern speaking on the phone and the incessant beeps of the heart monitor alarms located right outside my door.

"Are we talking about the same patient? His legs are really swollen, and I think a diuretic is probably a good idea."

Were we talking about the same patient? One patient was supposed to get prednisone and the other patient a diuretic—that's what I ordered in the computer, wasn't it?

Right—unless I screwed up.

Unless I screwed up. I froze for a second or two, able to focus only on the unforgettable sensation inside my body, feeling as if my own heart had suddenly been teleported out of my chest.

I pulled up the patient's list of orders, and there it was: I had ordered prednisone for the patient with heart failure and a diuretic for the patient with exacerbation of COPD. I must have gotten distracted and mixed up the patients either in my head or on their charts, resulting in the wrong orders for the wrong patients. *I screwed up.*

By now, my heart had returned to my chest, and it was beating fast. *What did I just do?* Immediately, I canceled the order for the diuretic on the patient with exacerbation of COPD, which fortunately had not yet been given. But the patient with heart failure had already taken the prednisone; there would be no averting this mistake. While often the pharmacist reviewing a medication order or the nurse who gives the medication will catch errors like this one, because the patient had COPD in addition to heart failure, they likely assumed that by ordering prednisone, I wanted to treat the patient for an exacerbation of COPD *in addition* to his heart failure. They had no obvious reason to object. I had nobody to blame but myself.

Although it's a common medication, prednisone has side effects that could cause real harm to a patient who doesn't need it. One of them is fluid retention—the exact problem the patient was admitted for and that I might now have made worse. It can also raise the blood sugar levels of patients with diabetes, making it harder to safely dose their insulin. The other concerning side effect of prednisone in elderly patients is its ability to cause delirium—a state of confusion and disorientation that can be dangerous in its own right.

"How did this happen?" I thought. "Was I too distracted by my other patients, the discharges, pages, and phone calls? Was I rushing? Did I hurt this patient? If I can't keep my patients straight and do basic things like prescribe the right medications to the right patients, should I even be doing this job? Am I going to get fired? Am I going to get sued?"

I told my supervising resident and attending physician what had happened. They reacted calmly and explained that after we made sure we did everything to treat both patients appropriately, the next step would be for me to tell the patient what happened and to file a hospital safety report. They assured me that while it was possible the patient might be harmed by this error, a single dose of prednisone would be unlikely to cause significant harm. (Fortunately, they would be proven correct; the patient experienced no effects from my mistake.)

I wasn't looking forward to disclosing my error to the patient, but it was, of course, my duty to do so. So I went into his room, pulled up a chair next to the head of his bed, and explained what happened. He was relieved. He said that based on my demeanor when I came in, he was expecting to learn he had "cancer or something." He said I shouldn't worry about it since he wasn't worried about it—he'd taken prednisone several times before, and it didn't cause him any problems—and he knew I was just trying my best to help him. I apologized for the error and told him I would do everything I could to prevent such errors in the future.

"It's okay," he said, smiling wisely. "It happens."

—

While the details of this story are unique, the broader concepts and feelings will be familiar to anyone who has dropped the ball when things got busy. Workplaces are always rife with distraction, whether it's colleagues wanting to catch up about their weekend or the constant chime of phones and inboxes. The hospital is no different; it just has its own unique set of distractors.

Assuming that distraction played a role in the medication error, what could have prevented it? A few ideas come to our minds, but they come with trade-offs. The electronic health record could have prompted: "You are caring for two patients in the same room. Are you writing orders for the correct patient?" This sounds appealing on its face, but because the hospital environment has so many other alarms and alerts, most of which aren't actually indicative of a problem, it becomes, over time, all too easy to ignore (a problem known as "alarm fatigue"). We could find a quieter, less distracting work environment for doctors, but that could result in their being farther away from patients (the reason they're at the hospital at all) and their nurses, potentially worsening communication. Doctors could be granted "do not disturb" periods, when they are to be interrupted only by major emergencies, allowing them better focus (in the way that we were trained to *never* interrupt a nurse who is either preparing a medication for a patient or handing off a patient to another nurse). Of course, this could result in delaying non-emergent care, creating new problems down the road.

You could probably think of a few ideas to reduce such distractions yourself. Brainstorming commonsense solutions to problems is a critical step in how hospitals respond to an event like a medication error. Unfortunately, a solution that suits one hospital may not suit another—there could even be differences across units within the same hospital—making one-size-fits-all solutions to error avoidance exceedingly rare.

—

Avoiding distraction is important in all areas of medicine, but it's particularly important in the operating room. Justin Dimick, the chair of surgery at the University of Michigan, described the focused headspace he enters prior to operating on a patient on an episode of the *Freakonomics, M.D.* podcast: "You take off your outside clothes and put on scrubs. You put on a surgical cap, you get your OR glasses on, and you walk there, and you scrub.* And scrubbing—a lot of people will describe as kind of a pre-operative clearing of your head. You walk through the case. You visualize how it's going to go. It also allows you to just kind of set aside everything else." Once operating, he and other surgeons enter what's known as a "flow state"—similar to the concept in sports of being "in the zone."

"It really is like time melts away," he says. "You can look up at the clock and two hours has gone by in a flash. It's almost trance-like and probably different for different people, but the scrub techs† will often have to shake me to get me to respond to some question they have because I'm so focused on what I'm doing."

For all the attention surgery requires, operating rooms are full of distractions. A 1972 study found that noises in the operating room— the snapping of gloves, clanging of metal instruments, slurping of surgical suction—can regularly reach decibel levels as loud as a small aircraft and high enough to elicit subconscious physical responses. Surgeons can also have their attention drawn away by events happening to their patients outside the operating room. Dr. Dimick recalls times when people have come into the operating room to tell him there's a patient he has to see in the emergency department, or that one of the patients he previously operated on is having a complication. "Those things can be distractions," he says, since it can "pull you out of that flow state" when you are forced to think and make decisions about another individual.

It's not surprising that things happen in an operating room that could be distracting to a surgeon. But like anyone else, surgeons may also get distracted by things happening outside work, things unrelated to patient care, perhaps related to things happening in one's

---

* The physical act of scrubbing is the process of thoroughly and systematically washing your hands, fingers, nails, and forearms to remove any bacteria from your skin prior to putting on gloves and operating on a patient.

† A scrub tech, or a surgical technologist, is the member of the operating room team who is responsible for setting up the OR for surgery, providing and organizing the instruments the surgeons will use for the procedure, and helping maintain sterility in the OR.

personal life. *Stitch.* What movie should I see this weekend? *Stitch.*
Why is my ankle hurting today? *Stitch.* I wonder how my portfolio
is doing.* *Stitch.* Did I remember to lock the front door? *Stitch.* How
should I spend my birthday this weekend?

A birthday. Of course, most adults don't find their birthdays as
exciting as they once did, but the day is often an excuse for special treatment or to get together with friends and family. Could a
surgeon's birthday be distracting enough to affect the outcomes of
patients they operate on?

Once again, birthdays provide us with a natural experiment—not
to divide surgeons by the months of their birth, but this time to
study the effect of being distracted by things happening in a doctor's
personal life. Again, we can't just ask surgeons if being distracted
affects the care of their patients, but a natural experiment could shed
some light. A surgeon's birthday is as good as random as far as surgical patients are concerned—as long as the surgeon isn't purposefully
scheduling or avoiding certain surgeries on their birthday. But emergency surgeries, by definition, aren't planned in advance. Since surgeons performing emergency surgeries have no control over which
patients need treatment on their birthday, the surgeon's birthday is
as good as random. The conditions for a natural experiment are met.

In a study of patients undergoing emergency surgery over a four-
year period, we (Bapu, along with the UCLA researchers Yusuke
Tsugawa and Hirotaka Kato) linked Medicare data about patients
and their surgery to data about their surgeons, which included their
surgeons' birthdays. We wanted to see whether Medicare-age patients
who had emergency surgery[†] on their surgeon's birthday were any
more or less likely to be alive thirty days after surgery than patients

---

* Bapu once looked into surgical outcomes during the stock market crash in 2008,
wondering if surgeons might be distracted by their investment portfolios in the operating room, but there was no evidence of any differences in patient outcomes in the
weeks during and following the crash.

† Defined by one of seventeen common emergency surgeries—such as coronary
artery bypass grafting, hip fracture repair, or gallbladder removal—that were performed within three days of being admitted to the hospital for acute problems. This
did not include patients who were admitted for a planned surgery.

who had surgery *by the same surgeon* on any other day. As long as these patients were otherwise similar except for the timing of their surgery, patients who had surgery on other days would serve as a counterfactual group to those who had surgery on their surgeon's birthday.

We looked at about 980,000 surgeries, of which about 2,000 were performed on the surgeon's birthday. Considering the two groups, the procedures themselves and the characteristics of the patients, such as their age or chronic medical conditions, were effectively the same. Surgeons who operated on their birthday performed just as many procedures on similarly complex patients as they would on any other day. It appeared, therefore, that surgeons were not selectively choosing certain patients on which to operate on their birthday.

Looking at all of the surgeries together, the thirty-day mortality was 7.0 percent when it occurred on the surgeon's birthday compared with 5.6 percent on other days. In an analysis that used a statistical model to compare patients who were operated on *by the same surgeons,* the findings were similar: thirty-day mortality was 6.9 percent when the surgery was performed on the surgeon's birthday compared with 5.6 percent on other days.

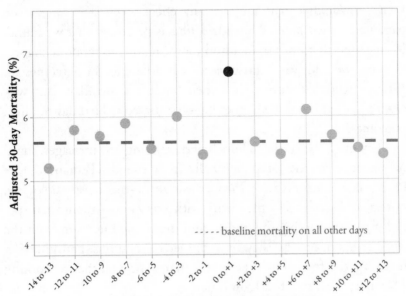

Days Relative to Surgeon's Birthday

We did a few extra analyses to make sure our main finding wasn't simply a statistical fluke. First, we repeated the analysis using the surgeon's *half* birthday and saw that there was no difference in mortality rates—as expected, since half birthdays are generally of no significance to adults, if they're acknowledged at all. Next, we looked at "milestone" birthdays—the big 4-0, 5-0, and 6-0—to see if the effect was any larger on birthdays where a bigger celebration might be in order; we didn't see any difference. We also looked at which day of the week birthdays fell on, hypothesizing that birthdays that fell on a Friday might be more likely to have a distracting celebration planned than birthdays that fell on Monday through Thursday, but again, we didn't see any day-of-week differences. The difference in mortality rate seemed to be confined to the birthday alone.

Using methods similar to those in the Joint Commission study, we also created a thousand computerized simulations in which we assigned randomly generated *pretend* birthdays to surgeons, linking the surgeon's pretend birthday to the real patients on which they operated on those days. If our initial findings were true—that the surgeon's actual birthday affects their performance in some way—then we wouldn't expect to see any effect when they operate on patients on their *pretend* birthday. This is precisely what we found. It suggested that our original finding wasn't due to random chance.

What we had was data suggesting a difference in outcomes for patients who had surgery on their surgeon's birthday. But why exactly? What might be happening on a surgeon's birthday to affect outcomes?

They might be getting a bunch of distracting text messages, social media notifications, or phone calls from friends. Perhaps they're having conversations with their co-workers—the anesthesiologists, nurses, and scrub techs they work with every day—about their special plans, distracting themselves and the whole OR team from the work at hand. Maybe they have dinner reservations, and knowing that surgeries frequently take longer than expected, they're working a bit more hastily to finish on time.

Whichever of these forces (or some combination) were at play, we can confidently assume the culprit was distraction.

—

What's the alternative? Should doctors leave their home lives at home, check their personal lives at the door of the clinic, hospital, or operating room, in the name of avoiding distraction?

In the sci-fi TV show *Severance,* employees of Lumon Industries undergo a (fictional) surgical procedure in their brain to completely separate their work and professional spheres. When they arrive at work, they have no memory of their personal lives outside work, allowing them to be productive without distraction. When they leave for home at the end of the day, they have no memory of what they did at work, free to lead their personal lives without work-related stress. The show explores what it might look like if a true, complete separation of work and home were somehow possible. (Without spoiling the show, we'll just say it's a recipe for problems.)

In light of the results of the Joint Commission and surgeon's birthday studies, it's tempting to think that a *Severance*-like scenario, while absurd, might be good for hospitals. Highly trained and knowledgeable doctors, nurses, and other staff could show up every day and care for patients without outside influence. After all, without personal lives, there are no birthdays, no social media notifications, no text messages, no chats about hobbies or weekend plans. Just work—right?

In reality, some degree of blending of personal and work life is probably a *good* thing for work performance, particularly in high-stress environments like the hospital. Personal connections with co-workers are considered critical building blocks for cohesive teams that trust one another and communicate well enough to be effective in the high-stakes situations that can arise during patient care, whether in the hospital or the outpatient clinic.

Take the medical staff at Nellis Air Force Base in Nevada, who participate in planned "team- and community-building activities throughout the year—for example, picnics or bowling—so that individuals can get to know each other on a personal level." The goal is to improve interpersonal dynamics, trust, and communication in a way that ultimately benefits patients—for instance, when team members feel comfortable speaking up to avoid errors.

Medical teams aren't the only ones on an air force base for whom team cohesion, trust, and communication can save lives. In aviation—where distraction and human error can have catastrophic consequences—reducing errors has always been a top priority. For example, checklists to remind pilots to follow every necessary step to maintain a safe flight have been a part of aviation protocols since the field's infancy in the 1930s.

In fact, the idea of avoiding errors by building trust and communication within health-care teams was borrowed from aviation. Recognizing that human fallibility was the biggest threat to aviation safety following a series of accidents in the 1970s—including a disaster on Tenerife in the Canary Islands, where a number of complicating and distracting factors, combined with team communication failures, led to 583 deaths on the runway—spurred the development of "crew resource management" training. At its core is the recognition that even the most highly trained experts and team leaders can fall victim to distraction, lapses in memory, and errors in judgment. By fostering open communication, where even a team's most junior member feels comfortable pointing out an unsafe situation or a mistake made by its most senior, a team can avoid errors by taking advantage of all of the group's human potential.

Crew resource management and its principles have been adapted from aviation to such environments as the operating room, emergency department, and ICU. We still struggle to quantify how much it helps patients, but we can only imagine that improving team dynamics is beneficial. Research on surgical teams who frequently work together has shown that higher team familiarity is associated with better communication, more efficient surgery, and, most important, fewer surgical errors and patient complications.

It could very well be, then, that the same interpersonal connections that might cause distractions in the OR on a surgeon's birthday are actually responsible for *improved* care through team cohesion every other day of the year—a net gain.

—

Should we just give surgeons their birthdays off, then? Should we have Joint Commission inspectors constantly roaming hospital hallways? These aren't the most outlandish ideas we've cast out so far. (We're still trying to figure out a way to have all babies be born in the fall.) But they are obviously extreme, and surely there are better ways to keep teams focused and mitigate the negative effects of distraction.

There are those "time-outs" in the OR that we mentioned earlier, used by surgeons and their colleagues to ensure the right procedure is done on the right patient. In the ICU, incorporating checklists as part of a "bundle" of equipment and reminders has proven enormously effective, too. In what would prove to be a practice-changing study published in 2004, researchers in Michigan recruited ninety-six different ICUs from around the state to introduce a new checklist to be used whenever doctors placed central venous catheters (also known as central lines, the large IVs inserted in the neck for critically ill patients). Because central lines go directly into the large jugular vein, bacteria on the tubing can work its way into the bloodstream and cause serious, life-threatening infections. Doctors have to perform the procedure under sterile conditions, which can be logistically difficult to achieve in the emergency department or ICU (especially when compared with the operating room, where sterile procedures are normally performed).

The checklist and bundle of equipment were meant to get doctors to follow steps that improved sterility but that were not always performed when inserting a central line: hand washing, use of sterile surgical gowns and patient covers,[*] choosing the ideal location for

---

[*] We use specially packaged sterile gowns, hair nets, sterile gloves, and face coverings for the doctor, while the patient is shrouded from above their head to below their toes in a sterile gown that covers everything except for a small circle about the size of a donut, in which the catheter (also sterilized) is placed into a large vein, typically in the neck, upper chest, or groin.

the central line, cleaning the skin with chlorhexidine,* and removing
the central line as soon as possible once it's no longer necessary. Each
day, ICU teams used checklists to ensure that every central line was
reviewed and removed as soon as it was no longer necessary, since
removing the central line removed with it the risk of infection.

The results were dramatic. Prior to the implementation of the
checklist, the group of hospitals had an infection rate of 2.7 infections per 1,000 "catheter-days"; this meant that if there were 1,000
ICU patients with a central line in place for 1 day, an average 2.7
of them developed an infection.† During the rollout period of the
checklist, the infection rate dropped to 1.6 infections per 1,000
catheter-days, a decrease of about 37 percent. Better still, in the time
period stretching to three, six, nine, and even eighteen months after
the implementation of the checklist, the infection rate dropped to
zero—as in no more infections.

"Dropping to zero" isn't something that happens often in medicine. So this study made quite a splash. Central line "bundles,"
including the checklist and necessary sterile equipment, have since
become widely used across the United States, and rates of central line
infections have predictably fallen when ICUs have adopted them.

Why was this intervention so successful while many others floun-
der? The physician and revered health-care-quality scholar Avedis
Donabedian, who spent much of his professional career at the University of Michigan until his death in 2000, viewed problems within
the health-care system through three lenses: the *structure* of care,

---

* Chlorhexidine is a powerful disinfectant that is extremely effective at killing the
bacteria and fungi that normally live on the skin—microbes that can cause infections by growing on central lines and spreading into a patient's bloodstream.
† Epidemiologists frequently measure rates like this to group together patients who
stay in the ICU with a central line for varying amounts of time. One patient who
has a central line for 1 day contributes 1 "catheter-day" to the analysis. A thousand
catheter-days could be 1,000 patients with a catheter for 1 day (1,000 x 1 = 1,000), 500
patients with a catheter for 2 days (500 x 2 = 1,000), 200 patients with a catheter for
5 days (200 x 5 = 1,000); in real-life analyses, it ends up being a mixture of patients
with the catheters in place for varying amounts of time.

or the physical environment, equipment, and people involved; the *processes* of care, or the actions that are taken to diagnose and treat patients; and the *outcomes* of care, or what actually ends up happening to patients. The development, implementation, and widespread adoption of research-backed central line bundles was one example of the kind of improvement effort that well covered all three of these areas. It addressed the *structure* of ICU care by giving doctors the tools at their fingertips, coupled with a few key reminders that work well in a busy ICU environment. It addressed the *processes* of ICU care by forcing busy and potentially distracted doctors to follow the steps necessary to prevent central line infections, not to mention empowering nurses and others to make sure these steps were followed. And, most important, the changes resulted in real, measurable, improved *outcomes* for patients: fewer bloodstream infections.

—

Unfortunately, central lines are only one small piece of the very large puzzle that is health-care quality and safety. Other pieces of this puzzle have been solved over the years. For example, the use of checklists and bundles for doctors treating patients admitted for heart failure has led to better outcomes.

However, it has proven difficult to replicate the story more broadly to make major improvements on a large scale. In 2020, two decades after the National Academy of Medicine published *To Err Is Human* and *Crossing the Quality Chasm,* highlighting the desperate need for improvement when it comes to errors in the hospital, the prominent leaders in the health-care-quality movement Donald Berwick, Harvard professor and founder of the Institute for Healthcare Improvement, and Christine Cassel, former chief executive of the National Quality Forum and president of the American College of Physicians, wrote,

> The key thesis that the best way to control costs is to improve the quality of processes, products, and services, while continually reducing waste, which is practically doctrinal now in many

industries, has never penetrated deeply into most health care organizations' strategies.

When a patient experiences a preventable adverse event in the hospital of the kind we've discussed—a surgical complication or a central line infection—the hospital will of course treat them for it and could then bill insurance for this additional treatment. If a hospital's ICU didn't use the optimal sterile technique while placing a central line, resulting in an infection, an insurer would be charged both for the central line procedure *and* for treating the infection. You can well imagine the problematic incentives this creates: hospitals could potentially make *more* money by providing *worse* care. While purposefully creating complications would be both unethical and criminal, under some payment models the financial incentives to innovate and improve upon the status quo simply aren't there.

With these forces at play, it's only natural to think that if we realign financial incentives for hospitals and insurers to the benefit of patients—pay more for high-quality care, pay less for low-quality care—we might get better results. A central line resulted in an infection? Let the hospital foot the bill. The hospital's surgical complication rate is lower than the national average? Give the hospital a bonus payment.

If we financially incentivize high-quality care, how many patients could we save from unnecessary death and disability?

Health-care providers have begun to find out. Payment structures that financially incentivize high-quality care and disincentivize low-quality care have been established in various ways that can be summed up for our purposes as "value-based payments," incorporating both quality and costs. Over the past several decades, we've seen value-based payment systems rolled out across the country, with "high value" care financially rewarded and "low value" care penalized. Has this approach improved quality?

As the cardiologist and national correspondent for *The New England Journal of Medicine* Lisa Rosenbaum wrote in 2022, "It's hard to know. Some early efforts—such as those focused on reducing [hospital-acquired] infections, improving surgical outcomes, and improving processes of care for patients with pneumonia, heart failure, or myocardial infarction—succeeded. But recently, there has been a growing recognition of the quality improvement movement's shortcomings."

Among those shortcomings: When financial incentives are tied to certain quality measures, hospitals are incentivized to improve their *scores,* not their patient outcomes—similar to how schoolteachers might be incentivized to maximize standardized test scores rather than improve true education. Billions of dollars have been spent on improving value scores without changing any of the underlying care, with health-care organizations going so far as to hire consultants to optimize their documentation practices, leading doctors to spend more time writing in charts and less time at the bedside with patients.

Moreover, tying financial incentives to improving scores has potentially led to patient *harm.* Safety-net hospitals, which generally care for more patients using Medicaid, have disproportionately been hit with financial penalties for their "low quality" care, likely due in part to not being as flush with funds (to pay for optimized documentation practices, for example) as nearby hospitals that collect more money from commercial insurance.

Suffice it to say that finding large-scale interventions to improve quality and reduce errors remains a vexing problem. Financial incentives can motivate change within a system, but they may not solve the problems we want them to and can potentially introduce new ones. At a minimum, history and evidence have taught us that simply tying care and payment together is no panacea. "Despite innumerable metrics and vast research assessing their worth," Rosenbaum writes, "it's still not clear that we're measuring what matters nor whether we have the methods to figure it out."

If attempts to realign financial incentives aren't leading to the large-scale improvements in quality that we would have hoped for, what would? If only the answer were clear. The Harvard physician and health economist J. Michael McWilliams has posited

that COVID-19 showed the power of another incentive. As he elo-
quently observed in 2020 of the pandemic response by health-care
professionals,

> [They] not only exhausted and imperiled themselves. . . .
> They embraced new responsibilities . . . They did not retreat
> from compassion. . . . No financial incentives or performance
> measures were required . . . a reminder that clinicians' unique
> training and intrinsic concern for their patients is our greatest
> resource, our best hope, for improving health care.

In other words, beyond dollars and cents, something else altogether can serve as an even greater motivator for health-care providers to achieve better patient outcomes: our sense of duty.

CHAPTER EIGHT

WHAT DO CARDIAC SURGEONS AND USED-CAR SALESMEN HAVE IN COMMON?

L ET'S SAY YOU'RE the proprietor of a grocery store. Gearing up for back-to-school season, you decide to start selling a new product: a family-size pack of mozzarella string cheese. Based on what you pay for it from the supplier and your other costs, you estimate that you need to sell the cheese for somewhere in the neighborhood of $8.00. How do you pick the specific price to charge?

You don't have to work in retail to know that you should probably set the price at $7.99. We're all aware of this commonplace pricing trick. Because even though $7.99 is only one cent less than $8.00, it subconsciously *seems* like a better deal: "seven-something" certainly *seems* better than "eight-something." It's evidence of a tendency our brains fall victim to, what is called "left-digit bias," one of our many cognitive biases (alongside the representative and availability heuristics we've previously covered).

Retailers of all kinds have been taking advantage of this bias for decades. Meanwhile, economists, psychologists, and linguists have been studying the phenomenon, looking for a scientific theory to explain it.

In English, we read numbers from left to right, starting with the biggest unit in the number and moving to the smaller units. So in a number like 43, we start our processing with the tens digit followed by the units digit. When we see a number like 43 and compare it with another number, like 78, our brains tend to place them on an "analog scale" or a "number line" that exists in our subconscious, helping us easily sort out bigger and smaller quantities and the differences between them. (Such a scale presumably would have been useful to our human ancestors when trying to assess and compare quantities of objects, before mathematics was developed.)

How can the brain speed up this process? Presented with these two two-digit numbers, we don't bother with the units digits (since all numbers in the 40s are smaller than all numbers in the 70s). Our minds process first digits, comparing 40-*something* with 70-*something.* Setting the two numbers on our subconscious number line, we quickly conclude that 78 is bigger than 43. When we are comparing two numbers with the same tens digit—for example, 53 and 55—it takes us ever so slightly longer, since we have to process both the tens digit *and* the units digit before placing them on our number line.

For these reasons, when we shop for string cheese, it's easier for our brain to tell us that $7.99 is less than $8.00 than it is to tell us that $8.01 is less than $8.02. More important, when the left digits are different, we tend to place them *farther away from other numbers on our analog number line,* even if, as in this example, the prices are only a cent apart in each instance. In the grocery store, this means that if we see an item on sale that usually costs roughly $10.00, we tend to place a sale price of $7.99 significantly farther away from $10.00 than a sale price of $8.00.

Let's shift gears, as it were, to a purchase a lot more significant than cheese.

Let's say you're in the market for a used car. What are the details you would need to know to make a purchase? Surely you would want to know if the car would generally suit your needs, if it was in decent condition. You also want to know roughly how many miles it's been driven—the mileage being a useful proxy for general wear and tear on the car's parts. Because many people buy a used car thinking about how long it will last them before they need to buy a new one, they would be willing to pay a lot more for a car with 30,000 miles on it than they would for the same car if it had 80,000 miles on it and was thus that much closer to the end of its life.

How much should that extra 50,000 miles of wear and tear drop the price of the car? Probably quite a bit—thousands of dollars, we'd think. What about a difference of 40,000 miles? Still a lot, but not as much as for 50,000 miles, we can reasonably stipulate. But what about small differences—of 100, 10, or even 5 miles?

Used-car buyers are forced to make subjective judgments in determining how much more or less they're willing to pay for a car based on its mileage (among other factors). Although more miles generally translates to a lower perceived value, *how much* that value changes based on mileage will be different for different people. Buyers may get assistance from tools like the Kelley Blue Book—which bases its estimates on transaction prices from prior car sales—but they ultimately have to make a judgment call when agreeing on a price with a seller, who brings their own set of interests and judgments to the negotiating table.

Where does left-digit bias fit into all of this? Well, based on what we know, a car priced at $8,999 will be slightly more likely to sell than that same car priced at $9,000—but that's not where we're going with this. Left-digit bias shows up pretty much anytime we're trying to compare quantities, not just price.

In a study examining more than twenty-two million used-cars sales, the economists Nicola Lacetera (University of Toronto), Devin Pope (University of Chicago), and Justin Sydnor (University of Wisconsin–Madison) set out to study the effect of left-digit bias when it came to a car's mileage and how it affected the perceived value of a car, as reflected in its sale price. They hypothesized that cars driven just under a major mileage milestone, like 20,000 or 50,000 miles, would be perceived to be disproportionately valuable. In other words, they wanted to see if a 2003 Toyota Camry with 39,993 miles would sell for significantly more than a 2003 Toyota Camry in the same condition with 40,019 miles.

Because we would expect the group of cars with just under 40,000 miles to be essentially the same as the group of cars with just over 40,000 miles, the groups of cars serve as counterfactuals to each other. The cars with just over 40,000 miles tell us what the cars with

39,900-ish miles would have sold for if they had just a few more miles on them, and vice versa. A classic natural experiment.

They divided the twenty-two million cars into groups based on their mileage, rounding down to the nearest 500 miles (so all cars driven between 22,000 and 22,499 were in one group, 22,500–22,999 in the next, and so on). They then took the sales price of the car and subtracted out the part of the price that was attributable to the baseline characteristics of the car—the make, model, model year—based on a statistical model they created. What they were left with was the "residual sales price," which essentially represents the portion of the sales price that could be attributed to the buyer's and seller's subjective judgment about the value of the car. Plotting out the residual sales price based on the number of miles the car was driven, here's what they found:

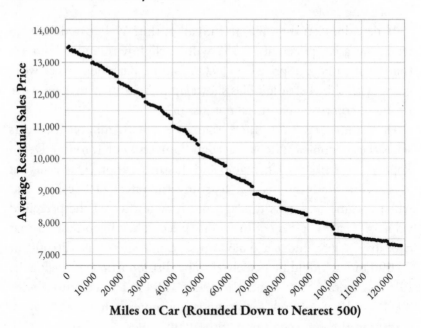

The more miles on a car, the lower the residual sales price. This is what we would expect, since each additional mile driven on a car adds to its wear and tear, decreasing its value. But at the "milestone" odometer readings every 10,000 miles, there are sudden drops in price: from the 9,500–9,999-mile group to the 10,000–10,499-mile group, and again from 19,500–19,999 miles to 20,000–20,499 miles, and so on.

The sudden drop in price occurring at these cutoffs is called a "discontinuity," because while we would generally expect there to be a steady and continuous decline in price as mileage goes up, something unique is occurring at these milestones that breaks the otherwise smooth decline. We have to presume that the discontinuous drop in price at these 10,000-mile marks must be due to something subjective, since there is nothing objectively different about a car as it passes the 10,000-mile mark compared with when it passes the 9,500-mile, 10,500-mile, or 11,000-mile mark.

The only thing that's meaningfully different as a car passes these milestones is the leftmost digit on the odometer. Left-digit bias is the only reasonable explanation for the findings.

This makes sense given everything we know about that subconscious analog number line—a car driven 49,999 miles will be perceived to have a longer remaining life than a car driven 50,000 miles, making it worth it to pay more for it.

So whether we're at the grocery store or on the used-car lot, left-digit bias wields influence over the way all of us perceive quantities. But consumers aren't the only ones comparing numbers. As physicians, we're constantly looking at them—whether it's a patient's age, the result of a laboratory test, the breathing settings on a ventilator, or the size of an abnormality on an X-ray—and we're constantly making rapid decisions based on our assessment of those values. This raises some questions: Are doctors' decisions affected by left-digit bias? And if so, how does it affect patients?

—

Remember Roberta, the seventy-seven-year-old woman who was rushed to the emergency room with a heart attack back in chapter 6, only to find out that the senior cardiologist was out of town at a research conference? Her story began when she developed shortness of breath and tightness in her chest while raking leaves. When an

ambulance arrived, the emergency medical team immediately suspected she might be having a heart attack, and they performed an
ECG to look for signs.

One of the reasons to immediately think Roberta was having a
heart attack was her age, since heart disease is common among sep-
tuagenarians. If an ambulance pulled up to a twenty-seven-year-old
complaining of shortness of breath and tightness in her chest, the
EMTs' first thought probably wouldn't be a heart attack, quite rare
among people in their twenties. Instead, they might think of a disease that's more common among twenty-seven-year-olds—asthma,
for example.

Doctors, paramedics, nurses, and others whose job involves
making rapid assessments generally get better at it through experience—an important reason we spend so much time in training. As
we see more and more patients, we hone our sense of what diseases
are common or uncommon, in which patients these illnesses tend to
occur, and what manifestations of those diseases are typical or atypical. With training and experience, doctors' minds eventually start
to put together "illness scripts": mental representations of various
diseases, with ideas for how to spot them.

An illness script for pneumonia, for example, might include the
epidemiology of who gets the disease (older patients, patients with
weak immune systems, patients with lung disease), typical signs and
symptoms of the disease (several days of cough, shortness of breath,
fevers), and common test findings (abnormality on a chest X-ray,
elevated white blood cell count). When we see a case with enough
of these features, the pneumonia illness script will "light up" in our
heads, suggesting a diagnosis with minimal cognitive effort on our
part.

These illness scripts are heuristics yet again, helping doctors with
the everyday task of making diagnoses. It would seem only natural
that these shortcuts would be prone to biases.

Intrigued to learn more about left-digit bias's potential effect on
medical care, the Columbia University economist Stephen Coussens, while still a graduate student, began examining diagnostic reasoning among emergency department doctors. He took advantage

of the heart attack illness script that most adhered to, based on the classic guidance that heart attacks tend to occur in patients over forty years old. A doctor would thus be more likely to suspect a heart attack for a patient in their 40s than for an otherwise-similar patient in their 30s.

Let's think about the natural experiment at play here. You might take two groups of randomly selected patients: a group who are *about to turn* forty years old, and a group that *just turned* forty years old. When it comes to their risk of heart attack, would we expect any difference between them? Although the risk of heart attack generally goes up as people get older, a few months of aging around age forty should lead to only a minuscule increase. Otherwise, medically and biologically speaking, these two groups of patients should be essentially the same. They're counterfactual to each other.

Patients who are *almost* 40 are, of course, technically 39. If left-digit bias is playing a role, an emergency doctor seeing a patient who is *almost* forty and comes in with chest tightness might be less likely to activate their subconscious "heart attack" illness script than if the doctor saw that same patient with the same symptoms a few months later when the patient was *actually* forty.

In an analysis that included 5.6 million patients who came to the emergency department for any reason within five years of their fortieth birthday—of which about a million were within one year of their birthday—Coussens looked to see whether left-digit bias might affect a doctor's decision to check for evidence of a heart attack using a blood test called troponin.* Categorizing patients by age in three-month blocks (for example, 39 years and 0–2 months, 39 years and 3–5 months, and so on), he was interested in quantifying the probability that a doctor ordered a troponin test based on the patient's age.

If there was no left-digit bias present, we would expect the chances

---

* Troponin is a protein that is found in muscle cells, including the heart. During a heart attack, the blood supply to the heart is cut off, resulting in damage to heart muscle cells that release troponin into the blood. So when doctors are concerned a patient might be having a heart attack, common practice is to check if troponin levels in the blood are elevated.

of testing for a heart attack to go up gradually and smoothly with age—just as we would have expected the value of a used car to go down smoothly with more miles. If left-digit bias was present, however, we would expect to see another discontinuity—a sudden "cliff" in the chart when the data points crossed age forty. Here's what he found:

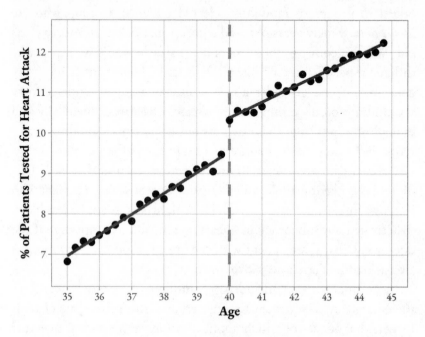

At age forty, patients suddenly started getting tested for a heart attack considerably more often in the emergency department. Just like with the sudden drop in price of used cars at the major odometer milestones, this jump suggested something unique was at play at 40 compared with 38, 39, or 41, where the probability of testing increased smoothly.

Of course, the only real difference at the age of forty is that the patient leaves their thirties and enters their forties. It's highly suggestive of a left-digit bias in the emergency department. Patients who were almost forty but still technically "in their 30s" were getting tested for a heart attack a little over 9 percent of the time, while those who are basically the same age but technically "in their 40s" were getting tested a little over 10 percent of the time. After accounting for the overall smooth trend of increased testing as patients get older, the sudden jump corresponded to a 9.5 percent relative increase in the probability—attributable not to the patients' *actual* age but to their *perceived* age. While this might seem like a small percentage, it suggests that thousands of these tests are being performed every year in the United States for a completely arbitrary reason unrelated to the patient's underlying biology.

Coussens also took this experiment one step further to see if this increase in *testing* translated into an increase in *diagnosis* of heart attacks and other forms of coronary artery disease. He found a similar pattern—a sudden increase at age forty, where the rate of diagnosis of heart disease was suddenly 19.3 percent higher. This difference could have been because doctors tested more often, making them more likely to find disease, or it could have been that doctors were more likely to label a patient as having coronary artery disease when they're "in their 40s"—or some combination of the two. It also meant that either patients just under forty might be systematically underdiagnosed with heart disease or patients just over forty were being overdiagnosed. Either way, the evidence was clear: left-digit bias was affecting physician behavior in the emergency department.

—

A patient's age is one of the single most important characteristics doctors have to consider when making diagnostic decisions. The probability that a patient's symptoms are due to a given illness can vary dramatically with age. One reason heart attacks are so uncommon in younger patients is that they are most often the result of decades of narrowing of the coronary arteries. Meanwhile, there are many conditions that are rare in adults—Kawasaki disease, for example, an inflammatory illness of the coronary arteries that tends to affect only young children. So age makes up a central part of those "illness scripts," which means our diagnostic accuracy is especially vulnerable to age-based biases like left-digit bias.

But age doesn't just help doctors narrow in on the right diagnosis. It also helps doctors decide what *treatments* they should recommend. A treatment that a doctor might find safe and effective for a 60-year-old may not be considered safe and effective for a 90-year-old. This raises the question: Could it affect more than just diagnosis? Could it affect doctors' treatment decisions too?

Let's turn to an area where treatment decisions are rarely black and white, and thus are prone to subjectivity and bias: open-heart surgery for elderly patients with heart attacks. When a patient comes in with a heart attack, cardiologists try to localize the coronary arteries that have become blocked. Sometimes heart attacks can be treated with medication alone. Other times, blockages can be relieved by placing stents in the coronary arteries, opening up blockages with a minimally invasive procedure performed in a cardiac catheterization, or "cath" lab (we heard about this procedure, the percutaneous coronary intervention, in chapter 6). In other situations, a cardiac surgeon might have to "bypass" the blockages by adding blood vessels to route blood around the blockage—a major open-heart surgery called coronary artery bypass graft, or CABG (pronounced "cabbage") for short.

As you might imagine, CABG carries with it a lot of risks. The procedure is performed when the short-term risk of complications is exceeded by the potential benefit: namely, longer life. In some patients, however, the risks of the surgery are higher than the risks associated with not having surgery, treating the condition with medication, or stenting alone. This means cardiac surgeons have to exercise discretion in figuring out which patients will benefit from surgery and which patients are more likely to be harmed by it—an often-difficult call. Just as an emergency doctor will rely on training and experience to develop subconscious probabilities of different diagnoses, a cardiac surgeon will use a similar process to estimate whether a patient is likely to benefit or be harmed by CABG surgery.

A patient's age, of course, is a key component in this calculation. Older patients, in general, are more likely than younger patients to struggle after a heart attack, and are at higher risk of death no matter what kind of treatment they get. Older patients are also more likely to struggle with complications from a surgery. They have lower overall survival in the postoperative period. On the flip side, when patients do well after CABG surgery, it can extend their life and improve the quality of their remaining life (however long that may be).

In a study published in *The New England Journal of Medicine* in 2020, we (Bapu, along with Andrew Olenski, the Harvard cardiologist and health policy researcher André Zimerman, and Stephen Coussens) examined rates of CABG surgery among elderly Medicare recipients who had been diagnosed with a heart attack. We hypothesized that left-digit bias might play a role around age 80; most patients in their 80s are in the last decade of their lives and might be considered less likely to benefit from surgery than patients in their 70s.

A surgeon's assessment is going to rely on both objective data from the patient's medical history and a somewhat subjective assessment of the potential risks and benefits to the patient. Importantly, guidelines don't push surgeons one way or another at this age milestone. This subjectivity, we hypothesized, might open the door for left-digit bias. If we think about the surgeon's subconscious analog number line, a patient who's 79 is going to feel further away from the end of their life than one who's 80, making the benefit of surgery—years of life with better heart function—seem greater for a 79-year-old than for an 80-year-old. Does it put a finger on one side of the risk/benefit scale, making the risk seem more worth taking?

To answer this question, we used data from Medicare to find patients who were admitted to the hospital with a heart attack within two weeks of their 80th birthday (in other words, patients who were between 79 years and 50 weeks old and 80 years and 2 weeks old when they were admitted). Our assumption was that patients who are 79 years and 50 weeks old are essentially the same as patients who are 80 years and 2 weeks old, the only difference being the broad label on their ages—70-something versus 80-something. Therefore, any difference between the groups could be attributable to differences in how patients labeled "79" are treated compared with those labeled "80."

Even though it's intuitive, the first thing we had to do, as always, was look for evidence that these groups were effectively the same and could serve as counterfactuals to each other. Looking at the baseline characteristics of the roughly 9,500 patients with heart attacks near their eightieth birthday, we found no differences in sex, race, disability, Medicaid eligibility, or rates of preexisting heart disease, lung disease, diabetes, high blood pressure, high cholesterol, stroke, cancer, and dementia. There were also no differences in the rate of hospitalization between the two groups, suggesting that left-digit bias wasn't influencing decisions in the emergency department to test for heart attacks or admit the patient to the hospital. Finally, we checked for differences in the severity of their heart attacks—those STEMI and non-STEMI types you may remember from our discussion of cardiology conferences. We found no difference between the two groups.

So yes, the evidence was there that these groups made good counterfactuals for each other. There was a valid natural experiment.

Here's what we found: patients who came in with a heart attack within the two weeks *before* their eightieth birthday underwent surgery 7.0 percent of the time, while those who came in within the two weeks *after* their eightieth birthday underwent surgery 5.3 percent of the time.* Because we determined that these two groups were otherwise similar, the difference between these surgical rates, 1.7 percentage points, represents the difference in how patients with an age *labeled* "79" are subjectively perceived compared with those *labeled* "80." This meant that for every fifty-nine patients who came in for a heart attack near their eightieth birthday, one of them wasn't getting surgery simply because they came in on the wrong side of their birthday.

How could we confirm that this difference was due to left-digit bias? If it really was the left digit leading to a change in perception of the risk of these patients, then there shouldn't be any difference in surgical rates across birthdays when the left digit didn't change. So we repeated the study across ages 77 to 83, studying patients who had heart attacks within two weeks of their birthday.

---

* After adjusting for potential confounding for baseline characteristics, the results were unchanged—presumably because the two groups were already so similar to each other.

For the birthdays where the left digit doesn't change, there were some small differences in CABG rates across the birthday, but none of them were statistically significant. Only the eightieth birthday was associated with a significant drop in surgical rates—which is what we would expect if left-digit bias was driving the difference.

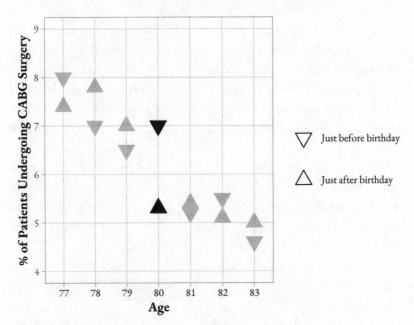

Just before birthday

Just after birthday

Just like some of our prior birthday-driven natural experiments, we assigned Medicare patients pretend birthdays and repeated the experiment by looking for patients who had a heart attack near their *pretend* 80th birthday. If the difference in CABG surgical rates was being driven by left-digit bias, we wouldn't expect to see any differences for patients with heart attacks within the two weeks before and two weeks after a pretend birthday—and we didn't.*

At this point, we had pretty convincing evidence that left-digit bias was affecting decisions about CABG, with patients just north of their eightieth birthday receiving surgery significantly less often.

---

* This analysis also demonstrated that the small amount of *true* age difference between the two groups—up to four weeks—didn't sway CABG decision making (unsurprisingly).

The next question to answer was this: Did it matter for the patients? On the one hand, they missed out on a surgery to improve blood flow to their hearts. On the other hand, they avoided major open-heart surgery that carries with it significant risks and a potentially difficult recovery.

To figure out whether left-digit bias's effect on surgical rates translated into meaningful differences in outcomes for patients, we looked to see whether, a year later, patients were still alive (their one-year mortality rate). Because we saw no differences in characteristics between patients just shy of 80 years old and those just over 80 years old other than the CABG surgery rate, we could attribute any differences in mortality between the two groups to their difference in surgery rates.

Doing a similar analysis, only this time for mortality rather than surgical rates, we found that there was no significant difference in one-year mortality between those hospitalized with heart attacks just before their eightieth birthday compared with just after. In other words, for patients approximately 80 years old, CABG surgery didn't always lead to improved one-year survival. (If it had, we would have seen reduced mortality for the patients just under 80 who were more likely to have surgery.)

This isn't to say that the procedure can't help some patients at that age; these are aggregate numbers, and there are some patients for whom deciding to operate is a clearer decision. But for patients who were "on the margin"—patients for whom a doctor thought surgery and no surgery were both reasonable options—it seemed that not operating could result in similar mortality rates, without the pain, inconvenience, and costs of open-heart surgery.

A grocery store shopper who fails to realize a retail item priced at $7.99 isn't as good a deal as it might seem could be dubbed penny-wise and pound-foolish. Left-digit bias in surgical decisions is something else, though. Surgeons know, correctly, that generally speaking older patients are going to be less likely to benefit from CABG surgery than younger patients; they were "pound-wise" in this regard, since patients "in their 80s" are in fact at higher risk than patients "in their 70s." But when it came to the smaller details, like the minute difference between 79-year-old and 80-year-old patients, they were "penny-foolish," led astray by left-digit bias.

—

Subsequent studies by others have found evidence that left-digit bias influences medical decisions in settings beyond emergency and surgical care for heart attacks. Multiple studies have found evidence of left-digit bias in kidney transplantation. Using data from the national organ donation database, containing data on tens of thousands of organs up for potential donation, researchers found that kidneys from potential donors who were 70 years old were substantially more likely to be discarded (not transplanted due to their perceived low quality) than kidneys from otherwise-similar 69-year-old patients. In an additional analysis of blood creatinine levels (a measurement of kidney function, where higher values correspond to worse kidney function), researchers also found that kidneys from potential donors with a creatinine level of 2.0 mg/dL were more likely to be discarded than kidneys from donors with a creatinine of 1.9 mg/dL, even though these two values are clinically quite similar.[*]

In another study of about 130,000 Medicare-age patients with acute cholecystitis—an infection of the gallbladder, most often caused by gallstones blocking the outflow of bile juices needed for digestion—researchers found that 79-year-olds and 89-year-olds were significantly more likely to have surgery than their otherwise-similar 80-year-old and 90-year-old counterparts. In patients who are considered low risk for surgery, the typical treatment is cholecystectomy, the surgical removal of the gallbladder. In high-risk patients, however, surgery may be deferred in favor of less invasive interventions.[†]

Finally, in a study of about 100,000 patients in the National Can-

* Anything that might be unnecessarily reducing the number of available organs for transplantation merits further investigation, and more research on the effect on transplant recipients will shed more light on how serious a problem this is.

† In this study, there was no difference in surgical rates between 69-year-olds and 70-year-olds, suggesting that surgeons didn't perceive patients "in their 60s" to be significantly different risk-wise from patients "in their 70s."

cer Database on rectal cancer, researchers wanted to see if left-digit bias might affect the probability that patients received "guideline adherent" care, meaning all of the surgery, radiation, and chemotherapy that guidelines recommended for each patient's individual type and stage of rectal cancer. They found that patients aged 58 or 59 were significantly more likely to receive guideline-adherent care than 60-year-old patients; meanwhile, there were no differences between 60-year-old patients and those aged 61 or 62. What the presence of left-digit bias might translate to in terms of important outcomes like survival or quality of life for these patients remains unknown.

We see that the age 60 cutoff seemed to matter for these cancer patients, the age 70 cutoff for kidney transplants, and the age 80 for gallbladder patients. In other words, there's not one magical decade marker at which doctors decide someone is "old." Rather, "oldness" is determined as a function of the specific disease.

—

Some medical errors are unpredictable. As with Chris's example of mixed-up medications from the last chapter, it's hard to know in advance which patient is going to fall victim to a mistake. So with medications we put systems in place to minimize the chance that these errors happen—like using barcode scanning every time a medication is given in the hospital to make sure the right drug goes to the right patient.

Other errors are more predictable, however, such as the ones due to left-digit bias that we've been discussing. That's not to say that we can see the future. But just as we could guess that, on average, you might get a better deal on a used car with 50,000 miles on it than one with 49,995, we can reasonably anticipate that 39-year-olds are at greater risk of underdiagnosis for heart disease in the emergency department than their 40-year-old peers. In both cases, a predictable cognitive error is at fault.

In the examples we looked at, left-digit bias, combined with representativeness bias, seemed to lead doctors to perceive patients in a way that influenced their practice. But the left digit isn't the only way patients get labeled and put into categories that affect their medical care. Age cutoffs are used in medicine constantly, and they sort patients into groups in all manner of arbitrary ways that can have real effects on patients.

For example, the U.S. Preventive Services Task Force (known by the clunky acronym USPSTF) recommends screening tests to detect early cancer in the general population. They advise that all adults undergo screening for colorectal cancer from age fifty to seventy-five—which would make forty-nine- or seventy-six-year-olds less likely to have a screening colonoscopy, even though their risk is going to be similar to the fifty- or seventy-five-year-olds'. They also recommend that fifty-to-eighty-year-olds who have smoked an average of at least one pack of cigarettes per day for twenty years be screened annually for lung cancer with a CT scan. A forty-nine- and eighty-one-year-old will have similar risk, but will be less likely to be screened (and so would someone who smoked slightly less than one pack a day for twenty years).

Of course, we can't blame the USPSTF for this—a line has to be drawn *somewhere*. No matter where it's drawn, though, there's going to be a cutoff, and that cutoff is going to divide patients on either side of it in an arbitrary fashion. This makes cutoffs of any kind excellent sources of natural experiments in many areas of research, medicine included.

One of the first meaningful age cutoffs Americans experience is age eighteen—the age of majority that, legally speaking, distinguishes an adult from a child. Age eighteen is a point along the continuous, gradual process of adolescence—the period of human development from a "child" into an "adult" that generally begins in the preteen years, extends into the twenties, and happens at different speeds for different people. Of course, there's no sudden biological change that occurs the day an adolescent turns eighteen. But the world does, suddenly, treat eighteen-year-olds differently, and medicine is no exception.

We (Chris and Bapu, along with Jaemin Woo and Harvard colleague Michael Barnett) wanted to see how this sudden change in labeling from "child" to "adult" could affect medical care. Because adolescents just under eighteen are labeled "children," they may be treated differently from those labeled "adults" for two primary reasons. First, the risks and benefits of a given treatment or intervention might be perceived differently when prescribed to a "child" versus an "adult." A doctor treating someone just shy of their eighteenth birthday might treat them closer to how they would treat a teenager, whereas the *same* doctor might treat someone who just turned eighteen as they would a young adult. The second reason has nothing to do with cognitive biases. A "child" who enters the emergency department may see different doctors and nurses, and be treated in a different area (a pediatric area, with specialized staff, decorated with colors and animals) from an adult (characteristically bland, no frills), or else be subject to different protocols within the emergency department—all of which could contribute to differential treatment.

We thought one way eighteen-year-olds might be treated differently was in the likelihood that they would be prescribed an opioid pain medication during an emergency visit. Because those just under age eighteen should be similar to those just over eighteen, other than being deemed a "child" or an "adult," differences in opioid prescribing between the two groups should be attributable to differences in how they're labeled. Doctors who may be reluctant to prescribe opioids to a "child" may be more likely to prescribe opioids to an "adult."

In a study using a database of commercial insurance claims, we found about 875,000 emergency department visits between 2006 and 2016 for kids who were either seventeen or eighteen years old. We started by examining whether adolescents just under eighteen in the ED were similar to those just over eighteen by comparing characteristics of kids aged seventeen years and nine to eleven months with those aged eighteen years and one to three months. Indeed, they were similar across a wide range of attributes, including sex, geographic location within the United States, rates of chronic illness (including diabetes, obesity, lung disease, alcohol use disorder), rates of *prior* opioid prescription, opioid use disorder, or overdose. They had similar reasons for coming to the emergency department as well, most of which were injuries and infections, typical for this age group.

Next, we wanted to see if the just-under-eighteen-year-olds were treated differently in the emergency department. This can be hard to do using insurance claims data, since it doesn't tell us the nitty-gritty, moment-to-moment details of what was happening in the ED, but we were able to glean some information on the types of doctors who saw these patients. We found that most patients near eighteen years old were cared for by emergency physicians who treat *both* children and adults. However, a smaller proportion of patients just over eighteen were cared for by emergency physicians who specialize in pediatric care and predominantly treat children, either in a specialized pediatric ED or in a pediatric area of a larger ED, compared with patients just under eighteen (5.4 percent and 1.7 percent, respectively).

Then we looked at the rate of opioid prescription following emergency department visits based on the age, in months, of the adolescent. Here's what we found:

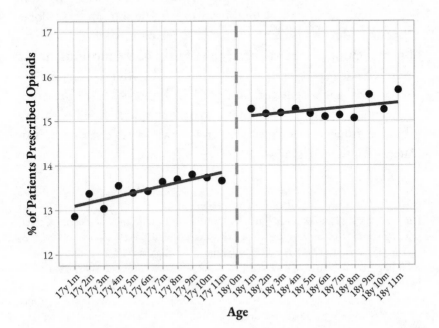

In general, as adolescents got older, there was a gradual increase in the probability of being prescribed an opioid—perhaps not surprising under the assumption that doctors would find opioids less risky to prescribe to an older adolescent. But there was a jump—a discontinuity—at age eighteen, the cutoff between "child" and "adult." Patients aged seventeen years and eleven months received an opioid 13.7 percent of the time, while those aged eighteen years and one month received an opioid 15.3 percent of the time—a 1.6-percentage-point increase. Under a statistical model* that accounted for the gradual increase in prescription rates as well as confounding factors, we estimated this to be closer to a 1.3-percentage-point increase.

In other words, this meant that for adolescents around age eighteen, being labeled an "adult" made them 9.7 percent more likely to receive an opioid than if they had been labeled a "child." With an estimated 20.2 million ED visits by patients aged fifteen to twenty-four annually in the United States, this difference corresponded to at least tens of thousands of arbitrary opioid prescriptions filled each year.

Opioid pain medications are dangerous, as we all know by now, placing patients at risk of long-term use, addiction, and overdose.[†] Of course, doctors prescribe them to treat pain when the benefits of pain control are felt to outweigh the risks of the medication. But when such drug prescriptions are influenced by arbitrary factors—in this case, an adolescent's proximity to adulthood—there's only risk, no benefit. And if indeed opioids were being prescribed with this arbitrary influence, we should see an increase in adverse events associated with them, right?

---

* We used a "regression discontinuity design" model, which helps determine the true size of the discontinuous "jump" that occurs at a cutoff. This model subtracts out changes due to broader trends (in this case, opioid prescription rates generally increasing as patients age) as well as any jump that might be due to measurable confounding from a change in composition of the groups on either side of the boundary (which wasn't a major factor here).

† Excessive prescribing of opioids also places patients' family members and community at risk when opioid pain medications end up in the hands of people other than the patient to whom the drug was prescribed, which happens frequently.

We looked at the same group of adolescents, but this time focused on the probability that any one of several major opioid-related adverse events occurred after an ED visit: new long-term opioid use, a new diagnosis of opioid use disorder, or overdose. Fortunately, these events are uncommon following ED visits. We found that in only 1.6 percent of all ED visits did one of these events occur in the year following the visit. But using a statistical model similar to the one used before, we found that being considered an "adult" rather than a "child," regardless of their true age, was associated with a 0.2-percentage-point increase in the rate of an adverse event, making patients around age eighteen who happened to have been labeled "adults" 12.6 percent more likely to have an adverse event than those labeled a "child."

Our results showed us a few important things. As noted, adolescents around eighteen were being treated differently in the ED depending on whether they were labeled a "child" or an "adult," resulting in differing rates of opioid prescriptions and subsequent adverse events. We can't say for sure what was driving the difference, but we believe it was some combination of representativeness bias on the part of physicians (treating "children" one way and "adults" another) coupled with differences in treatment protocols (when patients go through "pediatric" care systems versus "adult" care systems).

As we continue to grapple with the opioid epidemic, such results can be demoralizing. Opioids appear to be entering patients' homes and communities for arbitrary reasons (with adult/child labeling being just one). But at the same time, it's incredibly important that we understand the different drivers of well-intentioned prescribing behavior if we are to develop systematic changes—ways to treat patients' pain while minimizing risks. Our study suggested that perhaps there was some aspect of the "pediatric approach" that led to fewer prescriptions in this adolescent population—an approach that, if applied to "adults," could be beneficial in curbing the opioid epidemic.

—

Let's change gears again. Consider a local police department that has noticed a problem with cars speeding through town, including in areas where it's particularly dangerous, like school zones, resulting in car accidents and pedestrian injuries. To deter speeding, the department is considering installing cameras around town to take pictures of speeding cars and to issue tickets by mail. The question is, Where should they install the cameras?

One option would be to install a camera on every block of every intersection in the town—a move that would almost certainly curtail speeding but also be incredibly costly and impractical. Another option would be to install cameras at random intersections; drivers might generally slow down, since a camera could be around any corner, but if the cameras weren't in areas where speeding tended to take place, they might not catch too many speeders or prevent accidents in high-risk areas.

A third option (and perhaps the obvious choice) would be to install a handful of cameras in places where (a) people predictably tend to speed most often, such as at the bottom of a hill, and (b) curtailing speeding is most important, like those school zones. Issuing tickets for speeding in these locations would probably get you the most bang for your buck with a handful of cameras, maximizing the number of speeders who are caught while also addressing the important outcome of keeping pedestrians and schoolchildren safe.

Recognizing that doctors make errors and fall victim to cognitive biases in a predictable fashion, finding the places where they happen, and intervening to prevent them is the equivalent of that third approach. We're not implying that doctors are committing minor criminal offenses with their errors. On the contrary, they almost always happen to doctors who are genuinely trying to do their best by their patients. But finding and studying areas where these types of mistakes are most likely to happen is fundamental to our ability to make systematic changes, leading to better outcomes for all patients.

For example, looking at how care changes at specific ages due to predictable biases—like left-digit bias and representativeness bias—is like putting a speed camera at the bottom of a big hill. It's not hard to find potential errors there or to think of ways to prevent them. We reviewed several studies in medicine that show that left-digit bias leads to predictable errors in clinical judgment. We now have the opportunity to do something about them. At the very least, we can make doctors and patients aware of the role bias might be playing in the course of everyday medical care. We can also incorporate such knowledge into the digital health tools made possible by electronic health records (more on this to come).

There are other forms of predictable bias in medicine—errors that don't pop up randomly but occur systematically when you're looking in the right place. We've visited a few of them already in this book, like the study we discussed in chapter 4 where availability bias led doctors to check for a pulmonary embolism more often if they had just diagnosed one. But since doctors are human, too, we should be able to find evidence of bias in any situation in which we know humans, in general, would be subject to bias.

Let's take the example of the "win-stay/lose-shift" heuristic. This is a learning heuristic, a shortcut to help us get better at successfully completing a task. If we take one strategy when completing a task like solving a puzzle and are successful, we "win." Next time we're doing a similar puzzle, we tend to "stay" with that previously successful strategy. But if a strategy is unsuccessful and we "lose," we're inclined to "shift" the strategy, since it's evidently not a winning one. The win-stay/lose-shift heuristic is helpful in a lot of situations, like solving a new problem through trial and error or optimizing a player's strategy in a game. But it can also lead to problems if what you learn from a "win" or "loss" in a prior case isn't relevant to a future one.*

Manasvini Singh, an economist at the University of Massachu-

---

* As you might have already gathered, the win-stay/lose-shift heuristic is closely related to other heuristics and biases we've talked about, such as the availability bias discussed in chapter 4 that led doctors to be more likely to check for a pulmonary embolism in future patients if one was recently diagnosed. It's also closely related to basic principles of positive and negative reinforcement: if you are rewarded with a "win" for a given behavior, you'll continue doing it; meanwhile, if you are punished with a "loss" for a behavior, you'll be less likely to repeat it in the future.

setts, thought the win-stay/lose-shift heuristic might influence the decision making of doctors in the delivery room. Because so many people have personal experience in labor and delivery units, it can be easy to overlook how many rapid, high-stakes decisions doctors make while overseeing the birth of a child—or sometimes multiple children at the same time. Uncertainty about how labor will progress, how a baby is doing at any given moment, and the risks of intervention or inaction—to both mom and baby—make for around-the-clock, high-pressure decision making. One of the most common decisions that doctors make with patients who were planning to deliver a baby vaginally but whose labor is not progressing as expected is whether to change course and deliver via cesarean section (C-section, a major surgical procedure) or to continue efforts to deliver vaginally.

Singh hypothesized that if a physician experienced a complication while delivering a baby—either vaginally *or* by C-section—they would perceive it as a "loss" and thus be more likely to "shift" on their next patient. Because what happened to a laboring mother in room 3 earlier in the day should have no bearing on what happens to the laboring mother in room 6 later in the day, the win-stay/lose-shift heuristic could cause doctors to alter their behavior when they shouldn't—making this a good place for Singh to set up a metaphorical speed camera.

There's a natural experiment here. Let's say a doctor delivers babies from two different mothers each shift. If we combine all of that doctor's shifts together, we can create a few groups of mothers: There are the mothers who delivered first. Then there are mothers who delivered second *after another mother's uncomplicated birth,* and mothers who delivered second *after another mother's birth with a complication.* The two groups of mothers who deliver second are counterfactual to each other: the mothers who delivered second following an uncomplicated birth earlier in the shift tell us what would have happened to mothers who deliver second following a complicated birth, and vice versa. Any differences between them we would attribute to changes in physician judgment brought on by the complications in the preceding birth.

In a 2021 study published in *Science,* using electronic health data from several hospitals over the course of a decade, Singh took a look at more than 86,000 deliveries performed by 231 different doctors, with an average of 390 babies delivered per doctor. For each delivery, she noted whether it was a vaginal delivery or a C-section, and for each one she totaled up the number of complications, including obstructed labor (baby gets stuck on its way out), postpartum hemorrhage and other maternal injuries, umbilical cord problems, and infant injuries and complications.

Looking at the sequence of deliveries performed by an individual doctor over time, she calculated the probability that the *next* baby would be delivered vaginally based on whether the *prior* delivery was either vaginal or a C-section *and* how many complications were associated with that prior delivery. Since the next birth should have nothing to do with the prior birth, we would expect that on average rates of vaginal delivery in the next birth shouldn't vary based on the number of complications in the prior.

She combined all of the doctors into a single analysis and adjusted for confounding factors like the patients' age, race and ethnicity, chronic medical problems, and number of babies delivered (singleton, twins, and so on).

If the *prior* baby was delivered vaginally, she found that as the number of complications with that birth increased, the probability that the *next* baby would be delivered vaginally decreased—consistent with the win-stay/lose-shift heuristic. If there were no vaginal birth complications, the next birth was vaginal 79 percent of the time; if there were three complications, the next birth was vaginal 78 percent of the time; if there were eight or more complications, the next birth was vaginal 76 percent of the time. If the prior birth was a C-section, when the number of complications increased, so did the probability that the next baby would be delivered vaginally. If there were no complications, the next birth was vaginal 76 percent of the time (since vaginal births are more common); three complications, 78 percent of the time; with eight or more C-section complications, the next baby was delivered vaginally 80 percent of the time.

The modest effect of the heuristic—a few percentage points—

meant that most of the time doctors appeared to be bringing a clean mental slate to their next delivery; the key drivers of whether a baby was delivered vaginally or by C-section were clinical factors, not whether a doctor succumbed to cognitive bias. But it also was clear that at least occasionally doctors were bringing mental baggage from the prior case to the next one, apparently employing the win-stay/lose-shift heuristic. If they weren't, we wouldn't have seen changes in vaginal birth rates based on the number of prior complications. Some laboring mothers, therefore, were delivering either vaginally or by C-section when, were it not for what had happened in the prior birth, they would have been delivered by the other mode.

In her next analysis, Singh estimated the effect of this way of thinking. In the patients who she predicted were affected by the switch, she saw small increases in the chances of a prolonged hospitalization, needing extra doctor visits after hospital discharge, and, most concerning of all, increases in maternal and fetal mortality. The win-stay/lose-shift heuristic seemed to be playing a small but predictable role with doctors, with demonstrable effects on patients. Her study suggests that thousands of the more than 3.6 million babies born each year had their care affected by the previous baby, some with devastating results.

—

Singh's study of C-sections was a remarkable addition to a number of studies that have shown how recent experience might influence how a doctor treats subsequent patients. One such study was a 2006 examination of Canadian physicians, in which the Harvard physician and health policy researcher Niteesh Choudhry and colleagues analyzed the health records of patients in Ontario with atrial fibrillation, a common chronic heart rhythm abnormality that places patients at increased risk of strokes from blood clots that form in the heart and travel to the brain. To prevent strokes, anticoagulation ("thinning of the blood") through medication is considered by doctors for any affected patient. But while anticoagulants decrease the risk of stroke, they *increase* the risk of bleeding, which means that in some patients the danger of hemorrhage (like internal bleeding in the brain or gastrointestinal tract) outweighs the potential benefits of stroke prevention. Despite the research and guidelines that support these decisions, weighing the risks of anticoagulation against its benefits can be challenging, involving a doctor's subjectivity. And where there's subjectivity, bias enters the frame.

Using data from patients with atrial fibrillation aged sixty-six and older, the researchers identified about twelve hundred doctors who had taken care of patients who either had a severe bleeding event while taking anticoagulants (in this study, the drug warfarin) or had suffered a stroke while *not* taking anticoagulants—in other words, patients with atrial fibrillation who had suffered a complication of the decision to anticoagulate or not anticoagulate. Their hypothesis was that after caring for a patient with a complication of either anticoagulation (namely, bleeding) or no anticoagulation (stroke), a doctor would be more likely to use the alternate strategy for future patients. Sound familiar? It's the win-stay/lose-shift heuristic all over again.

For each doctor who treated a patient with a bleeding or stroke complication, the researchers took the date of that patient's hospitalization and looked at the ninety days before and after. If the doctor's experience with that patient influenced future decisions, they would prescribe anticoagulants at different rates after the complication than before it. Because the timing of one patient's complication is as good as random with respect to the other patients the doctor treats, there's a natural experiment here: the group of patients the doctor treats *before* the patient with a complication is a counterfactual group to those patients the doctor treats *after;* they tell us how that doctor would have prescribed anticoagulants *had they not recently treated a patient with a complication.* (To check this assumption, the researchers again compared characteristics, like chronic medical conditions and their baseline risk of bleeding or stroke, of the patients and found the groups were similar.)

Can you guess the results of their main analysis?

After doctors cared for patients who had bleeding complications while taking anticoagulants, they became less likely to prescribe it for subsequent similar patients with atrial fibrillation—an effect that appeared to last for at least a year after the complication occurred. This meant that some patients were not receiving anticoagulants who otherwise would have if their doctor hadn't recently treated a patient with a bleeding complication. To check whether this was a finding specific to anticoagulants and not medications in general, they looked at rates of prescribing of a common blood pressure medication and found that, as expected, prescription rates of this medication, unrelated to bleeding, didn't change after doctors cared for patients with complications of anticoagulation.

Interestingly, they found different results in the inverse scenario when atrial fibrillation patients who weren't prescribed anticoagulants later had a stroke—the feared complication in that scenario. For those doctors, there was no difference in prescribing rates of anticoagulants before and after the complication.

So researchers saw a change in behavior when patients experienced a complication of their *active* treatment (giving a patient a pill), but they didn't see a change when patients experienced a complication from *nontreatment* (withholding a pill). Why the difference?

It's hard to say for certain based on data alone, but it may be related to the way doctors perceive complications of their *action* compared with their *inaction*. If we think back to our discussion in chapter 6 of doctors' and soccer goalkeepers' urge to do *something* over doing nothing, it might be that they feel more responsible for a complication from their choice to act, and thus change their behavior in the future, than in instances when they chose inaction.

Put differently, doctors may fear adverse consequences of their actions over consequences of their inaction, even if, as we've seen, either path can lead to serious harm.

Another example of how doctors' decisions are influenced by their recent experiences comes from a type of doctor who never meets most of their patients: pathologists. Pathologists are doctors who specialize in the examination and analysis of tissues, fluids, and other materials taken from patients to help make diagnoses. They're experts in getting answers; medical and surgical doctors alike frequently rely on a pathologist's examination of a patient biopsy* to make a complex or elusive diagnosis. By considering cells under a microscope or using advanced laboratory testing, they help make life-altering diagnoses with confidence. They carry the reputation of being a source of truth in a clinical environment rife with uncertainty, earning the pathologist the nickname "the doctor's doctor."

It's tempting to think that looking at tissues and cells under a microscope could be done without bias—that pathologists are just calling balls and strikes each time they report their findings on a biopsy. But interpreting a slide is not as objective a process as one might think. Pathologists don't always agree—a "strike" for one might be a "ball" for another—making "second opinions" a common practice for pathologists, especially when stakes are high.

We chose that baseball metaphor for a reason. Baseball umpires are human beings, so they must be prone to bias, right? In one study, the economists Daniel Chen (Université Toulouse) and Tobias Moskowitz and Kelly Shue (both at Yale) showed that home plate umpires, whose job it is to determine whether a pitch is thrown in the strike zone (and therefore a strike) or outside the strike zone (and therefore a ball), can be biased by the previous pitch. Using data generated during Major League Baseball games that measure pitch location within a centimeter, they analyzed 1.5 million called pitches (pitches at which the batter did not swing) from 12,564 games and 127 different umpires. They found that *for pitches in the same location* umpires were more likely to call that pitch a strike if they had called a ball on the prior pitch, and more likely to call a ball if they had called a strike on the prior pitch; the effect was even stronger when pitches were closer to the edge of the strike zone, where they would have more uncertainty in their call. In other words, umpires were biased toward "evening out" balls and strikes based on the prior pitch.†

---

* A biopsy is the removal from the body of a small sample of an organ (for example, skin, liver, lung, kidney) for the purposes of microscopic examination by an expert, typically a pathologist.

† The baseball umpires displayed a type of bias known as the "gambler's fallacy," part of our tendency to think that unrelated events—like two pitches or two flips of

Could pathologists display a similar type of bias? On the one hand, the studies of laboring mothers and patients with atrial fibrillation told us that recent events with one patient can influence a doctor's behavior with their next patient. But on the other hand, pathologists aren't trying to be "fair" like a baseball umpire, calling some in favor of the disease and some in favor of the patient. They're just trying to find evidence of disease—or lack thereof—to make a diagnosis.

In a rare turn of events for this book, we have the chance to look at a randomized controlled trial (not a natural experiment) to tell us how recent experience might bias pathologists. In a unique study published in 2022, a team of researchers led by the UCLA physician and professor Joann Elmore relied on the common practice for a pathologist to see the first opinion before offering their second one to look for evidence of bias. They set out to find out how one pathologist's interpretation of a skin biopsy might affect another pathologist's interpretation of the same slide. Put another way, how does the "first opinion" affect a "second opinion" of the same biopsy?

While baseball umpires might be motivated to correct *themselves*, based on the prior pitch, researchers wanted to know how pathologists generating a second opinion might respond to their *peers* who were generating the first opinion.

In the trial, 149 dermatopathologists (pathologists specializing in the interpretation of skin tissue samples) were given a random slate of eighteen skin biopsies that were concerning for melanoma (a con-

---

a coin—are related. If you flipped a coin five times and it came up heads every time, what is the chance that it will be heads on the next flip? The answer, of course, is 50 percent. The gambler's fallacy is the gut feeling that tails is more likely because it's somehow "due" to come up. A baseball umpire might similarly have the subconscious impulse that their close calls in favor of the pitcher should even out with calls in favor of the batter if they're being a "fair" arbiter of events in a game. Casinos take advantage of this bias when they show the history of recent spins at a roulette table; even though what happened on the prior spin has no bearing on the next one, you might be tempted to bet big on black if the last few spins were red. The casino, of course, has an advantage no matter what color you bet on; they just want you to bet, and bet big.

dition that can be challenging for pathologists to diagnose; such biopsies are frequently sent out for second opinions). The pathologists were asked to grade the disease severity of each slide along the spectrum of invasiveness for melanoma. These measurements were recorded as their phase 1 interpretations.

Researchers then waited one to two years—enough time for the pathologists to have completely forgotten the slides and their diagnoses—and gave them the exact same eighteen digital slides, without telling them they were doing so. For this phase 2, however, a random selection of the slides came with a "first opinion" from another pathologist appended to them. Participants were essentially, in these instances, being asked to give a second opinion on those slides.

The first opinions, however, had been manipulated by the researchers. Knowing how the pathologists initially graded each slide at phase 1, they generated a "first opinion" in phase 2 that was (randomly) either more or less severe than their initial diagnosis.

The pathologists in phase 1 were therefore serving as counterfactuals to themselves in phase 2, telling us how they would have interpreted the slide *had they not been exposed to the differing first opinion.* If there was any difference in the way pathologists interpreted the slides, it could reasonably be attributed to the bias introduced by the first opinion provided by the researchers.

What did they find? When pathologists saw a first opinion in phase 2 that was more severe than their initial diagnosis from phase 1, they were swayed toward a more severe diagnosis, being 58 percent more likely to grade the same slide as more severe in phase 2 than they did in phase 1. When they saw a first opinion in phase 2 that was less severe than their initial diagnosis from phase 1, they were swayed toward a less severe diagnosis, being 38 percent more likely to grade the same slide as less severe in phase 2 than they did in phase 1. In either case, they tended to be swayed *toward* what a random "first opinion" suggested and *away* from what they'd initially thought. Moreover, the bias toward agreement with the first opinion was often swaying pathologists away from the "correct" diagnosis (as determined by a consensus of a panel of experts). That is, often they were right the first time, but were swayed to make the wrong diagnosis the second time when primed by "another pathologist's" first opinion. While baseball umpires' bias seemed to balance out their prior calls, pathologists were biased toward reinforcing opinions.

This is an example of what's called "anchoring bias." Anchoring bias is so named because once humans have a starting point on our way to figuring out an answer, we tend to want to stay close to it like a ship to its anchor. It applies to doctors offering second opinions but also to the way moviegoers judge a film after reading a critic's review. It's closely related to confirmation bias, our tendency to favor and prioritize new information that conforms to our initial conclusion and de-emphasize information that refutes it.

When a pathologist picks up a slide and sees the first opinion, they're not starting from scratch when they peer down the microscope; they're anchored to the first opinion, which influences the way they interpret what they see under the microscope, whether they know it or not.

———

As ever, the question arises: What should we do about all this?

First, let's not forget that many cognitive biases come about with good cause as humans gain experience and learn to recognize patterns that help them predict the future. Yes, recent experience can contribute to biased decision making, but *cumulative experience* over many years is what allows doctors to do their job effectively (more on this in chapter 9). Mental shortcuts develop in the first place because they often get doctors to the right place. Without heavily relying on pattern recognition and rapid thinking, doctors wouldn't be able to care for nearly as many patients as they do.*

Of course, cognitive biases and heuristics can also be very effec-

---

* We also wouldn't be able to take advantage of these biases and heuristics to study natural experiments and answer questions that are otherwise difficult to answer. Left-digit bias gave us the opportunity to study the risks and benefits of CABG surgery in roughly eighty-year-olds, while the representativeness heuristic allowed us to estimate the effects of unnecessary opioid prescriptions in roughly eighteen-year-olds.

tive at getting doctors to the *wrong* place, leading patients to harm and, in some cases, even death. But completely eliminating cognitive biases simply isn't possible, since the brain mechanics that lead to them are deeply wired and so heavily relied upon for much of the good care we provide.

It behooves us, then, to figure out what types of guardrails should be put in place to prevent patients from being harmed by biases, while still allowing mental shortcuts to offer us benefit. This is much, much easier said than done. We currently don't have many tools to eliminate the adverse effects of cognitive bias on a large scale, in part because until recently we didn't really know the extent to which such biases were affecting doctors and patients.

Still, the likely first step is "debiasing" doctors: making them aware of the cognitive biases we know exist and the effects they can have. Medical schools and residency programs have increasingly included training in cognitive biases, the threats they pose to patients, and strategies to mitigate them.

For example, as a resident at Boston Medical Center, I (Chris) participated in a weekly teaching session called a Clinical Reasoning Exercise (C-REX for short, and yes, the conference reminder emails featured a dinosaur). The purpose of this group was not to learn about advancements in treatments for various diseases or the nuanced details of managing rare diseases—that was saved for other teaching sessions—but rather to learn about how we, as doctors, think as we care for patients, make diagnoses, and decide on treatments. The idea was to improve our metacognition—our understanding of our own thought processes—so we could become more aware of how cognitive biases and other thought processes might be influencing our practice. If we could see biases coming around the corner, we might better avoid the pitfalls they create.

One way to avoid cognitive biases is through "cognitive forcing strategies," which encourage doctors to take a moment to reevaluate their own line of thinking. As described by the Dalhousie University emergency physician and patient safety expert Pat Croskerry, "In contrast to heuristics, cognitive forcing strategies are a specific debiasing technique that introduces self-monitoring of decision making. They are designed to prevent clinicians from pursuing a pattern-recognition path that typically will lead to error. . . . They are rules that depend instead on the clinician consciously applying a metacognitive step and cognitively forcing a necessary consideration of alternatives." In other words, when doctors are faced with a clinical decision, this strategy forces them to actively consider—and then actively reject—alternative courses of action. It is a strategy that, while more time consuming, is designed to bypass precisely the types of mental shortcuts we've been discussing.

What does a cognitive forcing strategy look like in practice? Let's say an elderly patient has come to the emergency department after falling at home. His memory of the fall is hazy, but he has substantial pain in his right leg, a wrist injury, and injuries to the nose and cheek—all presumed to be due to the fall. X-rays show a hip fracture, but no fractures in the wrist or face. The orthopedist has seen the patient and plans to pin the fracture in the operating room the next day. The doctor caring for this patient could simply assess and diagnose the injuries, provide pain control, and prepare the patient for surgery the next morning.

A doctor using a cognitive forcing strategy, however, will recognize that while traumatic injuries are important and require immediate care, they can also be distracting: wounds and blood and pain tend to absorb our attention. The doctor might think (or say out loud to their team), "Let's back up for a second. For every patient who comes in with a fall, we have to ask *why* they fell. Could this elderly patient have had a drop in his blood pressure, causing him to briefly lose consciousness and fall from a heart attack, or an abnormal heart rhythm?" By forcing themselves to think about alternatives or underlying explanations, doctors take their brains off the "highway," where biases and heuristics keep them moving quickly, and instead take the "scenic route" for a while, where a more deliberate consideration of the patient can more easily occur. In this case, taking that moment of extra time could result in checking an ECG, which could in turn reveal the onset of an abnormal heart rhythm that led to the fall (and that also needs to be treated).

Simulation is another opportunity for doctors to learn about cognitive biases and heuristics, because it allows us to *make* errors without exposing patients to harm. We've both been though many simulations in our training, and most doctors undergo them periodically to maintain certification in certain skills (like the management of cardiac arrest). Good simulations might involve high-tech mannequins, trained actors, real-time data (like vital signs), and real hospital rooms and medical equipment; they're about as close to real life as is reasonably possible. Following a simulation, we undergo a "debriefing" where we review the case with teammates and observers, scrutinize our own decisions and actions, and consider what we might have been able to do better.

In a study of thirty-two resident anesthesiologists (doctors who had completed medical school and were in residency training to become anesthesiologists), participants underwent a videotaped simulation of a set of common emergencies that anesthesiologists encounter—situations like anaphylaxis, pulmonary embolism, and difficulty placing a breathing tube, all of which are high stakes and require rapid decision making. Meanwhile, experts watching the simulation monitored for nine common cognitive biases. In what might not come as a surprise at this point, cognitive errors were common; for example, anchoring bias was observed in 62 percent of simulations, premature closure bias (similar to anchoring bias, a tendency to home in on a diagnosis before all information is known) was seen in 80 percent of simulations, and sunk-cost bias (a tendency to continue with a course of action, even if you have evidence showing it is wrong, because you have already invested resources in it) was seen in 68 percent of simulations. The study suggested both that cognitive biases were pervasive in simulation—even though participants knew they were being watched—and that simulation is a viable way for doctors to learn about their own cognitive biases in a safe setting.

While education and training can certainly raise awareness of cognitive bias, they can take us only so far. Other tools—some of which we have discussed previously—can help too. The surgical time-out, for example, is likewise designed to take surgical teams' brains off the "highway" and put them on the "scenic route," if only for a minute, to make sure they're doing the correct surgery on the correct patient.

Research-based guidelines and other tools to aid in decisions (sometimes referred to as clinical decision support) can help too. For example, risk calculators are one way to avoid the type of heuristic thinking we saw in the left-digit bias study of CABG surgery. Using data from millions of patients to predict the probability of adverse outcomes following surgery, the American College of Surgeons' online risk calculator can estimate the risk of many procedures, without the human influence of left-digit bias. It processes age along a continuous number line, rather than placing patients "in their 70s" or "in their 80s" the way we automatically do. Or take primary care doctors, who can use the American College of Cardiology's online risk calculator to help them decide if patients would benefit from taking a statin medication to lower their cholesterol and prevent heart attacks.

Other digital tools in the electronic health record could monitor data generated by patients and help avoid cognitive errors in real time. Digital nudges remind doctors and nurses in the hospital that a central line or urinary catheter has been in place for too long and needs to be removed to avoid infection, something it's all too easy to forget to do. We can also create "order sets" for patients with a certain condition that serve as checklists to remind us about easily overlooked aspects of their care; an order set for a patient with heart failure, for example, might prompt doctors to prescribe an ACE inhibitor, a beneficial blood pressure medication in these patients. Other, more sophisticated algorithms can scan the data and alert doctors that they might have missed a diagnosis of sepsis, a serious condition that requires immediate treatment but can easily be missed.

While digital tools like these are not, in principle, prone to cognitive bias the way we humans are, it bears remembering that they have been *programmed by humans.* Algorithms may crunch numbers dispassionately, but algorithm designers might unknowingly put their fingers on the scale. For example, what if an electronic alert was set up to remind emergency doctors that patients over 40 are at risk for heart attack? Such an alert would probably cause doctors to check for heart attacks much more often in 40-year-olds than in 39-year-olds, thus creating or even exacerbating a left-digit bias.[*]

Alternatively, if a surgical risk calculator didn't factor in smoking status in its risk prediction, a meaningful factor for many health outcomes, it's not going to accurately assign risk differently to smokers and nonsmokers. (The calculators we mentioned above both do.) Or if the millions of patients upon which an algorithm's predictions are based don't include certain groups of people, the predictions they generate won't be accurate across diverse populations. If a sepsis detection algorithm is based on data from patients in a large urban hospital with a thousand beds, it may not perform as accurately in a small, rural hospital with only sixty beds, one that treats a completely different population of patients and a different set of medical conditions.

While there are many other strategies to avoid the adverse effects of cognitive biases and heuristics that we haven't discussed, there's no silver bullet. Most strategies come with drawbacks or limitations: they may take too much time to be practically incorporated at the bedside or may be prone to other, unrelated biases. As we continue to identify more roles cognitive bias is playing in everyday medical care, it's critical that we continue to find ways to mitigate the harm they can do without introducing new harm along the way.

For now, this means that doctors *and patients* need to be aware of the cognitive bias they may encounter in their treatment. Simply taking the time to reflect on this possibility may do a lot to mitigate harm.

Now, with all this talk of "bias," you might have noted that cer-

---

[*] If they actually existed, such alerts or other reminders that led to doctors treating 40-year-olds differently than 39-year-olds might have contributed to that study's results.

tain types were conspicuously absent from our discussion. What about the kind of bias based on gender or race or other personal characteristics, the type so pervasive in American society? In the next chapter, we're going to explore some of the ways these types of biases can influence physicians and medical care—in some not-so-obvious ways.

CHAPTER NINE

WHAT MAKES A GOOD DOCTOR?

W HEN HE WAS a medical student, the University of Michigan physician and professor Elliot Tapper was interested in TV doctors. He noticed that doctors on modern shows were portrayed differently than those from earlier decades. Curious to understand the discrepancy, he became a connoisseur of medical TV programming, watching and studying shows when he wasn't busy doing his course work, dissecting in the anatomy lab, or rotating in the hospital. His research started in the 1950s with *Medic*—arguably the first popular medical drama on TV—and moved forward through time with shows like *Marcus Welby, M.D., ER, Scrubs, House,* and *Grey's Anatomy.* This was in the early years of the twenty-first century—a now-unimaginable time before the rise of streaming services—meaning he had to watch *M*A*S*H* in the library media room and had Netflix send him *St. Elsewhere* DVDs through the mail.

He reported his observations in an article, one that he initially had trouble publishing. "When I submitted the paper somewhere, the [peer] review said, 'Elliot Tapper is not a historian, and it shows,'" Tapper recalls, twelve years later. "I chuckle to myself about that from time to time." Though indeed he was not and is not a historian, few (if any) young doctors in training could claim such extensive exposure to TV doctors.

"We began with doctor shows sanctioned by medical associations wherein a doctor could do no wrong," Tapper wrote in 2010, speaking of shows that featured highly idealized doctors. Marcus Welby, the titular character of a popular 1970s drama, is perhaps the best example of this phenomenon. He was an older, dedicated family physician who never seemed to fail his patients.* But this superhuman portrayal of doctors was unsustainable; it simply wasn't consistent with the health-care experiences of patients seeing "real doctors who were constrained by time and their own human foibles," Tapper noted.

Patients and doctors alike struggled to reconcile TV-based expectations with their lived reality. The disconnect was bad enough that medical malpractice insurers coined the term "Marcus Welby syndrome," according to a 1985 article in *The New York Times* titled "Physicians Have an Image Problem—It's Too Good." The character Marcus Welby, through his near-flawless clinical acumen and access to modern advancements in medical technology, was creating a standard no doctor could meet.

Insurers felt that real doctors weren't helping matters. "Many doctors reinforce Marcus Welbyism with a reassuring, ever-confident air designed to convince patients they have nothing to worry about," the *Times* wrote. "Then, when something goes wrong, the patient is shocked; and in more and more cases, a malpractice suit is filed." The American Medical Association (AMA) agreed. "We're too damned confident with our patients. We've got to work on patient expectations. We've got to be more candid in letting them know that things can go wrong," an AMA official said for the story, noting that in order to do this, "a massive change in public attitudes would be required."

Over time, the doctors who appeared on-screen became more recognizable to us. Their flaws, complexity, and imperfect judgment—

---

* The show *Marcus Welby, M.D.* and the character have been the subjects of criticism—even during the show's original airing. The show's portrayal of homosexuality, for example, was criticized during its run; in 1974, a number of ABC affiliates across the United States refused to air one episode in response to protests. Nevertheless, Marcus Welby is remembered fondly by many patients who watched the show. It is generally considered a compliment to compare your doctor to Marcus Welby today. O'Connor, "Pressure Groups Are Increasingly Putting the Heat on TV."

their humanity—became prominent features of their TV characters (as fans of *House* would agree). With accuracy generally taking a backseat to drama—one analysis of *ER, Chicago Hope,* and *Grey's Anatomy* found diagnoses skew toward dramatic conditions that carry a mortality rate almost nine times higher than in real life— multidimensional, flawed TV doctors caught in unlikely scenarios seemed to become the winning formula for prime-time entertainment. "The persistent demand for doctors on TV . . . represents a persistent fascination with the doctor's craft, science, and character," Tapper concluded.

Some doctors have trouble watching medical shows altogether. They can be so inaccurate that it's distracting, or they fail to offer enough of an escape from work to qualify as entertainment. But many of us would have to admit that medical shows have had a hand in making us the doctors we've since become.

For Chris, the TV doctor that most made a lasting impression is the Emergency Medical Hologram from *Star Trek: Voyager,* played by the actor Robert Picardo and referred to often as simply "the Doctor." The Emergency Medical Hologram was a walking, talking, human-appearing, sentient computer program designed to serve as an emergency medical assistant in the event of a mass casualty event aboard the starship *Voyager.* But when *Voyager* is marooned on the other side of the galaxy without any living medical staff, he becomes the ship's sole medical provider. He's programmed with an extensive library of medical knowledge and technical skill—more than any "real" doctor could ever know. But as a computer program, he has terrible bedside manner and lacks the empathy and ability for human connection we expect of our medical professionals. Over the course of the show, the Doctor's patients and shipmates end up teaching him some of what it really means to be a doctor—and what it means to be human—as they journey across the galaxy.

We hope by this point in *our* journey together, we've sold you on the idea that doctors are humans, too. If we haven't, perhaps it's because your favorite modern TV doctor made the case first.

—

We've spent much of this book exploring how doctors' humanity makes them flawed—prone to mistakes and susceptible to bias. Of course, humanity is also essential to our profession. It's what allows us to connect with patients, help them understand their health, and take steps to improve their lives. It's what allows us to see and treat a patient as a whole person—with values, priorities, hopes, and fears— far more than the sum of the cells, tissues, and organs targeted by our treatments. It's also what makes us confident that doctors won't be replaced by artificial intelligence like in *Star Trek: Voyager* any- time soon.

In a famous 1927 essay to medical students that, in many ways, is as relevant today as it was a century ago, the Harvard Medical School professor Francis Peabody wrote from Boston City Hospital:

> When one considers the amazing progress of science in its rela- tion to medicine during the last thirty years, and the enormous mass of scientific material which must be made available to the modern physician, it is not surprising that the schools have tended to concern themselves more and more with this phase of the educational problem. And while they have been absorbed in the difficult task of digesting and correlating new knowledge, it has been easy to overlook the fact that the application of the principles of science to the diagnosis and treatment of disease is only one limited aspect of medical practice. The practice of medicine in its broadest sense includes the whole relationship of the physician with his [or her] patient. It is an art, based to increasing extent on the medical sciences, but comprising much that still remains outside the realm of any science. The art of medicine and the science of medicine are not antagonis- tic but supplementary to each other.

Despite the standardized scientific training every doctor goes through and is tested upon when earning their medical credentials, the way we connect with and care for patients—an important part of the *art* of medical practice as Peabody describes it—is shaped by many factors. Some of them are taught; others are determined by a physician's innate strengths, background, personality, and unique perspective.

If the quality of our doctoring depends upon how we apply both the science and the art of medicine, surely there must be some who are "better" than others. We put "better" in quotation marks because despite what the existence of a magazine's "Top Doctors" list might suggest, there's no universally accepted way to recognize one doctor as "better" than another.* We've both had patients who think we're wonderful doctors and other patients who think we're terrible. We also have physician colleagues who trust our clinical judgment more than others, just as we might have differing opinions of their judgments.

However, there surely must be *some* objective measure by which one doctor can be deemed "better" than another. For example, compared with their peers, some emergency doctors must get to the right diagnosis faster or more often; some surgeons must have lower complication rates for a given procedure; and some primary care doctors must have a higher fraction of patients whose diabetes is well managed. If we measured enough of the right variables and defined "good," "bad," and "average" in defensible ways, surely some patterns would emerge to help us differentiate between the quality of care that doctors provide.

When the *British Medical Journal* asked its readers, "What makes a good doctor and how do you make one?" more than a hundred letters came in from doctors, nurses, patients, and others in twenty-four countries. A few themes emerged. One was the idea that training isn't everything; there's more to being a doctor than knowing the latest science and techniques (just as Francis Peabody wrote in 1927). Another was that the way a doctor listens to and communicates with their patients, nurses, and team members is critical for cooperation and advancing patient care. Good doctors must have

---

* It's worth being very skeptical of any "Top Doctors" list you read. These lists can amount to little more than paid advertisements for physician practices, as one ProPublica reporter found out when the nonphysician journalist was able to secure himself a Top Doctor designation (he listed his specialty as "investigation"). Allen, "I'm a Journalist. Apparently, I'm Also One of America's 'Top Doctors.'"

compassion and empathy for patients; they must be interested in their lives beyond the exam room and be able to advocate on their behalf. They should be comfortable with uncertainty and the feelings that can accompany it. They must be humble—willing to hear alternative viewpoints, to admit when they are wrong, to accept their limitations, and to be honest when they don't know something.

Try as we might, most doctors are going to have trouble embodying everything that makes a good doctor, by these definitions or any other. We will inevitably excel in one area and fall short in another. Much of what matters is hard to teach, or it takes time and experience to learn. It's not surprising, then, that writers to the *British Medical Journal* had a lot less to say about how to *make* a good doctor; their views were summarized this way: "All we can hope to do is select [medical] students with the right gifts (not the right exam results)."

—

To begin to address the matter of what makes a good doctor, let's start with a basic question: If doctors hone their craft through their years of experience, does that mean older doctors are inevitably better than younger ones?

If we look beyond the initial "hump" that is residency—when young doctors see and treat patients with various conditions for the first time—two obvious, competing hypotheses emerge. If doctors learn from experience, which they surely do, more senior doctors with decades of experience ought to be better than younger doctors fresh out of their training. Alternatively, because residency is a time when doctors are trained based on the latest advances in medical research, young doctors just out of residency should be more familiar with the latest treatments and techniques than their more senior peers, and thus should have better patient outcomes. (More senior doctors could hardly be blamed for failing to keep up with the ever-expanding research landscape—particularly challenging when more than a million biomedical research articles are published every year.)

In a study published in 2017, we (Bapu, along with the UCLA

researcher Yusuke Tsugawa and Harvard colleagues Joseph New-house, Alan Zaslavsky, and Daniel Blumenthal) set out to shed some light on the role of age when it came to internists who treat patients in hospitals. These physicians, called hospitalists (to reflect their specialization in treating hospitalized patients), provide the majority of care for patients hospitalized in the United States with some of the most common acute illnesses such as serious infections, organ failure, cardiac problems, and more.

Aside from offering a broad data set, there was another benefit to studying hospitalists. In much of medical care, patients choose their doctors—based on things like bedside manner, perceived expertise, responsiveness, and attributes that are impossible to deduce. This means, for example, that patients whose conditions are more serious may choose doctors who are more experienced, assuming they'll get more effective care. And if that occurs, we may falsely conclude (because of confounding) that older, more experienced doctors have worse outcomes for their patients, simply because the patients they treat were at higher risk of worse outcomes to begin with.

Patients who are hospitalized, however, don't get a say in which hospitalist will treat them; they're cared for by whichever doctor happens to be on duty at the time. Those doctors tend to be scheduled to cover the hospital in blocks—perhaps one or two weeks at a time. With their focus, hospitalists quickly become experts in hospital care, which comes with a different set of considerations from the outpatient care that most of us more typically experience.

Conveniently for us, this creates a bunch of natural experiments. Patients who are hospitalized are assigned to hospitalists in as-good-as-random fashion, based on which hospitalist happens to be on duty when a patient is admitted.* As long as we have enough patients to represent the variety of different conditions that result in hos-

---

* In the first few years after his residency, Bapu used to work from 7:00 p.m. on Thursday to 7:00 a.m. on Friday as a hospitalist, thus creating a natural experiment that could measure the effect on patients of being treated by one particular doctor/economist.

pitalization, the patients cared for by different hospitalists serve as counterfactuals for one another; any difference between patients can be attributed to differences between the hospitalists themselves.

Using data from Medicare on patients over age sixty-five and a database containing doctors' ages, we identified about 737,000 non-elective hospitalizations managed by about nineteen thousand different hospitalists from 2011 to 2013. We divided patients into four different groups based on the age of the doctor who treated them: doctors aged less than forty, aged forty to forty-nine, aged fifty to fifty-nine, and aged sixty and above.

As a first step (one that by now you can probably guess), we had to compare the characteristics of patients in each of the four groups. If hospitalized patients were being assigned to doctors in an as-good-as-random fashion, the groups should be similar, irrespective of their doctor's age. Indeed, that was the case across sex, age, race, rates of chronic medical conditions, and Medicaid-eligibility status (a proxy for socioeconomic status). We could reasonably say that they were counterfactuals to one another.

The hospitalist doctors in each group, however, were not similar. Older doctors obviously had more years of experience since completing residency, with doctors under forty having an average of 4.9 post-residency years of experience, increasing to 28.6 years for doctors over sixty. Older doctors were also more likely to be men (under-forty doctors were 61 percent men compared with 84 percent of over-sixty doctors), reflecting the shift in gender makeup that has occurred in our profession in recent decades. There were also differences in how many patients the doctors treated; doctors under forty and over sixty tended to treat fewer patients than doctors in the intermediate age-groups. The data didn't tell us the reason for those differences; perhaps younger doctors were pursuing additional training or busy with young families, older doctors were nearing retirement, and thus both groups were simply working fewer hospital shifts. Regardless, we had a valid natural experiment on our hands.

We were only halfway there, though. If we wanted to answer the question of whether older doctors were "better" than younger doctors, we'd have to define in what way they were better. In other words, by what measure should we compare them? For doctors who treat patients with life-threatening conditions that require hospitalization, an obvious and simple metric would be patient mortality rates. Some percentage of hospitalized patients will survive or die no matter who their doctor is, but for others their doctor's clinical judgment, decision making, and technical skill could be the difference between life and death.

The next step, therefore, was to compare mortality rates—specifically thirty-day mortality rates—between the four different groups. In a statistical model that accounted for differences between certain characteristics of patients and doctors,* and that compared outcomes of patients treated by doctors of varying ages within the same hospital,† we found that as doctors got older, their patients had higher mortality rates. The rate for under-forty doctors was 10.8 percent, increasing to 11.1 percent in the group of forty-to-forty-nine-year-olds, 11.3 percent in the group of fifty-to-fifty-nine-year-olds, and 12.1 percent in the over-sixty group. To put these numbers in perspective, the results suggested if the over-sixty doctors took care of a thousand patients, thirteen of the patients who die in their care would have survived had they been cared for by the under-forty doctors.

To make sure that these mortality differences were a result of differences between doctor ages and not some other factor, we ran a few additional tests. Older doctors might have been more likely to care for patients who were at high risk of death at baseline, so we redid our analysis after removing patients hospitalized with cancer or who

* Because we wanted to study the effect of age—and age alone—we have to account for other differences we might see due to other factors, such as gender-related differences (more on this later). Since older doctors are more likely to be men, we had to adjust for gender to prevent bias from confounding due to any difference between male and female hospitalists.

† Doing a "within hospital" analysis like this is particularly important. While we are assuming that patients get randomly assigned to a doctor within the hospital, we *can't* assume that patients are getting randomly assigned to hospitals; in fact, we know they're not. Certain patients with certain characteristics tend to be hospitalized at certain hospitals. So to avoid bias related to which hospitals patients go to, we compared patients with other patients who were hospitalized *in the same hospital.*

were known to be at the end of their life and discharged from the hospital to hospice care (in the event that older doctors might care for these patients differently). The pattern of mortality rates between age-groups remained the same. We also repeated the analysis limiting to patients aged sixty-five to seventy-five, who were less likely to die because they were younger than their older Medicare patient peers. The pattern remained. We repeated the analysis using sixty- and ninety-day mortality rates, in case longer-term outcomes might have been different, but again the pattern persisted.

The relationship between a doctor's age and patient mortality seemed real. Younger doctors had better outcomes than their more experienced peers. The inevitable question followed: Why?

There are two possible explanations. The first is that there is a true age effect, wherein simply being older leads to changes in how a doctor practices, resulting in higher mortality. Perhaps older doctors are overly confident in their experience—succumbing to things like anchoring bias when they've "seen a case like this a million times," and thus missing tricky diagnoses. The other, which we think is more likely, is that there are things that older doctors and younger doctors do differently simply because they were trained at different times—things that older doctors would do if they had been trained the same way younger doctors were, and vice versa. During their training, doctors are exposed to contemporary medical thinking, notions that cement themselves in their minds. Younger doctors would thus possess clinical knowledge that is more current. If older doctors haven't kept up with the latest advances in research and technology, or if they aren't following the latest guidelines, their care may not be as good as that of their younger peers.

The data can tell us only so much about what doctors of different ages might be doing differently, making this question hard to answer definitively. But there are some clues.

One way that doctors stay up to date is simply by taking care of patients. When patients come to us with a given diagnosis, it may prompt us to check out the latest research, guidelines, or recommendations for that condition. Older doctors might have higher patient mortality rates not because of their age per se but because they see fewer patients.

To see if this might be the case, we repeated the analysis but this time divided doctors based on both age *and* case volume. We found that for "low volume" doctors (doctors who didn't treat that many patients in any given year), older doctors still had higher mortality. For "medium volume" doctors, the pattern was less pronounced. And for "high volume" doctors, the pattern went away altogether. Mortality was similar across doctors of all ages.

What do we make of all this? Overall, older doctors had higher mortality rates than younger doctors, but there seems to be a relationship between doctor age, case volume, and mortality outcomes. In practical terms, as long as a doctor is seeing a sufficiently large number of patients, the doctor's age is irrelevant to the care they give. If they're not seeing enough patients, however, their younger peers seem to be outperforming them.

Does this mean that on balance younger doctors are "better" than older ones? This study suggests that if "better" is defined as a hospitalist having lower thirty-day patient mortality, then we would have to say yes, the *average* younger doctor is better than the *average* older doctor.

Jack Sobel, dean of the Wayne State University School of Medicine and a senior physician himself, reflected on the study's findings. As doctors age, he says, "It could be that high-volume doctors are experiencing no decrease in their skills or expertise. Maybe low-to-medium-volume doctors just don't see enough patients to have to keep up [with the latest advancements]. Or maybe those doctors are less knowledgeable, so they see fewer patients. It's not clear what comes first. . . . It's not that clinical skills deteriorate. People over age 65 are just not as familiar with the new methods. That's what gives younger doctors the edge. It's access to newer technology and knowing the newer drugs."

But just because the average mortality rate is higher for low-to-medium-volume older doctors, that doesn't mean there aren't both older doctors who are better than the average younger doctor and younger doctors who are worse than the average older doctor. What's more, there will be some doctors who may be below average overall, but who are above average in managing certain conditions or caring for specific groups of patients. The challenge, as a patient and as a researcher alike, is that it's hard to know who is who.

One way for an older doctor to mitigate the apparent effect of low case volume would be to make up for it with extra efforts to stay up to date by reading medical journals, by participating in continuing education (some of which is required to maintain board certification), and by teaching younger physicians, who often have plenty to teach more senior physicians. Jack Sobel reads medical journals and teaches students on a daily basis to stay sharp. "I happen to be addicted to keeping up to date," he says. "But I'm not the norm."

We tried, in our research, to hew to objective measures of doctor performance—hard-and-fast numbers that are difficult to refute. Of course, there are also *subjective* measures of doctor performance— our assessments of how good we are or other doctors are relative to their peers. These are of course prone to bias. When comparing ourselves with others, humans tend to overemphasize our own skills and de-emphasize the skills of others—a form of anchoring bias in which we anchor at our own skill level and try to evaluate others based on their relative strength. We tend to think we're "above average" on the objectively easy things, forgetting that if something is easy for us, it's probably easy for others.* This "above-average effect" has also been dubbed the "Lake Wobegon effect," named after the town from Garrison Keillor's radio program, *A Prairie Home Companion,* in which it is said that "all the women are strong, all the men are good looking, and all the children are above average."

Ask a bunch of doctors whether they're better than average at treating pneumonia—an "easy" condition that inpatient doctors treat all the time—and the Lake Wobegon effect would predict that a majority of them will think they're "above average." This means

---

* Similarly, for things that are difficult, we tend to think we're "below average" because we forget that if it's hard for us, it's probably hard for others, and the average skill is actually lower than we might think.

that a good number of below-average doctors may be out there providing lower-quality care with the confidence of someone who thinks they're among the best.

———

So far we've talked about hospitalists—internists who focus on diagnosis and medical treatments for hospitalized patients. But what about surgeons, who in addition to their diagnostic skills require technical abilities that depend on experience and muscle memory? Do surgeons get better over time as they gain experience? And if so, are older surgeons best? Or do younger surgeons, more recently trained on the latest techniques and closer to their physical peak, get better patient outcomes?

We (Bapu, along with Yusuke Tsugawa, Harvard colleagues John Orav, Daniel Blumenthal, and Thomas Tsai, the UCSD surgeon Winta Mehtsun, and Ashish Jha) sought to find out, in a study similar to the last one. This time, we looked at about 900,000 Medicare patients who underwent common nonelective major surgeries (for example, emergency hip fracture repair or gallbladder surgery) performed by about forty-six thousand surgeons of varying age. We chose nonelective surgery since patients don't have a whole lot of control over their surgeon when they come in with an urgent or emergent problem; like with hospitalists, they'll end up assigned to the surgeon on duty in an as-good-as-random fashion.

Just as before, patients were divided into four groups based on the age of their surgeon: under forty, forty to forty-nine, fifty to fifty-nine, or over sixty. Also as before, patients in the different groups were found to be similar to one another. And again using a statistical model that accounted for patient differences and that compared outcomes of patients treated by surgeons of varying ages within the same hospital, we calculated the adjusted thirty-day mortality rate following surgery.

Any guesses as to the results?

Unlike hospitalists, surgeons got *better* with age. Their patient mortality rates had modest but significant declines as they got older: mortality was 6.6 percent for surgeons under forty, 6.5 percent for surgeons aged forty to forty-nine, 6.4 percent for surgeons aged fifty to fifty-nine, and 6.3 percent for surgeons over sixty.*

Just as with the hospitalists, we repeated the analysis by dividing surgeons into groups based on their surgical volume. This time, we found that patient mortality continued to fall with surgeon age among high- and medium-volume surgeons, but no such relationship could be found among low-volume surgeons.

Clearly something different was happening here. When *hospitalists* got older, they got, on average, "worse"—unless they saw a high volume of patients. When *surgeons* got older, they got on average "better"—unless they operated on a low volume of patients.

Why? Hospitalists and surgeons are both doctors, but their jobs are very different. A hospitalist's job—broadly speaking—is to prevent, diagnose, and treat acute and chronic medical problems. To do this well, they need to have a broad working knowledge of a wide variety of diseases and the best treatments for them. Surgeons—again, broadly speaking—evaluate patients for surgical procedures, operate on those who they think would benefit, and then care for patients as they recover from surgery. While many doctors would quibble with these reductionist definitions—internists perform procedures, and surgeons diagnose and treat diseases, too—the emphasis of each job is by necessity quite different.

It may be that for hospitalists the benefit of steadily increasing experience starts to be outweighed by their waning knowledge of the most up-to-date care. If experience alone led to higher quality, we would still expect low-volume hospitalists to get better with age, but at a rate that was slower than the high-volume hospitalists since they would be seeing fewer patients over time. Instead, high-volume hospitalists held on to their skills as they aged, while lower-volume

---

* You might have noticed that postoperative mortality rates for surgeons were, in general, substantially lower than post-hospitalization mortality rates for hospitalists. The primary reason is patients who are very sick and at high risk of death following surgery are much less likely to undergo surgery in the first place; lower-risk options are often pursued in these patients. So among patients who might be considered for an urgent surgery, surgeons will often choose to operate only on those who are healthy enough to tolerate surgery.

ones seemed to lose them. This makes sense if being up to date on the latest advances is what most determines the quality of a hospitalist's care. Medications are the internist's primary tool; since newer and better drugs are developed at a (relatively) rapid pace, seeing a high volume of patients is a good way to keep up.

It's different for surgeons, though, who hone many of their skills in the OR. Surgeons build muscle memory through repetition, working in confined spaces with complex anatomy. They learn to anticipate technical problems before they happen and plan around them based on prior experience. Because of this, surgeons often spend several years longer in residency than internists,* to make sure they've had enough experience building their skills in the OR. To complete their general surgery residency, surgeons must take part in at least 850 major surgical cases. Eighty-five of those 850 have to have been surgeries of the gallbladder and biliary system. Even though that sounds like a lot, 85 cases represent only a slice of the variation in patient characteristics, anatomy, and clinical situations a doctor might confront across a career. The best way to build skills in gallbladder surgery is to operate on more gallbladders.

It makes intuitive sense, then, that surgeons get better with age as long as they're still operating a lot. Over time, they build greater technical skills across a wider variety of scenarios, learn how to best avoid complications, and choose better surgical strategies. At risk of stating the obvious, technical skills do matter for surgery outcomes.

If we take studies of hospitalists and surgeons together, it's clear that a doctor's age isn't something that can be dismissed out of hand—age does matter—but nor can it be considered in isolation.

What does this mean for all of us as patients when we meet a new doctor? If we're concerned about the quality of care we're receiving, when it comes to matters of age, the questions worth asking

---

* General surgery residency is usually five years (after graduating from medical school), while general internal medicine residency is three years. Subspecialized surgeons and internists will spend additional years in training depending on the field, and research is often a component of this extra training. Chris, for example, spent three additional years after his internal medicine residency in a fellowship to subspecialize in pulmonary and critical care medicine.

aren't "How old are you?" or even "How many years of experience do you have?" but rather "Do you have a lot of experience caring for patients in my situation?" or "What do you do to stay current with the research?"

———

There's one important characteristic of the surgeons in the mortality studies that we purposefully glided past: gender. Of the 45,826 surgeons included, only 10.1 percent of them were women—20.1 percent of surgeons under forty and just 3.1 percent of those over sixty. Overall, there were no differences in mortality between male and female surgeons, and the connection between higher surgical volume and lower mortality that we observed was equally present for male and female surgeons.[*]

Like many professions, medicine has historically been dominated by men for many years and for many reasons, none of which are rooted in producing the best possible care for patients. Even with more women entering the field in the past decades,[†] the misogynistic question of whether women are "up to the job" unfortunately comes up to this day, both explicitly and more subtly, among patients and physicians alike.

Explicit bias can take the form of harassment, stereotyping, and unequal treatment, the kind of harmful and inappropriate behavior

———

[*] It's worth noting that a smaller study of about 100,000 patients in Ontario, Canada, that included both emergent and elective procedures found that mortality was lower for *elective* surgery performed by women surgeons than by men surgeons, while there were no surgeon gender differences in *emergent* surgery. See Wallis et al., "Comparison of Postoperative Outcomes Among Patients Treated by Male and Female Surgeons."

[†] Although medical schools were taking woman students in the United States as early as the 1840s, by 1950 only 6 percent of doctors were women. Title IX of the Education Amendments of 1972 then prohibited medical schools' discrimination against women, substantially increasing enrollment. By 2007, 28.3 percent of physicians were women, a figure that increased to 36.3 percent in 2019—the same year that women first made up a majority of medical school students at 50.5 percent. See Nilsson and Warren, "Fight for Women Doctors"; and Boyle, "Nation's Physician Workforce Evolves."

toward women physicians that occurs with disheartening regularity. There's also implicit bias. In a study of such subconscious tendencies, health-care workers themselves associated men with career and women with family. Surgeons associated men with surgery as a specialty and women with family medicine as a specialty (not surprising given the "boys' club" perception that dogs the field).

One study of referrals showed that male physicians preferred to refer their patients to other men for surgery, and were more likely to send cases that would not require a surgical procedure to women surgeons. Another study by the University of British Columbia economist Heather Sarsons found that if a patient dies following surgery, other doctors are less likely to refer patients to that surgeon again if she was a woman, compared with if the surgeon was a man. Similarly, if a surgeon has a good outcome, other doctors are more likely to refer more patients to that surgeon if they are a man than if they're a woman.

In other words, compared with men, women were "punished" more harshly by their peers after a bad patient outcome and "rewarded" less after a good one. Bad surgical outcomes can happen to any surgeon, but when they occurred for men, referring doctors viewed them as the "cost of doing business," whereas bad outcomes for referred-to women suggested something negative about the surgeon's quality.

Women physicians are also impacted by the inequities that affect professional women across many industries. They are paid less than men, such that over the course of their entire careers, women have been estimated to make an average of $2 million less than their male counterparts.* Family and domestic obligations are often disproportionately shifted onto career-oriented women physicians, who

---

* This is after statistical adjustment for a number of differences between male and female physicians, such as physician specialty, hours worked per week, and volume of patients seen. Gender disparities in salaries of academic doctors at public medical schools showed significant differences even after accounting for age, experience, specialty, faculty rank, and measures of research and patient care productivity. In sum, this figure isn't about choosing lifestyle factors that result in women being paid less; it's less pay for the same work.

are more likely to have a spouse who works full time than men are. During the COVID-19 pandemic, when demands on physicians and parents were high, women doctors with children reported more stressors and were more likely to consider leaving or reducing their employment.

Nikki Stamp, an Australian heart and lung surgeon, wrote about what goes through her mind when she talks with young girls who want to be doctors when they grow up. It's hard, she says, to warn an ambitious child about the biases she will likely one day face. "No matter how much we tell her she can do anything," Stamp wrote in *The Washington Post*, "I worry we're misleading her on all the obstacles she's bound to face along the way. We never tell her the reality of life as a female surgeon in a profession where the boys' club is alive and well."

The cumulative effect of bias against women in medicine has led to a host of problems, some of which Stamp outlined. According to the Association of American Medical Colleges, as of 2019 women made up 51 percent of medical school applicants but only 48 percent of medical school graduates, 46 percent of residency graduates, 41 percent of medical school faculty, 25 percent of fully promoted medical school professors, and 18 percent of medical school deans. Failing to promote academic woman physicians with the same or better qualifications has been shown to be common.

If we take a look at the young physicians in residency training, we can get a sense of what the future gender makeup of the field looks like. In 2019, women made up 83 percent of residents training in obstetrics and gynecology, 71 percent of pediatrics residents, and 54 percent of family medicine residents. But they made up only 41 percent of the residents in the large group of general surgery and internal medicine (and their subspecialties), 36 percent of emergency medicine residents, and even smaller fractions of surgical subspecialty residencies (for example, 18 percent for neurosurgery and 15 percent for orthopedic surgery).

Suffice it to say that though progress has been made, there is plenty of room for more.

As in other fields, gender bias plays roles both measurable and more elusive. The surgeon study showed that when it comes to an important outcome, like postoperative mortality, there were no meaningful differences between male and female surgeons. What about internists? We know the job is a lot different; technical skill is less central than diagnostic and treatment skills, communication with patients and other health-care providers, and complex decision making. Are female and male hospitalists equally good?

In a separate study, we (Bapu, along with Yusuke Tsugawa, Ashish Jha, John Orav, Daniel Blumenthal, and the Harvard physician and policy researcher Jose Figueroa) took a look again at hospitalized Medicare recipients, this time dividing them up by whether the general internist[*] who admitted them to the hospital was a man or a woman. We looked again at thirty-day mortality outcomes, but we also looked at the rate of hospital readmission. Readmission—coming back to the hospital within thirty days of being discharged—is another common measure of quality, since a readmission often signals ineffective care or errors during a hospitalization.[†]

Studying more than 1.5 million hospitalizations, we found records for more than fifty-eight thousand different doctors, of which 32.1 percent were women. Women doctors were, on average, about five years younger than the men.

Overall, 11.3 percent of the elderly Medicare patients died within thirty days of being hospitalized. Using a statistical model to adjust for patient and physician differences, and again comparing outcomes between male and female doctors in the same hospital, women internists had a mortality rate of 11.1 percent, while male internists had a rate of 11.5 percent. When it came to hospital readmissions, women internists had a readmission rate of 15.0 percent while male internists had a rate of 15.6 percent.

---

[*] This could be a hospitalist or an internist who sees patients in both the outpatient and the hospital settings.

[†] While some readmissions are preventable and potentially due to errors, many would occur no matter how well the patient was cared for during their initial hospital admission.

These differences sound small, but they're meaningful. Let's put them in perspective. There are more than ten million hospitalizations of elderly Medicare patients for medical conditions each year. This difference suggests that if male internists were performing at the level of women, there would be thirty-two thousand fewer deaths following hospitalization of Medicare patients each year.

We did a few more analyses to try to paint a fuller picture of what we were seeing. First, we redid the analysis among just hospitalists, who care only for patients in the hospital, instead of general internists, who might work in both inpatient and outpatient settings. The pattern was the same: female hospitalists had lower mortality rates than male hospitalists.

Next, we looked at individual conditions. Turns out women internists had lower mortality rates than men when treating sepsis, pneumonia, kidney failure, and heart arrythmias. For other conditions, like heart failure, urinary tract infections, exacerbations of chronic obstructive pulmonary disease, and gastrointestinal bleeding, there were no differences in mortality rates between the genders.

Using the diagnoses available in the database, we then divided patients into five groups of illness severity, to see if the difference between male and female internists might be specific to patients with higher or lower overall risk of death. The pattern persisted: women internists had lower mortality rates and lower readmission rates across the board, regardless of how sick their patients were.

So when it came to mortality and readmissions of hospitalized patients treated by internists, it appeared that, on average, women doctors *were* better than men. And while this pattern wasn't present for every individual condition we looked at, the discrepancies were consistent enough to suggest that, from a thirty-thousand-foot view, women internists must be doing things differently than men, in a way that benefited patients.

———

This was not the first study to show differences between male and female physician outcomes. Over the past several decades, researchers have associated women internists with higher fractions of patients receiving guideline-recommended care for issues like diabetes, heart failure, and healthy diet and weight management. Patients of women primary care doctors have been found to be less likely to end up in the emergency department or hospital in one study, though this may not translate to decreases across the board in mortality or health-care costs.

You have to wonder: What exactly are women physicians doing, on average, that men aren't? It's not an easy question to answer, given how hard it is to measure subtle differences in the ways doctors practice in one-on-one interactions with patients. But an evolving research base has shed some light on what's happening in the exam room and at the bedside.

For starters, women physicians seem to be spending more time with their patients. In a study of more than twenty-four million primary care office visits in 2017 using data from electronic health records, women primary care doctors conducted an average of 10.8 percent fewer visits than their male colleagues. However, over the course of a year, women spent *more* overall time with patients—meaning each of their patient visits was longer.*

The nature of the time doctor and patient spend together is different, too. Women physicians, on average, tend to spend more time building partnerships with their patients, more time focusing on their patients' emotions, and more time counseling them on healthy living. Compared with patients of male physicians, patients of women report higher levels of participation in their own health care and decisions. While the connection between "building partnerships" with patients and mortality rates may not be intuitive, trust and mutual understanding between doctor and patient are key factors in motivating healthy behaviors—such as taking a new medication, getting a screening mammogram, or losing weight.

The challenge with interpreting these studies is figuring out what

---

* In the United States, doctors are often paid for each patient they see, creating a financial incentive to see as many patients as possible and thus spend less time with each one. Women physicians spending more time with their patients therefore contributes to gender disparities in physician income.

to do with the information. If women internists tend to both spend more time with their patients and end up with lower mortality rates, would making men spend more time with patients result in the same outcomes? If women internists were to spend less time with their patients, would their mortality outcomes get worse?

There are limits to what natural experiments can (so far) tell us. But we do know about more than just minutes spent. One small study of obstetricians seeing pregnant patients at their prenatal visits showed that it was *male* obstetricians who spent more time with their patients, spent more time making sure they understood their patients, and expressed more concern for their patients. Nonetheless, pregnant patients reported higher satisfaction with women obstetricians, who, despite spending less time with their patients, were found to spend more of their visits connecting with them emotionally.

It's quite possible that for pregnant patients, there may be something that's important, but difficult to measure, about having a doctor who shares your gender—who, if they haven't experienced pregnancy themselves, may be more likely to relate to your experience. Studies of gender concordance (doctors and patients being the same gender) have found that it can play a role in other aspects of medicine. A large study of patients undergoing one of twenty-one different surgeries in Ontario found that patient-doctor gender concordance was associated with reduced mortality rates and complications, particularly for women. Gender concordance has also been associated with improved quality measures for a variety of conditions, including management of chronic diseases, preventive care, and even acute care for heart attacks.

The reality is that we don't fully understand all the differences between how male and female doctors care for their patients. But what we do know is that women physicians face a host of challenges that men do not, and yet the evidence shows that in many settings they're getting better outcomes for their patients. This makes solving gender inequities in medicine all the more urgent.

—

As of 2018, although Black people constitute about 14 percent of the U.S. population, Black physicians of any gender made up only 5 percent of the physician workforce. Americans of Hispanic or Latino backgrounds made up about 19 percent of the overall population yet only 5.8 percent of physicians. Why do we bring this up now? Beyond equity within the profession—a worthy goal in and of itself—what does the absence of equal representation in the physician workforce mean for *patients*? Does racial and ethnic diversity make for better patient care?

In 2017, the Harvard economist and physician Marcella Alsan, the physician Owen Garrick, and the economist Grant Graziani recruited 637 Black men in Oakland, California, to see how the race of the doctor they saw might affect their decision to seek preventive medical care. Their findings were stark. Compared with seeing a non-Black doctor, when a Black man saw a Black doctor, he was 27 percent more likely to accept services related to weight management, 49 percent more likely to accept screening for diabetes, and 71 percent more likely to accept screening for high cholesterol. Even though the focus of the study was on preventive services, the Black men randomly assigned to a Black doctor were also more likely to bring up other, unrelated health questions with their doctor.

Another randomized trial asked 107 Black and 131 white patients to view videos of a vignette of a hypothetical patient with a cardiac problem (similar to the story we told of Roberta in our chapter on medical conferences). Study participants watched a discussion between a patient and a doctor from the point of view of the patient. In the video, the doctor explains the patient's coronary artery disease and recommends the patient undergo CABG surgery—the risky open-heart surgery we discussed earlier, designed to restore blood flow to the heart. Black participants who were randomly assigned to watch a video featuring a Black doctor were more likely to view the CABG surgery as necessary, and were more likely to say they would undergo such surgery if they were the patient, compared with Black participants who watched the same scenario play out with a white doctor. Meanwhile, white participants in the study felt the same about CABG surgery regardless of whether the doctor was Black or white.

Language and culture are important, too. This was most clearly on display in a natural experiment of 1,605 adults who had diabetes and whose preferred language was Spanish. The study focused on patients who switched doctors—an event whose timing is as good as random when it comes to measures of diabetes control like blood sugar levels. They found that when patients switched from a doctor who spoke only English to a doctor who spoke Spanish (the majority of whom were of Hispanic background themselves), they were more likely to see improvement in their blood sugar control and cholesterol levels than patients who switched from one English-speaking-only doctor to another English-speaking-only doctor.

These studies' results were in keeping with decades of research showing that patients from racial and ethnic minority backgrounds consistently experienced poorer communication with their doctors than white patients, and that having a doctor of similar background can help minimize disparities faced by minority groups. Findings like these have led many to suggest that if doctors focused on improving their communication skills with patients from backgrounds different from theirs, patients would benefit. This may be true to some degree, but no amount of training can replace a shared background or shared experience. Recall, for example, the male ob-gyns who had lower satisfaction scores than their woman peers, despite excelling in objective measures of communication.

We both like to think of ourselves as affable guys, doctors who can connect with patients from any backgrounds with relative ease. And we've had years of training and practice to bolster our communication skills. But we can only come to our patient encounters with the vantage points of our respective backgrounds and experiences, which, in one way or another, shape the way we view, interact with, and interpret the people around us.

In a 2020 issue of *The New England Journal of Medicine*, the Harvard neurosurgeon and bioethicist Theresa Williamson shared a story of how her biracial background helped her connect with the family of a young Black patient with a catastrophic gunshot wound to the head. She was called to the bedside as a team of white doctors were struggling to guide the family through care at what would be the end of the patient's life. She shared her thoughts on the patient's prognosis and what care options moving forward might look like with his family, and came back over several days to help conduct family conversations.

"I became an interpreter," Williamson wrote. "Why could I establish trust that White clinicians could not? Was it just the color of my skin? I believe that in this patient, I saw someone I knew, a story I recognized . . . I *saw him,* and his family knew that."

The ever-evolving research base suggests that having a shared background can provide one of the most important components of a good doctor-patient relationship: trust. "It's often impossible to find a physician like me to participate in a goals-of-care conversation with a family of similar background," Williamson added, "and even with similar backgrounds, systemic or personal factors may inhibit development of trust. . . . Increasing trust is challenging, but it may start with movements like the one we're seeing on the news these days—reflecting a burgeoning effort to better understand what it's like to be Black in American society."

Good health care is only as strong as the foundation of trust it's built on. If you don't trust your doctor, are you going to take the pill they recommend you take every day for the rest of your life? Are you going to go for the uncomfortable mammogram or colonoscopy they want you to get? Are you going to let them near you with a scalpel while you're unconscious for several hours?

Doctors are generally afforded a degree of trust when we walk in the door. Most patients assume we take our job seriously and are genuinely interested in trying to help them. But the threshold of trust needed for a patient to participate in a doctor's appointment or go to an emergency department is a lot lower than the threshold needed to act upon a doctor's advice—especially if that advice requires altering their life in a meaningful way.

One survey study of 401 patients in Baltimore found that those who have high levels of mistrust in their doctors and the healthcare system are less likely to take medical advice, keep follow-up appointments for ongoing medical issues, and fill prescriptions. Patients high in mistrust still sought medical care when they felt as if they really needed it, but they were more likely to delay that care. Another survey study, this one of 704 non-Hispanic Black adults, 711 Hispanic adults, and 913 non-Hispanic white adults, found that Black and Hispanic patients were significantly more likely to report mistrust of their health-care providers. Mistrustful patients were also more likely to have reported feeling discrimination in the health-care system based on their race; when asked "Have you ever felt judged or treated differently by a health care provider because of your race or ethnicity?" 30 percent of Black patients and 11 percent of Hispanic patients answered yes, compared with just 3 percent of white patients.

The origins of many minority patients' mistrust in the medical system are rooted in shameful aspects of American history—events that extend far beyond the infamous Tuskegee syphilis study where U.S. government physicians experimented upon several hundred Black men by deceptive means. The glaring inequities in health and health care that have resulted from this mistrust may be best summed up with a single statistic: in 2020, the life expectancy at birth of a Black American was estimated to be about six years less than that of a white American. How this mistrust manifests itself in the medical system and its effects on patient health are being actively investigated by researchers; the understanding they yield may benefit all patients. While we continue to deepen our understanding of these complex issues, the available evidence makes clear that a diverse physician workforce is the one best suited to care for a diverse set of patients.

—

So far we've talked about qualities of doctors that are simply inherent to them as people—their age, their gender, their background—but that nevertheless seem to play a role in the way they practice medicine. But when many patients are looking for the "best" doctor, they may not be all that interested in their personal characteristics. They might focus instead on their training. Did this doctor go to a prestigious medical school? Did they do their residency or fellowship at a top hospital?

It's logical to think that if one medical school or one hospital is better than another, then the doctor who trained at one might, on balance, be better than a doctor who trained at the other. After all, prestigious medical schools get a lot of applicants; they have the luxury of choosing to accept only the very best premeds. The faculty members teaching these doctors-to-be might also be particularly good educators, with greater resources at their disposal.

But these are all conjectural. We wondered, Do "better" schools graduate better doctors?

Let's return to our natural experiment that examined the quality of hospitalists. Using a similar approach as before, we (Bapu, along with Yusuke Tsugawa, Daniel Blumenthal, Ashish Jha, and John Orav), took a look at about a million Medicare patients who were hospitalized for urgent conditions and cared for by more than thirty thousand different hospitalists. This time, though, we looked up both where these doctors went to medical school and the *U.S. News & World Report* rankings of those schools. *U.S. News* ranks medical schools in two different ways: a "research ranking" that factors in the funding and productivity of the medical school, and a "primary care" ranking that factors in the number of graduates going into primary care specialties (family medicine, pediatrics, and internal medicine).

In what by now is a familiar approach, we divided patients into groups based on the *U.S. News* ranking* that applied to their hospitalist: patients cared for by doctors who attended schools ranked 1–10, 11–20, 21–30, 31–40, and 50 and above. For each of these five groups, we measured—once again—patients' thirty-day rate of mortality. There weren't any meaningful differences between patient characteristics in the various groups. As before, we used a statistical

---

* We looked at patients hospitalized between 2011 and 2015; so in order to determine the rank of the medical school at the time the doctors attended it, we used the *U.S. News* rankings from 2002. The rankings tend not to change very much over time, and the idea here was to use rankings from near the time many of these doctors would have been attending medical school.

model that compared outcomes of patients treated by different doctors within *the same hospital,* to avoid the bias introduced if doctors who graduated from top medical schools were more likely to practice at better-performing hospitals. Any guesses as to what we found?

There was no difference in thirty-day mortality rates across the groups of patients treated by doctors who'd graduated from differently ranked medical schools, regardless of whether we used the "research" or the "primary care" ranking scheme.

Why? The data didn't tell us, but it's not hard to think of some potential explanations. Perhaps you've worked with someone who, despite having been educated at a prestigious institution (as they're sometimes quick to mention), just isn't all that great at what they do. Meanwhile, there's no shortage of examples of brilliance in business or the arts from people who received little to no formal education or training.

Of course, to even be included in this study, doctors had to have made it through a few important checkpoints. They must have graduated from medical school, completed residency, and passed licensing exams. If these gatekeeping steps are stringent enough, the small differences in the medical education needed to pass through them are going to be irrelevant—at least as those differences in education pertain to patient outcomes.

It's also worth mentioning that there is no shortage of controversy over the schemes used to rank medical schools. *U.S. News's* current ranking system includes the reputation of the medical school, how residency program directors rate the quality of their graduates, average standardized test scores, and college GPAs of the graduates, among many others. These types of metrics are not necessarily indicative of the quality of the medical education, and they are prone to a host of biases. But for as long as these rankings matter to patients, premed students, and doctors, they will continue to have some bearing on health care.

—

Of course, not every doctor who practices medicine in the United States even attended an American medical school ranked by *U.S.*

News. As of 2016, an estimated 29.1 percent of physicians in the United States weren't born here; 6.9 percent of them were noncitizens. Doctors who immigrate to the United States have to jump through even more hoops than domestic medical school graduates before they can practice medicine. First, they must spend some time familiarizing themselves with the complex U.S. health-care system. Then, even if they have completed residency programs and practiced in their country of origin, they must complete a U.S. or Canadian residency program. They have to pass the same licensing exams as domestically trained doctors, with additional tests for English-language proficiency, and they have to apply for licensure in the state in which they will practice, many of which have yet more training and experience requirements. This means that while most patients of an immigrant physician will never have heard of the medical school they attended, immigrant physicians often bring with them years of training and experience beyond what your typical American medical school graduate has.

Especially given their prevalence in the American health-care system, you have to wonder, How do graduates of international schools stack up against those who attended U.S. schools?

We (Bapu, Yusuke Tsugawa, John Orav, and Ashish Jha) took a look at about 1.2 million Medicare hospitalizations treated by about forty-four thousand internists, of whom 44.3 percent were international medical graduates. Using similar statistical models as before, we found the thirty-day mortality rate for international medical graduates to be approximately 11.2 percent; the mortality rate for domestic graduates was 11.6 percent. This absolute difference of 0.4 percentage points—about the same size as the difference between male and female internists—translates to potentially thousands of fewer deaths every year among hospitalized Medicare patients if domestic graduates were achieving outcomes similar to those of international graduates.

Why might internists who trained abroad have better mortality rates than domestic graduates? Many of the internists who learned abroad would have gone through residency twice—once in their home country and again in the United States—so they would have benefited from both additional experience *and* additional instruction. What's more, because there are limited numbers of visas available for international medical graduates, residency programs get to take the very best applicants from around the world. It's also possible that because visa status may be dependent on their employment, international graduates may work harder to stay up to date on the latest developments and perform at a high level.

———

Now that you've seen all these studies, let's do a little exercise. Imagine you've been admitted to the hospital with pneumonia and you're meeting the physician taking care of you for the first time. Who are you hoping walks through that door?

Would you rather they be in their fifties with a good amount of gray hair, or in their thirties just a few years out of residency?

Would you rather see a man or a woman walk through the door?

Would you trust them more if you shared a background?

Would you prefer if they went to Harvard? A medical school in the United States, at least? Or do their training credentials not matter much to you?

If we're being honest, when *we* answer these questions, our answers don't always line up with what the data just showed us. As the readers who wrote into the *British Medical Journal* attested at the beginning of the chapter, most of us want knowledgeable, compassionate, communicative, and trustworthy doctors taking care of us. Because these kinds of metrics aren't available to us when we're looking at insurance directories or the online profiles of doctors, we inevitably come to the table with preconceived notions of what a good doctor looks like. These might be based on our upbringing, our culture, our experiences, our biases, or even the doctors we see on TV.

It's possible that our gut guides us to the best doctor for us. But the studies we looked at tell us that our gut is capable of leading us astray. Of course, there's no need to go ditch your male doctor for a woman doctor, swap your young surgeon for an old, a domestic grad for an international one. But we hope that the studies we've looked at in this chapter stick with you, and that they make you more conscious of the impressions being subtly made on you when you meet a new doctor.

We've considered a lot of the variables that distinguish one doctor from another, but there's one area we haven't so much as glanced at yet, one that is more and more salient in our divided world. With the next chapter, it's time for us to touch the third rail of modern American life: politics.

CHAPTER TEN

POLITICS AT THE BEDSIDE

THERE'S A DEFINITE difference in the tone of the phone—the White House phone," recalled a George Washington University Hospital emergency department staff member of the events of March 30, 1981. "This voice just said that the presidential motorcade was en route to the hospital."

Shortly before, gunshots had been fired at Ronald Reagan. The president was rushed by Secret Service agents into his limousine, which hightailed it to the hospital as three others lay wounded: the White House press secretary, James Brady; the police officer Thomas Delahanty; and the Secret Service agent Tim McCarthy, who had used himself as a shield for the president.

In the limousine, the Secret Service agent Jerry Parr, who had moments before jumped onto Reagan to further protect him, ran his hands over the president's body looking for a wound. "He claimed that I had hurt his ribs in landing on top of him, so I told the driver to head to the White House, the safest place," Parr recalled. "Shortly after that, I would say in a space of 10 or 15 seconds, he started coughing up a little blood. . . . As soon as I saw the blood, indicating a wound in the lung, I told the driver to head for GW."

"I still can't get over the fact of the delay between when—I know now that I was shot, but didn't know then—and the feeling of pain," Reagan recalled in the 1982 documentary *The Saving of the President.* "I always just assumed that if you were shot, you felt it and felt it right then. . . . I remember very well walking into that emergency room, not even knowing that I had been shot. I only learned afterward in reading I wasn't quite as well as I thought I was at the time."

Despite walking in of his own accord, Reagan collapsed shortly after telling staff, "I feel like I can't catch my breath." He was carried to the trauma bay and soon surrounded by hospital staff. His personal physician stood at the foot of the bed, monitoring his pulse in his feet. As a nurse began trauma protocols, cutting off the president's clothes, the president complained of shortness of breath and pain in his chest. Meanwhile, others placed IVs into his arms. His skin turned pale.

Pagers had summoned a swarm of surgeons—many of them young residents—to the ED. They began examining the president from head to toe. Listening to his lungs, they noticed that breath sounds were diminished on the left; air wasn't moving in and out properly. It was then that they discovered a small slit-like wound in the president's left armpit, presumably where he had been shot. His left chest cavity was filling with blood and compressing his lung. Surgeons placed a tube in the president's chest to drain the blood—1.3 liters of it—giving blood transfusions to replace the losses.

As all this played out, teams tended to the other three victims. James Brady had a severe gunshot wound to his head and was rushed to surgery. Tim McCarthy had taken a bullet that appeared to have entered his abdomen, and he was rushed for exploratory surgery. Thomas Delahanty, the third victim, had been taken to Washington Hospital Center, where he also underwent emergency surgery (in multiple-casualty situations, it is common to spread victims to different hospitals to avoid overwhelming emergency departments).

Back at the president's bedside, a thoracic surgeon named Benjamin Aaron approached. He watched the blood continue to flow out of a chest tube, suggesting that beyond simply collapsing it, the bullet had seriously injured the president's lung—and the blood vessels inside it. He too would need emergency surgery.

Reagan was rolled down the hallway into the operating room with his wife, Nancy, at his side. "Honey, I forgot to duck," he told her. Secret Service agents accompanied the president to the operating room, clumsily putting on scrubs and surgical masks to help maintain a sterile environment. (One agent arrived barefoot before being told to put his shoes back on.)

Treating gunshot wounds is, sadly, a routine part of trauma care. But operating on the president with a cast of strangers in the operating room was atypical, to say the least. As Aaron and the rest of the surgical team prepared Reagan for surgery and moved him to the operating table, it seemed the president could sense the tension in the room. Shortly before being placed under anesthesia, he lifted his head from the operating table.

"Please tell me you're all Republicans," he said to the OR team.

They laughed. Joseph Giordano, the surgeon—and a Democrat—who was evaluating for possible abdominal injuries to the president, replied, "Today, we're all Republicans, Mr. President."

Reagan's surgery was successful; surgeons were able to repair his wounds and ensure that no critical structures had been hit. The other three victims of the assassination attempt survived too, though two suffered long-term disability, preventing them from doing their jobs again. Press Secretary Brady's brain injuries left him paralyzed. He died of complications of the injuries in 2014 at age seventy-three.

Ronald Reagan was known to make such quips, and given the gravity of the situation, we're sure the doctors were grateful for his willingness to break the ice. But there is a kernel of truth to every joke, and there might have been some truth to this one. It's enough to make you wonder: Does your doctor's politics affect the care they give?

———

At risk of stating the obvious, health care in America is intensely political. Republicans and Democrats in Washington routinely disagree on matters such as how to pay for care or balance the interests of patients and businesses, not to mention hot-button topics that affect health: gun rights, marijuana, abortion. Given today's political landscape, it's hard to imagine a time, many decades ago, when abortion and end-of-life care *weren't* political wedge issues.

So it's not unreasonable for a patient—even the president of the United States—to wonder how their doctor's views might affect the care that they provide. Putting aside questions of actual medical practice, patients may simply be more comfortable with doctors whose beliefs and value systems align with theirs. Doctors aren't generally in the habit of announcing their political beliefs in the exam room, though you'd be surprised at how easily and how often their beliefs arise in the course of conversation. Some patients ask outright. (Trust us—it happens.)

To answer the question of whether a doctor's politics are relevant to the care they provide, we would have to first assess two factors: how political doctors are, as a class, and whether those politics bleed into the way they treat patients.

The first we can easily dispense with: Doctors can and do often get involved in politics. Physician groups like the American Medical Association, state medical societies, and specialty societies regularly advocate for policies at the state and local levels. As a group, they also donate to political campaigns and causes just like everyone else. A study of publicly available political campaign data showed that campaign contributions from physicians themselves increased 9.5-fold from 1991 to 2012, from $20 million[*] to $189 million. The percentage of physicians who contributed to campaigns rose from 2.6 percent to 9.4 percent over this period—a trend similar to that of the overall population, which has become more likely to donate to political causes over the past decades. Physicians, on average, have historically supported the Republican Party, though that tendency has waned. In the 1990s, a majority of physicians who contributed to political campaigns contributed to Republicans; by 2012, a majority were contributing to Democrats. As a rule, physicians practicing in certain specialties—particularly higher-income surgical specialties—lean more Republican than internal medicine specialists and pediatricians.

A 2016 survey study shed some light on whether doctors' political beliefs could affect the way they care for patients. Conducted by the Tufts University political scientist Eitan Hersh and the Yale psychiatrist Matthew Goldenberg, the study asked around 230

* Inflation adjusted to 2012 dollars.

Democratic and Republican primary care physicians to read a short vignette about a hypothetical patient and rate the "seriousness" of various medical issues the patient presented. The researchers purposely included both politically charged and nonpolitically charged issues. For example, one vignette focused on tobacco use, a non-charged issue. It described a patient who "acknowledges engaging in social smoking, consuming ~15–20 cigarettes per week (2–3 per day), a habit that began at age 18." A charged vignette said that the patient "acknowledges having had two elective abortions in the last 5 years. She denies any physical complaints or complications associated with these procedures. She is not currently pregnant." If politics were influencing doctors, we ought to see a difference in their views of the "seriousness" of charged issues and no difference when it came to non-charged issues.

That's precisely what researchers found. Republican doctors perceived patients who had had prior abortions—also who had used recreational marijuana—to have more serious medical issues than Democratic doctors. Democratic doctors perceived patients who had firearms in the home to have a more serious medical issue than Republican doctors. Meanwhile, non-wedge issues—like tobacco and alcohol use, obesity, and depression—were viewed as similarly serious.

The differences extended beyond their assessments to their recommendations. Republican doctors more often said they would encourage the patient in the above vignette not to have more abortions and would discuss abortion's effects on mental health. Republican doctors were also more likely to recommend that patients using marijuana quit and to discuss the health and legal risks associated with its use.

Survey responses are one thing, but how might those differences in beliefs translate to *actual* differences in care? In a natural experiment that took advantage of the Roman Catholic Church's well-established views on contraception, the economists Elaine Hill of the University of Rochester and David Slusky and Donna Ginther of the University of Kansas looked at what happened when hospi-

tals changed ownership between Catholic and non-Catholic enti-
ties from 1998 to 2013. They found that after hospitals switched
to Catholic ownership, rates of tubal ligations (the procedure commonly referred to as "getting your tubes tied") fell. Meanwhile, when
hospitals were sold from Catholic owners to non-Catholic owners,
the rate of tubal ligations went up. Taking the data together, they
estimated that Catholic ownership was associated with a 31 percent
decrease in tubal ligation procedures.

This was a study of institutional beliefs, rather than those of individual physicians. It's altogether possible that many women ended
up seeking tubal ligation elsewhere, at non-Catholic facilities. But
given what we've observed about patient and doctor behavior in
previous chapters, it offers persuasive evidence that the beliefs and
values of someone *other* than the patient could very well affect their
options for care.

So doctors as a group tend to be as political as everyone else if
not more so. And politics do seem to bleed into the care they give.
With these basic ideas established, let's dive in: How might doctors'
personal views affect their individual patients?

—

There are few subjects in health care in the last few decades that have
risen to such national prominence as end-of-life care. It wouldn't
be an exaggeration to say that the subject was launched into the
national conversation by the story of one woman, Terri Schiavo.

In 1990, twenty-six-year-old Schiavo suffered a cardiac arrest at her
home in Florida, leaving her in a persistent vegetative state from the
severe brain injury caused by lack of blood flow to her brain. Some
patients recover from such injuries, and Schiavo's family and doctors
wanted to give her the best chance possible of being one of the lucky
ones. Unfortunately, after several months, she wasn't showing signs
of meaningful improvement. Scans of her head showed severe loss of
brain tissue. Electrical tests showed loss of high-level brain activity;
her chances of making a meaningful recovery were deemed low.

This was still the case fully a decade later, and Schiavo was kept alive by a feeding tube. Her husband felt that had she been able to express her wishes, she would not want to continue this way. He asked to have her feeding tube removed. However, Schiavo's parents objected in a series of court battles in Florida, and artificial nutrition continued for several more years, as judges and appellate courts heard testimony from each side. Schiavo's parents eventually found support among Republican legislators and Governor Jeb Bush, who tried to intervene. But Florida courts ruled that Schiavo should have her feeding tube removed and be allowed to die.

With legal options exhausted in Florida, Schiavo's story gained national attention from politicians and the public alike. President George W. Bush, speaking in terms consistent with his party's long-held stance on abortion, felt they should "err on the side of life" and thus keep Schiavo alive. Efforts were made by Republicans in Congress to prevent the removal of Schiavo's feeding tube. Media coverage in the ensuing months was ample, though often divorced from the medical realities of Schiavo's condition.

Ultimately, the courts had the final say, and Schiavo's feeding tube was removed for the final time in 2005—fifteen years after her initial brain injury. She passed away about two weeks later. On autopsy, her brain showed extensive damage to critical areas. It weighed about half of what would be expected for a woman her age. Schiavo's case would spark debate in political, legal, and academic circles. To those in the medical realm, one thing was clear: death was not exempt from politics.*

---

* End-of-life issues have prominently entered the political sphere on other occasions. The Michigan physician Jack Kevorkian assisted dozens of patients with serious illnesses in ending their own lives in the 1990s. In one instance, he videotaped himself providing a lethal injection to a patient with amyotrophic lateral sclerosis (ALS), airing the tape nationally on *60 Minutes* with the intention of creating debate; he was later found guilty of homicide and imprisoned. (See "60 Minutes Archives: An Interview with Dr. Jack Kevorkian," CBS.) In 2009, the former Republican vice presidential candidate Sarah Palin referred to a provision in President Obama's proposed health-care plan—which allowed Medicare to pay for doctors to have discussions about end-of-life issues with their patients—as a government "death panel." No such panels were ever proposed or have ever existed; however, public fears of death panels became pervasive enough that Obama addressed them: "The notion

—

Sometimes, figuring out the best path forward for someone who is extremely ill is straightforward. Other times, particularly at the end of life, it can be very difficult to assess how much time is left for a patient, and how to best proceed. Of course, patient preferences matter: some patients may want to pursue more aggressive options to extend life, while others may focus on comfort and quality of remaining life. In situations such as these, though, where there is no "right" path, one could reasonably wonder, Are a doctor's personal views toward end-of-life care reflected in the care they give?

In a study that surveyed doctors and patients, the Harvard economists David Cutler and Ariel Stern and the Dartmouth economist Jonathan Skinner and physician David Wennberg asked questions about care at the end of life to determine what components of care were provided out of medical necessity, patient preference, or physician preference. After accounting for other factors, such as regional patterns of care, they estimated that for Medicare patients 35 percent of health-care spending in the last two years of life went toward care that doctors *believed* would be helpful but that didn't have proven benefit. In other words, a substantial portion of end-of-life care seemed to reflect doctors' preferences.

But these preferences were general, likely reflecting the overall uncertainty surrounding end-of-life care. The study did not answer the more specific question of how a physician's politics may influence the care they provide.

We (Bapu, along with Andrew Olenski, the Stanford political scientist Adam Bonica, the late NYU political scientist Howard Rosenthal, and the Cornell physician and health policy researcher Dhruv Khullar) thought an approach might exist to study that question. Specifically, we wanted to consider if the hospital care provided to

that somehow I ran for public office or members of Congress are in this so that they can go around pulling the plug on Grandma? I mean when you start making arguments like that, that's simply dishonest," he said in 2009. See Gonyea, "From the Start, Obama Struggled with Fallout from a Kind of Fake News."

patients at the end of life was different when provided by doctors affiliated with the Democratic Party versus the Republican Party. If the Terri Schiavo case was still representative, would Republican doctors "err on the side of life," as President Bush had put it, and provide more aggressive care for terminally ill patients than Democratic doctors?

Like the studies we looked at in the last chapter, we took advantage of the natural experiment that is created when patients come to the hospital and are assigned to whichever hospitalist happens to be on duty—meaning our results wouldn't be skewed by patients seeking care from particular doctors. Using Medicare data, we identified patients who died either in the hospital or within a few months of leaving the hospital (that is, patients who were terminally ill), then divided them into two groups: patients whose hospital care had been provided by doctors who were Democrats and those who had been cared for by Republicans.

You might be asking, How could they possibly know the political affiliation of the doctors involved? Medicare doesn't keep track of this data. But they do keep track of the identity of the doctors[*] who are billing them for services and providing care. And since individual donations to political campaigns in the United States are matters of public record, we could identify the doctors who were passionate enough about politics that they had donated to either Democratic or Republican candidates.[†]

Since our goal was to determine differences between Democratic and Republican doctors' practices for patients at the end of life, we focused on measures like time spent in the ICU and use of intensive treatments for organ failure like CPR, placement of a breathing

* While the specific identity of *doctors* is included in the Medicare data used for research, the specific identity of *patients* is not.

† Although the data is publicly available, putting it all together is no simple task. The Database on Ideology, Money in Politics, and Elections (the DIME database) was built by Adam Bonica, one of the study's authors, who has made it available for research purposes. See Bonica, "Database on Ideology, Money in Politics, and Elections."

tube, dialysis, and artificial nutrition. We also looked at total spending on end-of-life care and how frequently patients were transitioned to hospice care, where treatment is focused on comfort rather than resolving the underlying illness.

We ultimately identified about 1,500 Democratic physicians and about 770 Republican physicians, as well as more than 23,000 who had not made any donations. The patients they treated were hospitalized between 2008 and 2012 (a few years after Terri Schiavo passed away). The characteristics of the patients were similar across these three groups, supporting our natural experiment. (There were differences in the doctors themselves, though: Republican doctors were, on average, older and more likely to be male.)

In a statistical model that accounted for differences in patient and doctor characteristics and compared outcomes between Democratic and Republican doctors working within the same hospital, we found no difference in the intensity of end-of-life care provided to patients between Democratic, Republican, and non-donating doctors: no differences in costs, ICU use, mechanical ventilation, artificial nutrition, or hospice.

So at least when it came to this one question at the intersection of medicine and politics, we could offer a concise answer: a doctor's political affiliation, it seemed, wasn't influencing the care provided to hospitalized patients at the end of their life.

In other words, as Ronald Reagan's surgeon suggested, a doctor's politics can take a backseat.

—

Having arrived at the final chapter of this book, you might be wondering, Where, in all this discussion of hidden causes and effects, is COVID-19? For a book about doctors, patients, and health care, discussion of the biggest global health crisis in a century has thus far been strangely muted.

You'd be right to wonder. Unfortunately, many of the underlying drivers of public health behavior during the pandemic are still not fully understood. Studies have begun to emerge, though, and they've shed light—often in surprising ways—on why, despite the presence of a theoretically controllable disease, we as a nation lost so many fellow citizens to COVID-19.

Since the earliest days of the pandemic, many have lamented the "politicization" of public health as parties criticized one another for the decisions enacted by political officials across the country. This language is misleading: The practice of public health is *inherently* political. It requires governments—run by elected politicians—to educate diverse populations about pressing health issues while appealing to their varying concerns and values. It involves science, yes, but it also involves measuring the potential costs of a policy against the potential benefits of such action. It has to consider how the people who elected governmental leaders may value and respond to whatever trade-offs governments make. In other words: politics!

There were certainly memorable occasions (to put it mildly) in which prominent elected officials made factually incorrect assertions about COVID-19 and how we might manage it. Setting aside conspiracy theories and misinformation, most of the political debate centered not on the basic facts of the disease but on the trade-offs we as a nation should be making to manage it. Staying home from work would reduce transmission of a deadly virus, but it would have clear negative economic consequences. Closing schools could reduce spread of the virus, but it could leave children with suboptimal education and harm their social development. Instituting vaccine mandates would increase vaccination rates and temper the damage done by the virus, but it would also limit the choices people could make about what does and doesn't enter their bodies.

In other words, where should we draw lines in the sand: How *much* social distancing is necessary? How *long* should businesses be shut down? How *do* we balance the public health benefit of wearing masks against the imposition it places on citizens?

As the threat of COVID-19 became a reality in early 2020, politicians began dividing into opposing camps. Democrats tended to emphasize reducing the direct damage from COVID-19 over preserving the familiar rhythms of modern life. Republicans tended to take stands in favor of preserving the normal way of life over interventions that might reduce the spread and direct health effects of the virus. These debates played out in varying forms across our TVs, newspapers, and social media.

Unlike other health-related issues such as abortion and gun control, where popular opinion doesn't necessarily mirror the political debate, the rift in the population over COVID-19 policies more or less matched the politicians espousing them. The Pew Research Center estimated that in April 2020, 47 percent of Republicans said the coronavirus "has been made a bigger deal than it really is," compared with only 14 percent of Democrats. In that same month, 38 percent of Republicans said that public health officials had "greatly or slightly exaggerated the risks about the coronavirus outbreak," compared with only 11 percent of Democrats.

But people's actual behaviors don't always reflect their answers to polls, or even their closely held beliefs. As we've seen, behaviors that affect our health can be motivated by factors outside our control, and even our knowledge. So yes, Democrats and Republicans were *saying* different things about the threat of the pandemic. But did their behavior reflect them?

In a study using data from 2020, before COVID-19 vaccines were available, we (Bapu, along with the Rand economists Christopher Whaley and Jonathan Cantor and the data scientist Megan Pera) took a look at the relationship between political affiliations and COVID-19 behavior by the public. This was the time when health officials most discouraged social gatherings, as they might spread the virus. We wanted to know if people living in Democratic-aligned areas of the country avoided such gatherings, as their politics might imply, more than people living in Republican-aligned areas. And if so, were they successfully avoiding COVID-19?

The first question we would need to address was whether people were *actually* social distancing. It's no easy query. Sure, we could ask them in surveys, but survey data is often unreliable, and we wanted measures of their behavior, not their intended or reported behavior. Some companies collected location data from mobile phones; they could estimate the degree to which movement patterns changed within a region. But they couldn't tell us what people were doing in a particular location—grocery shopping or sipping cocktails among friends. And critically, their data weren't linked to COVID-19 outcomes.

Even if we had these data, we'd have to be able to account for differences in other behaviors. For example, if those who chose not to socially distance were also less likely to wear masks or wash their hands, we couldn't tease out the effects of social distancing specifically.

To create a natural experiment, we would need a social gathering whose timing was reliably *random*. We could then look at differences between people living in Democratic-leaning areas and those living in Republican-leaning areas and, assuming that there were no obvious, material differences between the groups, trust that COVID-19 infections after such gatherings were attributable only to their political alignment.

To find that random event, we turned to our ever-dependable source of natural experiments: birthdays. Or, more specifically here, birthday parties.

Birthday parties aren't completely random in their timing: they're more often held on weekends than on weekdays. But they obviously tend to occur *near* someone's birthday and are thus randomly timed throughout the year. Someone who gathered with others for a birthday party in the time before vaccines were available would presumably be at greater risk of getting infected with COVID-19 in the next few weeks than someone who didn't. Using commercial insurance claims data—where family members on the same insurance plan are linked to one another—we could see the birthdays of everyone in a family, and thus determine the times when they might be gathering for a birthday. We could also observe if and when a family member was diagnosed with COVID-19.

If, in the early stages of the pandemic, Democratic-leaning households were less likely to socially gather than Republican-leaning ones, as their politics suggested, we would expect to see lower COVID-19 infection rates in the two weeks following birthdays in Democratic-leaning households than in Republican-leaning households. (Two weeks allows for a few days' gap between the birthday and the party, as well as time for the viral infection to incubate and make someone sick.)

So with all this in mind, we looked at more than 6.5 million individuals in 2.9 million households from January 1 to November 8, 2020, and measured rates of diagnosed COVID-19 infections* in the weeks surrounding a household birthday. We examined the data in a few different ways, but the overall pattern was clear: COVID-19 diagnosis rates increased after a birthday in a given household.

But which households?

First, we considered counties across the United States where circulating levels of COVID-19 were highest—places where we would expect there to be more birthday-party-related transmission. In counties in the top 10 percent of COVID-19 circulation, households that had a birthday in the previous two weeks had a COVID-19 diagnosis rate that was 31 percent higher than households with no birthday in the previous two weeks. There were no differences, however, between households in those counties with the *lowest* levels of circulating COVID-19—which makes intuitive sense. A birthday party is less likely to increase transmission when there's relatively little circulating virus to begin with.

Even more telling than the "birthday party effect," as we came to refer to it, was whose birthdays, within a household, were most associated with COVID-19 infection rates. In counties with the highest circulation, the effect of a child's birthday was nearly three times higher than that of an adult's birthday. It's obvious enough that parties were more likely to be held for kids than adults. There are some birthday-loving grown-ups out there, but as a rule kids' birthdays are treated as party-worthy, whereas many adult birthdays come and go without event, even outside a pandemic.

Finally, the subject we were most interested in: we looked for differences in this birthday party effect in counties that leaned Republican (defined by having voted for Donald Trump in the 2016

---

* Because these infections had to be *diagnosed* in order to show up in insurance claims data, we likely were able to reliably detect only moderate or severe cases of COVID-19—ones that were bad enough to warrant seeing a doctor.

presidential election) and those that leaned Democratic (having voted for Hillary Clinton). There we arrived at perhaps the most surprising finding of all: there was no significant difference in the birthday party effect in different counties. Republican or Democratic leaning, the effect remained the same.

When so much of the discourse surrounding pandemic response suggested a stark divide between Republicans and Democrats—groups that seemingly couldn't see eye to eye on mask mandates, school closures, business closures, or vaccines—the finding was almost comforting. It suggested that when it came to what Americans hold most dear—celebrating their families—the differences between political parties simply fell away.

———

Doctors often found themselves in an uncomfortable position during the early phases of the pandemic. Some patients worried deeply about COVID-19 infection and rarely left the house. Others said people were exaggerating how serious the virus was (even as they came into the hospital, struggling to breathe from their own infection). Working with limited information, we treated patients with the goal of maximizing potential benefit of our treatment and minimizing potential harms.

We learned early that much of the damage wreaked by COVID-19 pneumonia was due to the body's inflammatory response, in some cases so strong that it damaged the lungs. Powerful anti-inflammatory medications of the corticosteroid family, such as dexamethasone and prednisone, had previously been studied as treatments for pneumonias caused by other viruses, though results were somewhat inconclusive. Still, in the absence of definitive remedies, these became some of our most promising potential treatments against this novel virus. A landmark randomized trial performed in the U.K. in 2020 showed a mortality benefit from dexamethasone, making it an early fixture in the treatment of severe COVID-19.

Corticosteroids weren't the only early therapy, though. Hydroxychloroquine, used to treat malaria and autoimmune diseases like lupus, and ivermectin, used to treat parasitic infections, were likewise considered in the first months of the pandemic, although neither had been used to treat viral infections.

Research performed after the emergence of SARS-CoV-1—the virus responsible for the severe acute respiratory syndrome outbreak in the early years of the twenty-first century—suggested that drugs in hydroxychloroquine's class could prevent spread of the virus from one cell to another in the laboratory. The drug was familiar and available. Absent studies suggesting otherwise, it seemed reasonable to try it in patients with severe, life-threatening cases of COVID-19 pneumonia from SARS-CoV-2.

So, while awaiting new data, the FDA issued an emergency use authorization for hydroxychloroquine. Many doctors (ourselves included) used it to treat hospitalized patients with severe cases of COVID-19. However, studies later showed that hydroxychloroquine did *not* help patients with COVID-19, in mild or severe cases. Especially given the potential for adverse cardiac side effects, most doctors stopped treating patients with it.

Meanwhile, in a study published in June 2020, ivermectin was reported to show some activity in the lab against SARS-CoV-2. Most doctors rarely if ever use ivermectin; in the United States, parasitic infections in humans are quite rare. But because the drug is generally considered safe at normal human doses, some doctors began using it to treat patients with COVID-19, in the event that what researchers saw in the lab might help actual patients in the world. But as with hydroxychloroquine, it soon became apparent that ivermectin was ineffective against COVID-19, and it likewise could cause problems for patients, especially when given at high doses. It was never authorized by the FDA for COVID-19; mainstream guidelines consistently recommended against its use.

That might have been the death knell for these two treatments. But a study released in November 2020—since retracted—combined with congressional testimony in December by a physician running against the grain of the larger medical community reawakened interest in ivermectin. As for hydroxychloroquine, President Donald Trump promoted its use against COVID-19, even as yet more evidence stacked up showing it to be ineffective and potentially harmful (evidence that led the FDA to revoke its emergency use authorization). "Hydroxy[chloroquine] has tremendous support," President Trump said, "but politically, it's toxic because I supported it."

Given the public debate, it was only natural that patients infected with COVID-19 and their families might ask doctors about these treatments. Though the preponderance of evidence suggested that they didn't work, there were those outlying studies. And the side effect profiles, in the scheme of things, weren't horrible. So, some doctors continued to prescribe these drugs, even as they fell out of favor among most of their colleagues.

Given the political divide associated with these treatments, we (Bapu, along with Michael Barnett, Ateev Mehrotra, and the Harvard graduate student Marema Gaye) wanted to know if off-label use of these prescription drugs differed depending on patients' political affiliation. Were Republicans more likely to take these drugs than Democrats?

Using data from about 18.5 million insured adults coming in for outpatient visits with their doctors between January 2019 and December 2020 (prior to the large-scale introduction of vaccines), we looked at the number of new prescriptions per week for hydroxychloroquine and ivermectin. The data from 2019 gave us useful information about the typical use of these drugs during *non*-pandemic times, a baseline that made it easier to tell if there was, as we'd expect, a significant increase in their use over 2020 as COVID-19 spread. We also looked at prescription rates for other drugs used to treat the same conditions that hydroxychloroquine and ivermectin are indicated for. Those were our counterfactuals. If their use stayed stable as use of hydroxychloroquine and ivermectin increased, it would suggest to us that the COVID-19 debate (and not some unrelated prevalence of parasites or malaria) was influencing use.

As expected, the number of hydroxychloroquine prescriptions was fairly stable until the March 2020 announcement by the FDA authorizing its emergency use, when use increased dramatically. It dropped again after the FDA revoked the drug's emergency use authorization in June 2020, only to increase again to a level that was higher in December 2020, after it had been proven ineffective, than it was in April.

Ivermectin use was stable prior to the pandemic, increasing only slightly following the publication of the study suggesting it might have an ability to act against the virus in the lab. It increased dramatically, however, in December, following the publication of the now-retracted study and congressional testimony. Through all this time, prescriptions for the "control" drugs remained stable.

So far, the results were predictable to anyone following the news. Now we wanted to see how political alignment tracked with use of these drugs. Did counties with a higher Republican vote share in the 2020 election use them more than those with a lower Republican vote share?

In a word, yes. The Republican and Democratic counties trended similarly until June 2020, when the FDA withdrew its emergency use authorization for hydroxychloroquine. After this, heavily Republican counties saw the highest numbers of hydroxychloroquine prescriptions, peaking at 146 percent of the 2019 baseline prescription rate. The least Republican counties saw small increases in the same period, but they were much less pronounced.

A similar trend emerged with ivermectin. Counties trended along the same lines until December 2020. Then ivermectin prescriptions rose in *all* counties, but the increase was most pronounced in heavily Republican counties, where prescriptions soared to 964 percent of the 2019 baseline prescription rate.

There were clear conclusions to be drawn. First, because these were prescription drugs, we knew that at least some doctors felt that despite the medical consensus against them hydroxychloroquine and ivermectin were treatments worth trying.* (Whether the prescriptions were driven by doctors' urging or patients' request or

---

* For hydroxychloroquine, it's also notable that doctors were writing outpatient prescriptions—as opposed to orders for hospitalized inpatients. The FDA's emergency use authorization of hydroxychloroquine was limited to use in patients with severe disease in the hospital, meaning these prescriptions were written outside the FDA's authorization.

some combination of the two, our study sadly can't say.) It was also clear that, unlike the birthday party effect—which suggested that when it came to flouting social distancing protocols in the name of a birthday, Republicans and Democrats behaved more or less the same way—here Republicans were putting their money (or their health) where their mouths were. Also telling is the way differences seemed to emerge only *after* the mainstream medical consensus recommended against use of these drugs. The same messaging that suppressed their use in Democrats increased their use among Republicans.

While the information our study provides was illuminating, its limitation bears noting: it tells us only about the average patients in those counties, and not specific patients. For reasons that are good for our individual privacy but challenging for research, it's hard to link data about a person's political leanings to their health behaviors and outcomes.

Hard but not impossible. In a study reported in 2022, three Yale researchers—Jacob Wallace, Paul Goldsmith-Pinkham, and Jason Schwartz—took advantage of publicly available data in Ohio and Florida to link individuals' political affiliation with that gravest of health outcomes: death. Using public voter registration and death records, they were able to see if and when people who were registered to vote for a given political party died during the pandemic. They used data from 2019, before the pandemic, as a baseline; it served as a counterfactual, telling them the approximate number of deaths in each month and each county that would have been expected in 2020 and 2021 had there been no COVID-19.* Excess deaths could reliably be attributed to the virus.[†]

First they looked at overall excess deaths in Florida and Ohio. They found, predictably, that there were more deaths in 2020 and

---

* The researchers also compared 2019 with 2018, which served as a "placebo" year to ensure that 2019 was actually representative of a typical non-pandemic year. They found that there were no meaningful differences in deaths between 2019 and 2018.
† Excess deaths could represent any death resulting from the pandemic, including deaths directly attributable to COVID-19—likely the majority of excess death—and those indirectly due to COVID-19 (such as a heart attack due to pandemic-related stress or pandemic-induced delays in care).

2021, when COVID-19 was claiming the lives of thousands upon thousands, than in years prior. They then divided individuals into two groups based on their political affiliations, drawing from party registration in voter files. When they used a statistical model that compared mortality outcomes between registered Democrats and registered Republicans of the same age living in the same county, differences emerged.

During 2020 and the first few months of 2021—before vaccines were available to the general adult population—excess deaths were similar for Democrats and Republicans. But after the COVID-19 vaccines became available to the general adult population, in the spring of 2021, a divide emerged. The excess death rate of registered Republicans became significantly higher than that of Democrats: 153 percent higher between April and December 2021, researchers estimated.

Given the timing of the deviation, it isn't hard to guess a cause. It seems likely that the results could be explained, at least in part, by differences in vaccination rates, with Democrats in these states more likely to get vaccinated than Republicans. We know that vaccines are the best tools to prevent death from COVID-19; it's not surprising to see differences in excess deaths that coincide with differences in vaccination rates.

As we discussed back in chapter 3 when we considered flu shots, the underlying reasons for vaccine hesitancy are complex, but they can generally be reduced to three Cs: complacency, confidence, and convenience. One study that repeatedly surveyed U.S. residents during 2020 suggested that Republicans, on average, perceived the threat from COVID-19 to be lower than Democrats did (whether you call that "complacency" may be a question of your own political leanings). There were also differences in the degree of mistrust toward government, public health officials, the media, vaccine manufacturers, and the scientific community—questions of confidence, supported by the research into hydroxychloroquine and ivermectin showing persistent use despite the scientific evidence showing they were ineffective.

The study of excess deaths showed us something else. In emphasizing the differences between political parties in the post-vaccine phase, we risk ignoring the similarities in the *pre*-vaccine phase: excess deaths were shown to be more or less consistent between Democrats and Republicans in that time. This finding is somewhat surprising. Polls by Pew conducted in June 2020 showed that Republicans were more likely than Democrats to "feel comfortable" going to the grocery store (87 percent versus 73 percent), visiting family inside their home (88 percent versus 68 percent), getting a haircut (72 percent versus 37 percent), eating out at a restaurant (65 percent versus 28 percent), attending an indoor sporting event or concert (40 percent versus 11 percent), or attending a crowded party (31 percent versus 8 percent). In the same poll, 71 percent of Republicans said that masks should be worn in public places always or most of the time, compared with 86 percent of Democrats.

Shouldn't these findings have been reflected in COVID infection and mortality numbers? The fact that they weren't suggests one of two things: either social distancing and masking—the primary tools we had at our disposal at the time to fight infection—weren't as effective as we thought, or what Republicans and Democrats were *saying* wasn't, on average, what they were *doing*.

———

As doctors, it was heartbreaking for us to see so many life-threatening—and sometimes deadly—cases of COVID-19 among unvaccinated patients after the widespread introduction of vaccines. Many of these sick patients would tell doctors, including us, that they had underestimated the virus—that they thought it would be no worse than a cold. Chris, working in COVID-filled ICUs, took the opportunity to bring up the vaccine with patients when he could, to prevent similar illness for those patients or loved ones. Some unvaccinated patients and their family members, now face-to-face with the realities of what the virus could do, decided that vaccination would indeed be the course for them going forward.

It made us wonder: If people who were reluctant to get vaccinated for an illness were made more aware of just how harmful a disease could be through either first- or secondhand experience, would they be more likely to get vaccinated? Vaccine complacency could simply be the product of not recognizing how damaging an illness is. If people saw their own family member struggle mightily with an illness, would it motivate them to get vaccinated?

We (Chris and Bapu, along with Jaemin Woo, André Zimerman, and Charles Bray, our mighty research analyst) decided to find out by looking not at COVID-19, where data was still inconclusive, but at a different politically charged vaccine, to see what recent history could teach us about the role firsthand experience with a disease plays in vaccination decisions.

We looked at human papilloma virus, or HPV. The HPV vaccine works against a number of strains of the sexually transmitted virus, which are known to cause cervical cancer and genital warts. After its approval in 2006, however, the vaccine became "politicized." Various religious and conservative groups felt that to adopt the vaccine would be to promote more promiscuous sexual behavior (a concept that has since been debunked).* While HPV and COVID-19 are very different diseases, the similar milieu and decision-making process surrounding them made them interesting analogues and made the HPV vaccine worthy of examination.

Since HPV causes cervical cancer, we wanted to know whether mothers who themselves had experienced cervical cancer or had had a cancer "scare" (defined as having had a cervical biopsy) would be more likely to vaccinate their children against HPV than mothers who had not. Using data on about 750,000 children and their parents in an insurance claims database, we divided children up into three groups: kids whose moms had been diagnosed with cervical cancer (about 1,000 kids), kids whose moms had had a cancer "scare" but were not diagnosed with cervical cancer (about 38,000 kids), and those whose parents had had neither cancer nor a scare (our

---

* A 2015 study by Bapu and the USC economists Dana Goldman and Seth Seabury found that the rate of sexually transmitted infections was no different among female teenagers vaccinated against HPV compared with unvaccinated female teenagers of the same age, suggesting that vaccination was unlikely to be promoting unsafe sexual activity. See Jena, Goldman, and Seabury, "Incidence of Sexually Transmitted Infections After Human Papillomavirus Vaccination Among Adolescent Females."

controls, about 718,000 kids). We then followed the kids in the database over time to see if they were subsequently vaccinated for HPV, a treatment that the CDC recommends all kids get, in two shots, starting at age eleven.

Despite the recommendation, we found that only 54 percent of kids had received even one dose of the vaccine by their sixteenth birthday. When we looked at the vaccination rates for kids whose moms had been diagnosed with cervical cancer, had a cancer scare, or had neither, the results surprised us: there were no differences. Moms who had had cervical cancer or cervical biopsies—who had personal experience of the harm HPV can cause—were no more likely to vaccinate their children than moms who hadn't had those experiences.

It was a counterintuitive result, and we did additional analyses to see if there was anything we were missing. Were there differences between boys and girls, since the most feared outcome, cervical cancer, affects women? We found none. Were there differences in kids getting just one dose of the HPV vaccine versus two—did a mother's experience encourage them to finish a course of treatment? Still nothing.

We also checked whether mothers with a history of cervical cancer or a scare simply had different attitudes toward vaccination, in general, from the control group. If that were the case, we might expect to find differences in their children's uptake of the meningitis vaccine and tetanus boosters. But we found no difference, further suggesting that mothers' experiences with HPV simply did not make them more likely to vaccinate their children against the virus.

Why should this be? Wouldn't a mom who had experienced something as serious as cervical cancer do everything she could to help her child avoid something similar? Did these moms not understand the link between HPV and cervical cancer, despite having had the disease themselves?

Our study suggested that having personal experience with the most feared outcome that a vaccine tries to prevent simply isn't a significant driver of vaccine behavior—at least when it came to HPV and children.

What could this tell us about the behaviors surrounding COVID-19 vaccination decisions? Having a family member end up in the hospital with a severe COVID-19 infection might not be the motivator that we suspected. It tracks with data from Republican- and Democratic-leaning counties. Even as COVID-19 was disproportionately killing patients in counties with low vaccination rates, we saw no sudden uptick in vaccination. Intimate experience with the harms of a virus may not change minds as much as we doctors would think. It may simply be that as a population our vaccination decisions are more heavily motivated by a panoply of social factors than they are by any single event, even a life-or-death one.

If a near-death experience doesn't change minds when it comes to COVID-19 vaccination, what does? Vaccination rates among older Americans, at greatest risk of severe outcomes from COVID-19, have been very high—about 80 percent of U.S. adults over age sixty-five had received their first dose by April 2021. It suggests that your own conception of your personal risk may play a part. Incentive programs, like lottery drawings for which only vaccinated citizens are eligible, might have encouraged a few people to get vaccinated who otherwise wouldn't have, but they didn't seem to make a significant dent in overall vaccination rates. Negative incentive programs like workplace mandates did seem to work well; "get vaccinated or get fired" helped companies like United Airlines and our own hospital get to nearly universal vaccination. People rarely choose termination over staying unvaccinated. On balance, it seemed that "sticks" were more effective motivators than "carrots."

—

If we've so far treated politics as having a pernicious role in public health—steering patients away from the desired paths that we, their medical providers, would urge them along—it shouldn't be viewed only in that light. Politicians and appointed officials not only run the essential government response to any public health crisis; many have spent their careers learning to gain trust, to recognize and appeal to voters' values to motivate them. Politics and public health are inextricably intertwined; the party-line differences we've seen during COVID-19 tell us not that the two need to be disentangled, only that they could stand to work together better. The question, of course, is how?

Public health responses can and should be built on objective data and science. But where they often go wrong is not in determining the healthiest course for a population—such as wearing a mask, taking a vaccine, quitting smoking, eating right. These are often well established. It's in getting diverse groups of people to adopt those behaviors. That, after all, is the purpose of a successful intervention—not just innovation, but implementation. To do that, we have to better acknowledge the trade-offs involved in a behavior—the motivations to skip a birthday party or to get a vaccine—and the ways in which they can vary from person to person. As much as we might think we know what motivates health behaviors, people surprise us doctors and public health experts all the time. Working in the hospital, talking with patients to better understand what drives them to protect their well-being is eye-opening and always humbling.

It's been frighteningly easy for all of us to get caught up in the differences in how each of us has responded to the pandemic—to paint groups in broad strokes and lose sight of our shared experience. Yes, there were some who could have and should have been doing more to help their neighbors and communities. There were also those who suffered and died despite taking every precaution to protect themselves. Regardless of our individual decisions, we have all paid *some* price during the pandemic; we've made sacrifices, lost something or someone, had our lives upended.

We know that it's odd to view a pandemic that's been characterized by political polarization this way. But looking at our shared experiences of the last few years, we've come away cautiously optimistic about the future of public health in the United States. Take a step back for a moment: More than 90 percent of U.S. adults have taken the time, effort, and risk to get at least one COVID-19 vaccine. (Only about 70 percent of the adult population is up to date on their tetanus shot, which requires just one shot every ten years. Most years not even half of adults get a flu shot.) That tells us that despite our differences, getting vaccinated against COVID-19 became normalized, regardless of political affiliation. In fact, it's hard to find things we agree on more than getting vaccinated, though we found one: more Americans lack confidence in Congress (93 percent).

We've come to view the public health response to COVID-19 as a "successful failure," a term borrowed from the astronaut James Lovell. Lovell was commander of the Apollo 13 spacecraft, whose mission was to land on the moon. Completing that mission became impossible when one of their oxygen tanks exploded 200,000 miles from Earth, imperiling the lives of the three astronauts on board. Through tireless work and characteristic ingenuity, NASA was able to help the astronauts defeat the odds and make it back to Earth alive.

"Our mission was a failure," Lovell wrote, "but I like to think it was a successful failure."

With so many dead from COVID-19, it's clear that *our* larger mission—saving lives in the midst of a pandemic—has been a failure. More than a million Americans have died from the virus as we write this. Many of these deaths were needless, and our society will be paying the price for them for decades to come. But within these broader failures, the COVID-19 vaccine has been a resounding success. It's not just that it was developed extremely quickly, using novel technology. It's that this highly effective treatment became a fixture of American life and has saved more lives than we'll ever know.

A successful failure, indeed.

—

We started this book by telling you that chance occurrences change the course of our lives all the time. By braving some statistical concepts and exploring a range of natural experiments in medicine with us, you have, we hope, come to see the hidden role that chance plays in our health and in the practice of medicine. We've looked at how unconscious biases and accidents of fate sway doctors and affect patients, and we've found areas ripe for improvement within our complex health-care system.

But we've only scratched the surface—in this book and as researchers. There is an ever-growing pool of data available and an expanding set of digital tools for parsing it, which, when appropriately harnessed, stand to shed light and improve health outcomes for all of us.

Here's one example: In February 2021, a cold snap in Texas resulted in massive power outages across the state. On the news, we saw reports of hundreds of Texans being diagnosed with carbon monoxide poisoning, since the portable electrical generators that people often use to generate power during an outage release the toxic gas that can build up in poorly ventilated areas. We (Chris and Bapu, along with Jaemin Woo, the MIT economist Michael Kearney, and Charles Bray) were inspired to ask, How much does an as-good-as-random power outage increase the risk of carbon monoxide poisoning? Using data from the Department of Energy on major U.S. power outages and a national database of insurance claims, we found that for power outages lasting more than forty-eight hours, the risk of carbon monoxide poisoning was fully 9.3 times higher than the baseline; for children, it was 13.5 times higher. With inspiration from a single news story, we found a way to quantify the risk of an event—information that could materially improve public health as our power grid ages and such events (and such risks) become all the more common.

Another example: Hospital scuttlebutt has always said that when a motorcycle rally comes to town for "bike week," organ transplant teams should be at the ready. The thinking goes that if hundreds of thousands of motorcyclists descend on a location, there might be more fatal crashes, and thus more organ donors. Are the rumors true? Do bike weeks lead to greater organ donations? It's an admittedly odd question, and one that's next to impossible to study by conventional means. But since bike weeks are randomly timed with respect to the organ transplant system, there was a natural experiment just waiting for examination.

Using data from national organ transplant registries, we (Chris and Bapu, along with the Harvard surgeon and policy researcher David Cron, the Dell Medical School transplant surgeon Joel Adler, and Charles Bray) asked if the spike in organ donation during major motorcycle rallies in the United States was more than speculative.

We found that in fact it was. Looking at both organ donors who suffered motor vehicle collisions and the recipients of the donated organs, we found that, compared with the four weeks before and after a major motorcycle rally, the number of organ donors in a region increased by 21 percent and the number of transplant recipients increased by 26 percent. This translates to approximately one additional donor and six additional transplant recipients for every two major motorcycle rallies.* (There was no increase in donations during bike weeks from donors who died of causes other than motor vehicle collisions, corroborating our finding.)

You might well be asking, Does this really matter? Compared with blood pressure medications or cancer therapies, which can stand to improve the lives of millions, motorcycle rallies may seem like a trifle. But the organ donation and transplant system saves lives daily thanks to a complex network of transplant teams and highly choreographed procedures. Just like the study of marathons that we considered in chapter 5, what we learn about these rallies is valuable not only in itself but for the way it could point toward more and better transplantation broadly—a small notch in the greater effort of ensuring that as many lives are saved as possible in the wake of a tragic and otherwise senseless event.

Not all our ideas are winners; most aren't. For every fifty we come up with, only twenty might be practical for us to study, and of those only a handful might allow us to feel confident that our results reflect a genuine underlying phenomenon (because we're able to perform the sorts of supporting analyses that you've seen throughout this book). We like to think of the studies shared in this book as diamonds in the rough—good ideas that turned into (we think) good studies and that taught us something useful about patients, doctors, and the health-care system at large.

We hope that, having gone through dozens of natural experi-

---

* One organ donor can donate their major organs to multiple recipients, though each one has to be healthy enough to transplant. One donor can potentially donate two kidneys, a liver that can be divided to two patients, a heart, and two lungs. Other organs like the pancreas and intestines can be transplanted, and other body tissues can also be donated for medical use.

ments with us and having become familiar with the circumstances that create them, you too might come to see the way that chance affects your health—the way accidents of timing, birth date, gender, race, zip code, and political party might be bearing on you and your doctor at this very moment. At the very least, we hope you've gained insight into the ways one part of your life can spill over into another, to surprising and often profound effect. You might begin seeing the world as we do: ripe for study, a natural experiment always hiding in plain sight, waiting to be discovered.

You might even think up a slick natural experiment or two yourself. If you do, we'd love to hear about it. Who knows? Our next collaborator could be you.

—A.B.J. and C.W., January 2023

ACKNOWLEDGMENTS

When thumbing through books I frequently first turn to the acknowledgments, since they offer a window into the writer's life that the stories of a book sometimes cannot provide. I hope to give you that view here.

I have many people to thank. My wife, Neena Kapoor, an accomplished physician in her own right, whose friendship, love, and counsel have meant everything to me since our early days in Chicago. My children, Annika and Aiden, whose curiosity is pure and whose lives will always be a reminder that almost nothing is as important as it seems. My mother, Tripti Jena, who came to this country more than fifty years ago, trained in an era of medicine so different from what it is now, and devoted her life to her family, to her patients, and to the beautiful art of medicine. My father, who taught me that laughter is indeed the best medicine and to this day has taken more interest in my work than any person alive, including me.

My research has benefited greatly from many research assistants and collaborators over the years, too many to name here. They have taught me what they know and tolerated flurries of emails with hare-brained ideas, like whether doctors named Christopher are more likely to be cardiologists, doctors named Daniel are more likely to be dermatologists, and doctors named Gina are more likely to become gastroenterologists—they are not! Most important, though, many have become close friends. One colleague bears special note: Christopher Worsham. First a student, then a colleague, and now a friend. This book is because of him.

I consider myself to be extraordinarily lucky. Many of the studies in this book, and many of mine that did not make it into these pages, are unconventional for the field of medicine, yet were possible because of support from the right people. Barbara McNeil, a pioneer in health-care policy, gave me my first job at Harvard. She, Joseph Newhouse, and others built an intellectual environment and community that have allowed me to thrive there ever since. My Chicago advisers Tomas Philipson, David Meltzer, and Steve Levitt showed me how economics and medicine could be blended in ways that are creative, important, and sometimes both. But arguably no single person has had more impact on me than Dana Goldman, whose mentorship and friendship now serve as my model.

I am grateful to Stephen Dubner and the Freakonomics family, including my producer Julie Kanfer, for giving a voice to many of the ideas and themes in this book. Hosting the *Freakonomics, M.D.* podcast has been a joy and a privilege. It is also through Stephen that I ultimately found my way to my agents Jay Mandel and Alex Kane at WME, who early on helped shape the vision for what this book could be. But it is Yaniv Soha, my editor at Doubleday, who made that vision a reality. Special thanks also go to Emily Oster, David Epstein, Cass Sunstein, Steve Levitt, Katy Milkman, and Joshua Angrist, writers who I admire and who were kind enough to preview this work.

Lastly, professional accomplishments, like completing a book, are impossible without relationships and support in other parts of our lives. For the gifts of their time, their energy, and their friendship, I am grateful to Sakuntala Dhungana, Sabrina Dennison, and Elyse Fishkin.

—A.B.J.

This book focuses on the role chance can play in our health, but the book itself is also a product of chance—a result of Bapu Jena and I happening to cross paths at the right time. However, there are many, many people whose support made it possible for chance to play its role and to whom I owe many, many thanks.

My wife, Emily Worsham, has spent years supporting my training, research, and writing, all while working as an accomplished pharmacist caring for children with cancer. Her love, friendship, trust, good humor, and patience propel me forward every day. Our sons, Luke and Adam, are the greatest gifts we could ever have asked for. My parents, Donna Inserra Worsham, a television news producer, and James Worsham, a newspaper and print journalist, worked tirelessly to give me and my brother, Alex, every opportunity to thrive, grow, and be curious. In preparing this book, my mom generously leant her expertise in making complex concepts and stories approachable to anyone. My dad's influence is readily apparent in my writing, and while I wish he could have read this book, his fingerprints are all over it.

I'm also extremely grateful for the professional support given to me by educators, colleagues, and collaborators, throughout my education and training, particularly those at Boston University and Harvard. I want to thank Gopal Yadavalli, Tony Breu, Liz Klings, and James Moses for their mentorship launching my academic career at BU. Seeing that I wanted to do something a little different than a typical pulmonary and critical care doctor, Josalyn Cho, Asha Anandaiah, Ben Medoff, Kathryn Hibbert, Eric Schmidt, Woody Weiss, Rich Schwartzstein, Rob Hallowell, and Taylor Thompson at Harvard have supported me unflinchingly as a fellow and now faculty member. Forging enduring friendships during our training, my colleagues Lakshman Swamy, Rahul Ganatra, and Jason Maley are my go-to sounding boards for advice and perspective.

And then there's Bapu. A teacher, research collaborator, mentor, and friend, Bapu has changed the way I (and many others) think about the profession of medicine. Most important, he has taught me that thinking creatively about research is a skill to be practiced, honed, and shared. I will never be able to thank him enough for everything he has done for me, but I'm glad to have had the opportunity to share some of it in this book.

Finally, thank you to Jay Mandel and Alex Kane at WME for helping us develop a fuller vision of what this book could be, and to Yaniv Soha at Doubleday for working alongside us to bring that vision to life.

—C.W.

NOTES

Chapter One: Our Lives Are Woven in a Fabric of Chance

2   Because opioid-prescribing tendencies: Barnett, Olenski, and Jena, "Opioid-Prescribing Patterns of Emergency Physicians and Risk of Long-Term Use."

2   But if that person happens: Neprash et al., "Evidence of Respiratory Infection Transmission Within Physician Offices Could Inform Outpatient Infection Control."

4   In one study, the Princeton economist: Currie and Walker, "Traffic Congestion and Infant Health."

5   Here's another natural experiment: Deryugina et al., "Mortality and Medical Costs of Air Pollution."

7   Their work has been credited: Glied, "Credibility Revolution in Economics and How It Has Changed Health Policy."

7   Because the disease caused: Snow, *On the Mode of Communication of Cholera.*

Chapter Two: Natural Experiments

11   "With the stress of a financial meltdown": " 'More Gray Hair' for President Obama," CNN.

11   "Ten years ago": "Former President Obama Campaign Remarks in Gary, Indiana," C-SPAN.

15   A group of us: Olenski, Abola, and Jena, "Do Heads of Government Age More Quickly?"

18   Of course, Olympians: Clarke et al., "Survival of the Fittest."

18 "If I was an Olympic athlete": *Jerry Seinfeld: I'm Telling You for the Last Time,* directed by Callner.

18 In his 2018 study: Kalwij, "Effects of Competition Outcomes on Health."

20 While studies had shown: Baron and Rinsky, "Health Hazard Evaluation Report, National Football League Players Mortality Study."

20 The 1987 players' strike: Venkataramani, Gandhavadi, and Jena, "Association Between Playing American Football in the National Football League and Long-Term Mortality."

Chapter Three: Why Are Kids with Summer Birthdays More Likely to Get the Flu?

25 After all, influenza: Putri et al., "Economic Burden of Seasonal Influenza in the United States."

27 database containing insurance claims: Worsham, Woo, and Jena, "Birth Month and Influenza Vaccination in Children."

35 And as easy as: Towers and Feng, "Social Contact Patterns and Control Strategies for Influenza in the Elderly."

36 In a research study of deaths: Reichert et al., "Japanese Experience with Vaccinating Schoolchildren Against Influenza."

39 They call them the "3 Cs": MacDonald and Sage Working Group on Vaccine Hesitancy, "Vaccine Hesitancy."

40 Boston Medical Center: Bebinger, "Doctors Try Out Curbside Vaccinations for Kids to Prevent a Competing Pandemic."

40 These temporary solutions: Lerner, Newgard, and Mann, "Effect of the Coronavirus Disease 2019 (COVID-19) Pandemic on the U.S. Emergency Medical Services System."

41 A study by Bapu: Frakes, Gruber, and Jena, "Is Great Information Good Enough?"

41 The Nobel Prize–winning: Thaler and Sunstein, *Nudge.*

42 Researchers have looked: Hurwitz et al., "Studies of the 1996–1997 Inactivated Influenza Vaccine Among Children Attending Day Care"; Hurwitz et al., "Effectiveness of Influenza Vaccination of Day Care Children in Reducing Influenza-Related Morbidity Among Household Contacts."

42 In another study: King et al., "Effectiveness of School-Based Influenza Vaccination."

43 In the 2009–2010 influenza season: Chapman et al., "Opting In vs. Opting Out of Influenza Vaccination."

44 Still, as a nation: "Flu Vaccination Coverage, United States, 2020–21 Influenza Season," Centers for Disease Control and Prevention.

44 According to 2019 estimates: "National Health Expenditure Fact Sheet," Centers for Medicare and Medicaid Services.

44 A health-care system: Schneider et al., *Mirror, Mirror 2021*.

45 The cost of parents' time: Principi et al., "Socioeconomic Impact of Influenza on Healthy Children and Their Families"; Li and Leader, "Economic Burden and Absenteeism from Influenza-Like Illness in Healthy Households with Children (5–17 Years) in the US."

45 The idea that difficult-to-measure: Choudhry et al., "Full Coverage for Preventive Medications After Myocardial Infarction."

46 This is why for conditions: McClellan, "Does More Intensive Treatment of Acute Myocardial Infarction in the Elderly Reduce Mortality?"

Chapter Four: Tom Brady, ADHD, and a Really Bad Headache

48 A top high school player: Jenkins, "Self-Made Man."

49 Studies from the 1980s: Barnsley, Thompson, and Barnsley, "Hockey Success and Birthdate."

50 Researchers have found: Thompson, Barnsley, and Stebelsky, "'Born to Play Ball'"; Helsen, van Winckel, and Williams, "Relative Age Effect in Youth Soccer Across Europe."

50 A study of German: Ulbricht et al., "Relative Age Effect and Physical Fitness Characteristics in German Male Tennis Players."

51 Bapu, along with Harvard colleagues: Layton et al., "Attention Deficit-Hyperactivity Disorder and Month of School Enrollment."

51 A condition marked by inattention: "Data and Statistics About ADHD," Centers for Disease Control and Prevention.

52 Previous research had provided: Elder, "Importance of Relative Standards in ADHD Diagnoses"; Evans, Morrill, and Parente, "Measuring Inappropriate Medical Diagnosis and Treatment in Survey Data"; Morrow et al., "Influence of Relative Age on Diagnosis and Treatment of Attention-Deficit/Hyperactivity Disorder in Children"; Krabbe et al., "Birth Month as Predictor of ADHD Medication Use in Dutch School Classes."

56 A study from the U.K.: Root et al., "Association of Relative Age in the School Year with Diagnosis of Intellectual Disability, Attention-Deficit/Hyperactivity Disorder, and Depression."

56 A review of data in Alberta: Thompson, Barnsley, and Dyck, "New Factor in Youth Suicide."

56 A study in Norway: Black, Devereux, and Salvanes, "Too Young to Leave the Nest?"

56 A study by economists: Dhuey et al., "School Starting Age and Cognitive Development."

57 The Brown University economist: Oster, *Family Firm*.

58 And while one could interpret: Kazda et al., "Overdiagnosis of Attention-Deficit/Hyperactivity Disorder in Children and Adolescents."

58 Let's be clear: Wolraich et al., "Clinical Practice Guideline for the Diagnosis, Evaluation, and Treatment of Attention-Deficit/Hyperactivity Disorder in Children and Adolescents."

58 One study by Bapu: Barnett, Olenski, and Jena, "Opioid-Prescribing Patterns of Emergency Physicians and Risk of Long-Term Use."

58 In a similar study: Shi et al., "Association of a Clinician's Antibiotic-Prescribing Rate with Patients' Future Likelihood of Seeking Care and Receipt of Antibiotics."

59 ADHD is based: American Psychiatric Association, *Diagnostic and Statistical Manual of Mental Disorders (DSM-5)*.

61 A classic study: Tversky and Kahneman, "Availability."

61 A study by the UCLA: Ly, "Influence of the Availability Heuristic on Physicians in the Emergency Department."

62 While this is not a huge effect: "FastStats: Emergency Department Visits," Centers for Disease Control and Prevention.

62 "Without ever giving": Dhaliwal, "Piece of My Mind."

63 the relative age effect: Crawford, Dearden, and Meghir, "When You Are Born Matters."

63 In 2015, the National Academy of Medicine: Balogh, Miller, and Ball, *Improving Diagnosis in Health Care*.

66 One study estimated: Obermeyer et al., "Early Death After Discharge from Emergency Departments."

67 In a study designed: Doctor et al., "Opioid Prescribing Decreases After Learning of a Patient's Fatal Overdose."

Chapter Five: Are Marathons Hazardous to Your Health?

69 The modern marathon's checkered origin: "State of Running 2019," International Institute for Race Medicine.

70 Of course, the veracity: Lucas, "History of the Marathon Race—490 B.C. to 1975."

70 Featuring more than 50,000: "New York City Marathon Fast Facts," CNN.

70 With thousands of participants: American College of Sports Medicine, "Mass Participation Event Management for the Team Physician."

71 "The Pittsburgh Marathon": Perlmutter, "Pittsburgh Marathon."

72 Collapse is often treated easily: Kim et al., "Cardiac Arrest During Long-Distance Running Races."

72 "One nurse told me": Jangi, "Under the Medical Tent at the Boston Marathon."

73 The state police: Schoenberg, "Look Inside the Security Headquarters for the 2019 Boston Marathon."

76 If we were to only study: Baker-Blocker, "Winter Weather and Cardiovascular Mortality in Minneapolis–St. Paul"; Mohammad et al., "Association of Weather with Day-to-Day Incidence of Myocardial Infarction."

77 In a study published: Jena et al., "Delays in Emergency Care and Mortality During Major U.S. Marathons."

83 In 2004, the CDC: "CARES Fact Sheet," Emory Woodruff Health Sciences Center.

83 In one of their early studies: McNally et al., "Out-of-Hospital Cardiac Arrest Surveillance."

83 In a study using: Hasselqvist-Ax et al., "Early Cardiopulmonary Resuscitation in Out-of-Hospital Cardiac Arrest."

83 If patients living: Sasson et al., "Association of Neighborhood Characteristics with Bystander-Initiated CPR."

84 One of these factors is wealth: Dixon-Roman, Everson, and McArdle, "Race, Poverty, and SAT Scores."

85 In 2012, researchers in Stockholm: Ringh et al., "Mobile-Phone Dispatch of Laypersons for CPR in Out-of-Hospital Cardiac Arrest."

87 In a study led: Sanghavi et al., "Outcomes After Out-of-Hospital Cardiac Arrest Treated by Basic vs. Advanced Life Support."

89 In a separate study: Grunau et al., "Association of Intra-arrest Transport vs. Continued On-Scene Resuscitation with Survival to Hospital Discharge Among Patients with Out-of-Hospital Cardiac Arrest."

Chapter Six: What Happens When All the Cardiologists Leave Town?

97 According to the Events Industry: Events Industry Council, *Global Economic Significance of Business Events.*

99 We know, for example: Bell and Redelmeier, "Mortality Among Patients Admitted to Hospitals on Weekends as Compared with Weekdays"; Kostis et al., "Weekend Versus Weekday Admission and Mortality from Myocardial Infarction."

99 In a study that examined: Slater and Ever-Hadani, "Mortality in Jerusalem During the 1983 Doctors' Strike."

100 Surprising though they are: Cunningham et al., "Doctors' Strikes and Mortality."

101 We examined hospitalizations: Jena et al., "Mortality and Treatment Patterns Among Patients Hospitalized with Acute Cardiovascular Conditions During Dates of National Cardiology Meetings."

105 For a new analysis: Jena et al., "Acute Myocardial Infarction Mortality During Dates of National Interventional Cardiology Meetings."

106 For example, clinical trials: Keeley, Boura, and Grines, "Primary Angioplasty Versus Intravenous Thrombolytic Therapy for Acute Myocardial Infarction."

107 "Bottom line for us": "How Many Doctors Does It Take to Start a Healthcare Revolution?," *Freakonomics Radio*.

108 "How should we interpret": Redberg, "Cardiac Patient Outcomes During National Cardiology Meetings."

110 In a study of 286: Bar-Eli et al., "Action Bias Among Elite Soccer Goalkeepers."

110 "There are many reasons": Grady and Redberg, "Less Is More."

111 "My interest in healthcare": Park, "Interview with a Quality Leader: Dr. Ashish Jha."

112 In a widely discussed: Temel et al., "Early Palliative Care for Patients with Metastatic Non-small-cell Lung Cancer."

112 "promote conversations between": "Our Mission," ABIM Foundation.

113 "Perhaps the most accurate conclusion": Rosenbaum, "Less-Is-More Crusade."

Chapter Seven: Big Doctor Is Watching

116 Other than discovering: Wickström and Bendix, "Commentary."

116 "Insomuch as the interviewer": Roethlisberger et al., *Management and the Worker*, 529.

116 In the decades since: Adair, "Hawthorne Effect"; Jones, "Was There a Hawthorne Effect?"; Levitt and List, "Was There Really a Hawthorne Effect at the Hawthorne Plant?"; McCambridge, Witton, and Elbourne, "Systematic Review of the Hawthorne Effect."

117 Nevertheless, the idea: Levitt and List, "Was There Really a Hawthorne Effect at the Hawthorne Plant?"

118 With multiple layers: "Patient Safety 101," Agency for Healthcare Research and Quality.

118 "distractions that interfered": Ring, Herndon, and Meyer, "Case Records of the Massachusetts General Hospital."

118 "devastating": Cooney, "MGH Doctor Urges Safety After Mistake."

119   In a pivotal work: Hiatt et al., "Study of Medical Injury and Medical Malpractice"; Brennan et al., "Incidence of Adverse Events and Negligence in Hospitalized Patients."

120   More recent estimates: Rodwin et al., "Rate of Preventable Mortality in Hospitalized Patients"; James, "New, Evidence-Based Estimate of Patient Harms Associated with Hospital Care."

122   Inspectors perform "tracers": "All Accreditation Programs Survey Activity Guide," Joint Commission.

122   For example, inspectors will check: "Universal Protocol for Preventing Wrong Site, Wrong Procedure, and Wrong Person Surgery," Joint Commission.

122   "All of a sudden": "Mission: Achieve Continual Readiness for Joint Commission Surveys," American Nursing Association.

123   In a 2006 study: Eckmanns et al., "Compliance with Antiseptic Hand Rub Use in Intensive Care Units."

124   To answer these questions: Barnett, Olenski, and Jena, "Patient Mortality During Unannounced Accreditation Surveys at US Hospitals."

134   This sounds appealing: Cvach, "Monitor Alarm Fatigue."

134   You could probably: Swamy et al., "60-Minute Root Cause Analysis."

134   "You take off": "Bad News—It's Your Surgeon's Birthday," *Freakonomics, M.D.*

135   A 1972 study: Shapiro and Berland, "Noise in the Operating Room."

136   In a study of patients: Kato, Jena, and Tsugawa, "Patient Mortality After Surgery on the Surgeon's Birthday."

140   The goal is to improve: Mitchell et al., "Core Principles & Values of Effective Team-Based Health Care."

140   For example, checklists: Gawande, "Checklist."

140   Recognizing that human fallibility: Federal Aviation Administration, "FAA TV."

140   At its core: Helmreich, Merritt, and Wilhelm, "Evolution of Crew Resource Management Training in Commercial Aviation."

140   Research on surgical teams: Stucky and De Jong, "Surgical Team Familiarity."

141   In what would prove: Pronovost et al., "Intervention to Decrease Catheter-Related Bloodstream Infections in the ICU."

142   Central line "bundles": Furuya et al., "Central Line Bundle Implementation in US Intensive Care Units and Impact on Bloodstream Infections."

142   The physician and revered health-care-quality scholar: Donabedian, "Evaluating the Quality of Medical Care"; Donabedian, *Introduction to Quality Assurance in Health Care.*

143   For example, the use of checklists: Fonarow et al., "Influence of a Performance-Improvement Initiative on Quality of Care for Patients Hospitalized with Heart Failure."

143   "The key thesis that": Berwick and Cassel, "NAM and the Quality of Health Care—Inflecting a Field."

144   Payment structures that financially incentivize: Porter, "What Is Value in Health Care?"

144   "It's hard to know": Rosenbaum, "Reassessing Quality Assessment."

145   Billions of dollars: Casalino et al., "US Physician Practices Spend More Than $15.4 Billion Annually to Report Quality Measures."

145   Safety-net hospitals: Gilman et al., "Financial Effect of Value-Based Purchasing and the Hospital Readmissions Reduction Program on Safety-Net Hospitals in 2014."

146   "[They] not only exhausted": McWilliams, "Professionalism Revealed."

Chapter Eight: What Do Cardiac Surgeons and Used-Car Salesmen Have in Common?

147   Meanwhile, economists: Thomas and Morwitz, "Penny Wise and Pound Foolish."

147   When we see a number: Hinrichs, Yurko, and Hu, "Two-Digit Number Comparison."

148   Setting the two numbers: Dehaene, Dupoux, and Mehler, "Is Numerical Comparison Digital?"

149   Buyers may get assistance: "What Are Kelley Blue Book Values?," Kelley Blue Book.

149   In a study examining: Lacetera, Pope, and Sydnor, "Heuristic Thinking and Limited Attention in the Car Market."

152   With training and experience: Schmidt and Rikers, "How Expertise Develops in Medicine."

152   Intrigued to learn more: Coussens, "Behaving Discretely."

156   They have lower overall survival: Shahian et al., "Predictors of Long-Term Survival After Coronary Artery Bypass Grafting Surgery."

157   In a study published: Olenski et al., "Behavioral Heuristics in Coronary-Artery Bypass Graft Surgery."

157   Importantly, guidelines don't push: Hillis et al., "2011 ACCF/AHA Guideline for Coronary Artery Bypass Graft Surgery"; Lawton et al., "2021 ACC/AHA/SCAI Guideline for Coronary Artery Revascularization."

161   Multiple studies have found evidence: Husain, King, and Mohan, "Left-Digit Bias and Deceased Donor Kidney Utilization"; Jacobson

et al., "Left Digit Bias in Selection and Acceptance of Deceased Donor Organs."

161 In an additional analysis: Husain, King, and Mohan, "Left-Digit Bias and Deceased Donor Kidney Utilization."

161 In another study: Dalmacy et al., "Age-Based Left-Digit Bias in the Management of Acute Cholecystitis."

161 Finally, in a study: Melucci et al., "Assessment of Left-Digit Bias in the Treatment of Older Patients with Potentially Curable Rectal Cancer."

163 They advise that all adults: U.S. Preventive Services Task Force et al., "Screening for Colorectal Cancer."

163 They also recommend: U.S. Preventive Services Task Force et al., "Screening for Lung Cancer."

164 In a study using a database: Worsham et al., "Adverse Events and Emergency Department Opioid Prescriptions in Adolescents."

166 With an estimated 20.2 million: Rui and Kang, *National Hospital Ambulatory Medical Care Survey.*

169 the "win-stay/lose-shift" heuristic: Nowak and Sigmund, "Strategy of Win-Stay, Lose-Shift That Outperforms Tit-for-Tat in the Prisoner's Dilemma Game."

171 In a 2021 study: Singh, "Heuristics in the Delivery Room."

172 more than 3.6 million babies: "FastStats: Births and Natality," Centers for Disease Control and Prevention.

172 One such study: Choudhry et al., "Impact of Adverse Events on Prescribing Warfarin in Patients with Atrial Fibrillation."

174 Put differently, doctors may fear: Feinstein, " 'Chagrin Factor' and Qualitative Decision Analysis."

175 In one study: Chen, Moskowitz, and Shue, "Decision Making Under the Gambler's Fallacy."

176 In a unique study: Elmore et al., "Effect of Prior Diagnoses on Dermatopathologists' Interpretations of Melanocytic Lesions."

178 Anchoring bias: Tversky and Kahneman, "Judgment Under Uncertainty."

179 Still, the likely first step: Croskerry, Singhal, and Mamede, "Cognitive Debiasing 1"; Croskerry, Singhal, and Mamede, "Cognitive Debiasing 2."

179 For example, as a resident: "Categorical Training Program," Boston University School of Medicine.

179 "In contrast to heuristics": Croskerry, "Cognitive Forcing Strategies in Clinical Decisionmaking."

181 In a study of thirty-two: Stiegler et al., "Cognitive Errors Detected in Anaesthesiology."

182   Using data from millions: "ACS NSQIP Surgical Risk Calculator," American College of Surgeons National Surgical Quality Improvement Program.

182   Or take primary care doctors: "ASCVD Risk Estimator Plus," American College of Cardiology.

182   Other, more sophisticated algorithms: Umscheid et al., "Development, Implementation, and Impact of an Automated Early Warning and Response System for Sepsis."

Chapter Nine: What Makes a Good Doctor?

185   "We began with doctor shows": Tapper, "Doctors on Display."

187   With accuracy generally taking a backseat: Hetsroni, "If You Must Be Hospitalized, Television Is Not the Place."

188   "When one considers": Peabody, "Care of the Patient."

189   "What makes a good doctor": Rizo, "What's a Good Doctor and How Do You Make One?"

190   More senior doctors: Landhuis, "Scientific Literature."

190   In a study published in 2017: Tsugawa et al., "Physician Age and Outcomes in Elderly Patients in Hospital in the US."

191   These physicians, called hospitalists: Stevens et al., "Comparison of Hospital Resource Use and Outcomes Among Hospitalists, Primary Care Physicians, and Other Generalists."

195   "It could be that": Samuel, "Patients Fare Worse with Older Doctors, Study Finds."

196   When comparing ourselves: Kruger, "Lake Wobegon Be Gone!"

196   "all the women": Keillor, "News from Lake Wobegon."

197   Bapu, along with Yusuke: Tsugawa et al., "Age and Sex of Surgeons and Mortality of Older Surgical Patients."

199   To complete their general surgery: "Defined Category Minimum Numbers for General Surgery Residents and Credit Role," Accreditation Council for Graduate Medical Education.

200   Explicit bias can: Lim et al., "Unspoken Reality of Gender Bias in Surgery"; Viglianti, Oliverio, and Meeks, "Sexual Harassment and Abuse."

201   In a study of such subconscious tendencies: Salles et al., "Estimating Implicit and Explicit Gender Bias Among Health Care Professionals and Surgeons."

201   One study of referrals: Dossa et al., "Sex Differences in the Pattern of Patient Referrals to Male and Female Surgeons."

201 Similarly, if a surgeon: Sarsons, "Interpreting Signals in the Labor Market."

201 They are paid less than men: Whaley et al., "Female Physicians Earn an Estimated $2 Million Less Than Male Physicians over a Simulated 40-Year Career"; Jena, Olenski, and Blumenthal, "Sex Differences in Physician Salary in US Public Medical Schools."

201 Family and domestic obligations: Jolly et al., "Gender Differences in Time Spent on Parenting and Domestic Responsibilities by High-Achieving Young Physician-Researchers."

202 During the COVID-19 pandemic: Matulevicius et al., "Academic Medicine Faculty Perceptions of Work-Life Balance Before and Since the COVID-19 Pandemic."

202 "No matter how much": Stamp, "I'm a Female Surgeon. I Feel Uncomfortable Telling Girls They Can Be One, Too."

202 According to the Association: Lautenberger and Dandar, *State of Women in Academic Medicine, 2018–2019.*

202 Failing to promote: Bennett et al., "Gender Differences in Faculty Rank Among Academic Emergency Physicians in the United States."

203 In a separate study: Tsugawa et al., "Comparison of Hospital Mortality and Readmission Rates for Medicare Patients Treated by Male vs. Female Physicians."

204 Over the past several decades: Berthold et al., "Physician Gender Is Associated with the Quality of Type 2 Diabetes Care"; Baumhakel, Muller, and Bohm, "Influence of Gender of Physicians and Patients on Guideline-Recommended Treatment of Chronic Heart Failure in a Cross-Sectional Study"; Smith et al., "U.S. Primary Care Physicians' Diet-, Physical Activity–, and Weight-Related Care of Adult Patients."

205 Patients of women primary care doctors: Dahrouge et al., "Comprehensive Assessment of Family Physician Gender and Quality of Care"; Jerant et al., "Gender of Physician as the Usual Source of Care and Patient Health Care Utilization and Mortality."

205 However, over the course of a year: Ganguli et al., "Physician Work Hours and the Gender Pay Gap."

205 Women physicians, on average: Roter, Hall, and Aoki, "Physician Gender Effects in Medical Communication."

205 Compared with patients of male physicians: Cooper-Patrick, "Race, Gender, and Partnership in the Patient-Physician Relationship."

206 One small study: Roter, Lipkin, and Korsgaard, "Sex Differences in Patients' and Physicians' Communication During Primary Care Medical Visits."

206   A large study of patients: Wallis et al., "Association of Surgeon-Patient Sex Concordance with Postoperative Outcomes."

206   Gender concordance has also: Lau et al., "Does Patient-Physician Gender Concordance Influence Patient Perceptions or Outcomes?"

207   Americans of Hispanic: "Diversity in Medicine," Association of American Medical Colleges.

207   In 2017, the Harvard economist: Alsan, Garrick, and Graziani, "Does Diversity Matter for Health?"

207   Another randomized trial: Saha and Beach, "Impact of Physician Race on Patient Decision-Making and Ratings of Physicians."

208   This was most clearly: Parker et al., "Association of Patient-Physician Language Concordance and Glycemic Control for Limited–English Proficiency Latinos with Type 2 Diabetes."

208   These studies' results: Shen et al., "Effects of Race and Racial Concordance on Patient-Physician Communication."

208   In a 2020 issue: Williamson, "Goals of Care—Is There a (Black) Doctor in the House?"

209   One survey study: LaVeist, Isaac, and Williams, "Mistrust of Health Care Organizations Is Associated with Underutilization of Health Services."

210   Another survey study: Bazargan, Cobb, and Assari, "Discrimination and Medical Mistrust in a Racially and Ethnically Diverse Sample of California Adults."

210   Tuskegee syphilis study: Heller, "Black Men Untreated in Tuskegee Syphilis Study."

210   The glaring inequities: Elizabeth Arias et al., "Provisional Life Expectancy Estimates for 2020," Centers for Disease Control and Prevention, July 2021, dx.doi.org/10.15620/cdc:107201.

210   How this mistrust: Jaiswal and Halkitis, "Towards a More Inclusive and Dynamic Understanding of Medical Mistrust Informed by Science."

211   Using a similar approach: Tsugawa et al., "Association Between Physician *US News & World Report* Medical School Ranking and Patient Outcomes and Costs of Care."

212   *U.S. News*'s current ranking system: "Methodology: 2023 Best Medical Schools Rankings," *U.S. News & World Report.*

213   Doctors who immigrate: "Practicing Medicine in the U.S. as an International Medical Graduate," American Medical Association.

213   Bapu, Yusuke Tsugawa: Tsugawa et al., "Quality of Care Delivered by General Internists in US Hospitals Who Graduated from Foreign Versus US Medical Schools."

Chapter Ten: Politics at the Bedside

216   "There's a definite difference": Fine, "Saving of the President."

216   "He claimed that I had hurt": Pekkanen, "Saving of the President."

219   A study of publicly available: Bonica, Rosenthal, and Rothman, "Political Polarization of Physicians in the United States."

219   The percentage of physicians: "5 Facts About U.S. Political Donations."

219   A 2016 survey study: Hersh and Goldenberg, "Democratic and Republican Physicians Provide Different Care on Politicized Health Issues."

220   In a natural experiment: Hill, Slusky, and Ginther, "Reproductive Health Care in Catholic-Owned Hospitals."

222   President George W. Bush: Goodstein, "Schiavo Case Highlights Catholic-Evangelical Alliance."

222   Efforts were made: Babington, "Frist Defends Remarks on Schiavo Case."

222   Media coverage: Racine et al., "Media Coverage of the Persistent Vegetative State and End-of-Life Decision-Making."

222   Schiavo's case would spark: Perry, Churchill, and Kirshner, "Terri Schiavo Case"; Annas, "'Culture of Life' Politics at the Bedside."

223   After accounting for other factors: Cutler et al., "Physician Beliefs and Patient Preferences."

223   Bapu, along with Andrew Olenski: Jena et al., "Physicians' Political Preferences and the Delivery of End of Life Care in the United States."

227   The Pew Research Center: Mitchell et al., "How Americans Navigated the News in 2020."

227   In a study using data: Whaley et al., "Assessing the Association Between Social Gatherings and COVID-19 Risk Using Birthdays."

230   Still, in the absence: Prescott and Rice, "Corticosteroids in COVID-19 ARDS."

230   A landmark randomized trial: Recovery Collaborative Group, "Dexamethasone in Hospitalized Patients with Covid-19."

231   Research performed after the emergence: Vincent et al., "Chloroquine Is a Potent Inhibitor of SARS Coronavirus Infection and Spread."

231   However, studies later showed: Recovery Collaborative Group, "Effect of Hydroxychloroquine in Hospitalized Patients with Covid-19"; Self et al., "Effect of Hydroxychloroquine on Clinical Status at 14 Days in Hospitalized Patients with COVID-19"; Skipper et al., "Hydroxychloroquine in Nonhospitalized Adults with Early COVID-19."

231   Especially given the potential: Rosenberg et al., "Association of Treatment with Hydroxychloroquine or Azithromycin with In-Hospital Mortality in Patients with COVID-19 in New York State."

231   Meanwhile, in a study: Caly et al., "FDA-Approved Drug Ivermectin Inhibits the Replication of SARS-CoV-2 *in Vitro*."

231   But as with hydroxychloroquine: Siemieniuk et al., "Drug Treatments for Covid-19."

231   But a study released: Reardon, "Flawed Ivermectin Preprint Highlights Challenges of COVID Drug Studies."

231   congressional testimony in December: Senate Homeland Security and Governmental Affairs Committee, "Medical Response to COVID-19."

231   As for hydroxychloroquine: "Timeline: Tracking Trump Alongside Scientific Developments on Hydroxychloroquine," ABC News.

232   "Hydroxy[chloroquine] has tremendous support": "Remarks by President Trump in a Meeting with U.S. Tech Workers and Signing of an Executive Order on Hiring American."

232   Given the political divide: Barnett et al., "Association of County-Level Prescriptions for Hydroxychloroquine and Ivermectin with County-Level Political Voting Patterns in the 2020 US Presidential Election."

234   In a study reported: Wallace, Goldsmith-Pinkham, and Schwartz, "Excess Death Rates for Republicans and Democrats During the COVID-19 Pandemic."

235   We know that vaccines: "Red/Blue Divide in COVID-19 Vaccination Rates," Kaiser Family Foundation; "Unvaccinated Adults Are Now More Than Three Times as Likely to Lean Republican Than Democratic," Kaiser Family Foundation.

235   One study that repeatedly surveyed: Fridman, Gershon, and Gneezy, "COVID-19 and Vaccine Hesitancy."

236   Polls by Pew: "Republicans, Democrats Move Even Further Apart in Coronavirus Concerns," Pew Research Center.

237   We (Chris and Bapu): Worsham et al., "Association of Maternal Cervical Disease with Human Papillomavirus Vaccination Among Offspring."

239   Vaccination rates among older Americans: "COVID Data Tracker," Centers for Disease Control and Prevention.

239   Incentive programs: Law et al., "Lottery-Based Incentives and COVID-19 Vaccination Rates in the US"; Milkman et al., "Citywide Experiment Testing the Impact of Geographically Targeted, High-Pay-Off Vaccine Lotteries."

239   Negative incentive programs: "United Airlines CEO Discusses Holiday Crowds, Vaccine Mandates, Air Rage," NBC News; Lazar, "Threats of Termination Convince Many Hesitant Hospital Workers to Get COVID Vaccine, but Thousands of Holdouts Remain."

240   More than 90 percent of U.S. adults: "COVID Data Tracker."

240   Only about 70 percent: "Vaccination Coverage Among Adults," Adult-VaxView, Centers for Disease Control and Prevention.

241   more Americans lack confidence: "Confidence in U.S. Institutions Down; Average at New Low," Gallup.

241   We've come to view: Worsham and Jena, "'Successful Failures' of Apollo 13 and Covid-19 Vaccination."

241   "Our mission was a failure": Lovell, "'Houston, We've Had a Problem.'"

242   On the news: Treisman, "'Disaster Within a Disaster.'"

242   We (Chris and Bapu, along with Jaemin Woo): Worsham et al., "Carbon Monoxide Poisoning During Major U.S. Power Outages."

242   Using data from national organ transplant: Cron et al., "Organ Donation During Major U.S. Motorcycle Rallies."

BIBLIOGRAPHY

Abadie, A., and S. Gay. "The Impact of Presumed Consent Legislation on Cadaveric Organ Donation: A Cross-Country Study." *Journal of Health Economics* 25, no. 4 (July 2006): 599–620. doi.org/10.1016/j.jhealeco.2006.01.003.

ABC News. "Timeline: Tracking Trump Alongside Scientific Developments on Hydroxychloroquine." Aug. 8, 2020. abcnews.go.com.

ABIM Foundation. "Our Mission." www.choosingwisely.org.

Accreditation Council for Graduate Medical Education. "Defined Category Minimum Numbers for General Surgery Residents and Credit Role." May 2019. www.acgme.org.

Adair, J. G. "The Hawthorne Effect: A Reconsideration of the Methodological Artifact." *Journal of Applied Psychology* 69, no. 2 (1984): 334–45. doi.org/10.1037/0021-9010.69.2.334.

Agency for Healthcare Research and Quality. "Patient Safety 101." Sept. 7, 2019. psnet.ahrq.gov.

Allen, M. "I'm a Journalist. Apparently, I'm Also One of America's 'Top Doctors.'" ProPublica, Feb. 28, 2019. www.propublica.org.

Alsan, M., O. Garrick, and G. Graziani. "Does Diversity Matter for Health? Experimental Evidence from Oakland." *American Economic Review* 109, no. 12 (2019): 4071–111. doi.org/10.1257/aer.20181446.

American College of Cardiology. "ASCVD Risk Estimator Plus." 2021. tools.acc.org.

American College of Sports Medicine. "Mass Participation Event Management for the Team Physician: A Consensus Statement." *Medicine and Science in Sports and Exercise* 36, no. 11 (Nov. 2004): 2004–8. doi.org/10.1249/01.mss.0000145452.18404.f2.

American College of Surgeons National Surgical Quality Improvement Program. "ACS NSQIP Surgical Risk Calculator." 2021. riskcalculator.facs .org.

American Medical Association. "Practicing Medicine in the U.S. as an International Medical Graduate." Accessed Oct. 3, 2022. www.ama-assn.org.

American Nursing Association. "Mission: Achieve Continual Readiness for Joint Commission Surveys." *American Nurse,* accessed Dec. 7, 2022. www .myamericannurse.com.

American Psychiatric Association. *Diagnostic and Statistical Manual of Mental Disorders (DSM-5).* Washington, D.C.: American Psychiatric Association Publishing, 2013.

Andersen, J. J. "The State of Running 2019." International Institute for Race Medicine, July 16, 2019. racemedicine.org.

Annas, G. J. "'Culture of Life' Politics at the Bedside—the Case of Terri Schiavo." *New England Journal of Medicine* 352, no. 16 (2005): 1710–15. doi.org/10.1056/NEJMlim050643.

Association of American Medical Colleges. "Diversity in Medicine: Facts and Figures 2019." 2019. www.aamc.org.

Babington, C. "Frist Defends Remarks on Schiavo Case." *Washington Post,* June 17, 2005. www.washingtonpost.com.

Baker-Blocker, A. "Winter Weather and Cardiovascular Mortality in Minneapolis–St. Paul." *American Journal of Public Health* 72, no. 3 (March 1982): 261–65. doi.org/10.2105/ajph.72.3.261.

Balogh, E. P., B. T. Miller, and J. R. Ball. *Improving Diagnosis in Health Care.* Washington, D.C.: National Academies Press, 2015.

Bar-Eli, M., O. H. Azar, I. Ritov, Y. Keidar-Levin, and G. Schein. "Action Bias Among Elite Soccer Goalkeepers: The Case of Penalty Kicks." *Journal of Economic Psychology* 28, no. 5 (2007): 606–21. doi.org/10.1016/j.joep .2006.12.001.

Barnett, M. L., M. Gaye, A. B. Jena, and A. Mehrotra. "Association of County-Level Prescriptions for Hydroxychloroquine and Ivermectin with County-Level Political Voting Patterns in the 2020 US Presidential Election." *JAMA Internal Medicine* 182, no. 4 (2022): 452. doi.org/10.1001/ jamainternmed.2022.0200.

Barnett, M. L., A. R. Olenski, and A. B. Jena. "Opioid-Prescribing Patterns of Emergency Physicians and Risk of Long-Term Use." *New England Journal of Medicine* 376, no. 7 (2017): 663–73. doi.org/10.1056/nejmsa1610524.

——. "Patient Mortality During Unannounced Accreditation Surveys at US Hospitals." *JAMA Internal Medicine* 177, no. 5 (2017): 693–700. doi .org/10.1001/jamainternmed.2016.9685.

Barnsley, R.H., A. H. Thompson, and P. E. Barnsley. "Hockey Success and

Birthdate: The Relative Age Effect." *Canadian Association for Health, Physical Education, and Recreation* 51, no. 1 (1985): 23–28.

Baron, S., and R. Rinsky. "Health Hazard Evaluation Report: National Football League Players Mortality Study." National Institute for Occupational Safety and Health, Jan. 1994.

Baumhakel, M., U. Muller, and M. Bohm. "Influence of Gender of Physicians and Patients on Guideline-Recommended Treatment of Chronic Heart Failure in a Cross-Sectional Study." *European Journal of Heart Failure* 11, no. 3 (March 2009): 299–303. doi.org/10.1093/eurjhf/hfn041.

Bazargan, M., S. Cobb, and S. Assari. "Discrimination and Medical Mistrust in a Racially and Ethnically Diverse Sample of California Adults." *Annals of Family Medicine* 19, no. 1 (2021): 4–15. doi.org/10.1370/afm.2632.

Bebinger, M. "Doctors Try Out Curbside Vaccinations for Kids to Prevent a Competing Pandemic." WBUR, April 24, 2020. www.wbur.org.

Bell, C. M., and D. A. Redelmeier. "Mortality Among Patients Admitted to Hospitals on Weekends as Compared with Weekdays." *New England Journal of Medicine* 345, no. 9 (2001): 663–68. www.nejm.org.

Bennett, C. L., A. S. Raja, N. Kapoor, D. Kass, D. M. Blumenthal, N. Gross, and A. M. Mills. "Gender Differences in Faculty Rank Among Academic Emergency Physicians in the United States." *Academic Emergency Medicine* 26, no. 3 (2019): 281–85. doi.org/10.1111/acem.13685.

Berthold, H. K., I. Gouni-Berthold, K. P. Bestehorn, M. Bohm, and W. Krone. "Physician Gender Is Associated with the Quality of Type 2 Diabetes Care." *Journal of Internal Medicine* 264, no. 4 (Oct. 2008): 340–50. doi.org/10.1111/j.1365-2796.2008.01967.x.

Berwick, D. M., and C. K. Cassel. "The NAM and the Quality of Health Care—Inflecting a Field." *New England Journal of Medicine* 383, no. 6 (2020): 505–8. doi.org/10.1056/NEJMp2005126.

Black, S. E., P. J. Devereux, and K. G. Salvanes. "Too Young to Leave the Nest? The Effects of School Starting Age." *Review of Economics and Statistics* 93, no. 2 (2011): 455–67. doi.org/10.1162/REST_a_00081.

Bonica, A. "Database on Ideology, Money in Politics, and Elections: Public Version 2.0." Stanford, Calif.: Stanford University Libraries, 2016. data.stanford.edu.

Bonica, A., H. Rosenthal, and D. J. Rothman. "The Political Polarization of Physicians in the United States." *JAMA Internal Medicine* 174, no. 8 (2014): 1308. doi.org/10.1001/jamainternmed.2014.2105.

Boston University School of Medicine Internal Medicine Residency Program. "Categorical Training Program." Accessed Nov. 2, 2022. www.bumc.bu.edu.

Boyle, P. "Nation's Physician Workforce Evolves: More Women, a Bit Older, and Toward Different Specialties." Association of American Medical Colleges, Feb. 2, 2021. www.aamc.org.

Brennan, T. A., L. L. Leape, N. M. Laird, L. Hebert, A. R. Localio, A. G. Lawthers, J. P. Newhouse, P. C. Weiler, and H. H. Hiatt. "Incidence of Adverse Events and Negligence in Hospitalized Patients. Results of the Harvard Medical Practice Study I." *New England Journal of Medicine* 324, no. 6 (1991): 370–76. doi.org/10.1056/NEJM199102073240604.

Brinkley, J. "Physicians Have an Image Problem—It's Too Good." *New York Times,* Feb. 10, 1985, 6E. www.nytimes.com.

Callner, M., dir. *Jerry Seinfeld: I'm Telling You for the Last Time.* Aired Aug. 9, 1998, on HBO.

Caly, L., J. D. Druce, M. G. Catton, D. A. Jans, and K. M. Wagstaff. "The FDA-Approved Drug Ivermectin Inhibits the Replication of SARS-CoV-2 in Vitro." *Antiviral Research* 178 (June 2020): 104787. doi.org/10.1016/j.antiviral.2020.104787.

Casalino, L. P., et al. "US Physician Practices Spend More Than $15.4 Billion Annually to Report Quality Measures." *Health Affairs* 35, no. 3 (2016): 401–6. doi.org/10.1377/hlthaff.2015.1258.

CBS. "60 Minutes Archives: An Interview with Dr. Jack Kevorkian." www.youtube.com/watch?v=BiZKY6FSfwA.

Centers for Disease Control and Prevention. "COVID Data Tracker," accessed Oct. 11, 2022. covid.cdc.gov.

———. "Data and Statistics About ADHD." Updated Dec. 23, 2021. www.cdc.gov.

———. "Faststats: Births and Natality." Updated Sept. 6, 2022. www.cdc.gov.

———. "Faststats: Emergency Department Visits." Updated Sept. 6, 2022. www.cdc.gov.

———. "Flu Vaccination Coverage, United States, 2020–21 Influenza Season." Oct. 7, 2021. www.cdc.gov.

———. "Vaccination Coverage Among Adults." AdultVaxView. www.cdc.gov.

Centers for Medicare and Medicaid Services. "National Health Expenditure Fact Sheet." 2019. www.cms.gov.

Chapman, G. B., M. Li, H. Colby, and H. Yoon. "Opting In vs. Opting Out of Influenza Vaccination." *JAMA* 304, no. 1 (2010): 43–44. doi.org/10.1001/jama.2010.892.

Chen, D. L., T. J. Moskowitz, and Kelly Shue. "Decision Making Under the Gambler's Fallacy: Evidence from Asylum Judges, Loan Officers, and

Baseball Umpires." *Quarterly Journal of Economics* 131, no. 3 (2016): 1181–242. doi.org/10.1093/qje/qjw017.

Choudhry, N. K., et al. "Full Coverage for Preventive Medications After Myocardial Infarction." *New England Journal of Medicine* 365, no. 22 (2011): 2088–97. doi.org/10.1056/NEJMsa1107913.

Choudhry, N. K., G. M. Anderson, A. Laupacis, D. Ross-Degnan, S. L. Normand, and S. B. Soumerai. "Impact of Adverse Events on Prescribing Warfarin in Patients with Atrial Fibrillation: Matched Pair Analysis." *BMJ* 332, no. 7534 (2006): 141–45. doi.org/10.1136/bmj.38698.709572.55.

Clarke, P. M., S. J. Walter, A. Hayen, W. J. Mallon, J. Heijmans, and D. M. Studdert. "Survival of the Fittest: Retrospective Cohort Study of the Longevity of Olympic Medallists in the Modern Era." *BMJ* 345 (2012): e8308. doi.org/10.1136/bmj.e8308.

CNN. " 'More Gray Hair' for President Obama." 2010. www.youtube.com/watch?v=iuZkqemS7YI.

———. "New York City Marathon Fast Facts." 2021. www.cnn.com.

Cooney, E. "MGH Doctor Urges Safety After Mistake." *Boston Globe,* Nov. 12, 2010.

Cooper-Patrick, L. "Race, Gender, and Partnership in the Patient-Physician Relationship." *JAMA* 282, no. 6 (1999): 583. doi.org/10.1001/jama.282.6.583.

Coussens, S. "Behaving Discretely: Heuristic Thinking in the Emergency Department." *SSRN Electronic Journal* (2018). doi.org/10.2139/ssrn.3743423.

Crawford, C., L. Dearden, and C. Meghir. "When You Are Born Matters: The Impact of Date of Birth on Child Cognitive Outcomes in England." 2007.

Cron, D. C., C. M. Worsham, J. T. Adler, C. F. Bray, and Anupam B. Jena. "Organ Donation During Major U.S. Motorcycle Rallies." *JAMA Internal Medicine.* In press (2022).

Croskerry, P. "Cognitive Forcing Strategies in Clinical Decisionmaking." *Annals of Emergency Medicine* 41, no. 1 (2003): 110–20. doi.org/10.1067/mem.2003.22.

Croskerry, P., G. Singhal, and S. Mamede. "Cognitive Debiasing 1: Origins of Bias and Theory of Debiasing." *BMJ Quality and Safety* 22, no. S2 (Oct. 2013): ii58—ii64. doi.org/10.1136/bmjqs-2012-001712.

———. "Cognitive Debiasing 2: Impediments to and Strategies for Change." *BMJ Quality and Safety* 22, no. S2 (Oct. 2013): ii65—ii72. doi.org/10.1136/bmjqs-2012-001713.

C-SPAN. "Former President Obama Campaign Remarks in Gary, Indiana." Nov. 4, 2018. www.c-span.org.

Cunningham, S. A., K. Mitchell, K. M. Narayan, and S. Yusuf. "Doctors' Strikes and Mortality: A Review." *Social Science and Medicine* 67, no. 11 (Dec. 2008): 1784–88. doi.org/10.1016/j.socscimed.2008.09.044.

Currie, J., and R. Walker. "Traffic Congestion and Infant Health: Evidence from E-ZPass." *American Economic Journal: Applied Economics* 3, no. 1 (2011): 65–90. doi.org/10.1257/app.3.1.65.

Cutler, D., J. S. Skinner, A. D. Stern, and D. Wennberg. "Physician Beliefs and Patient Preferences: A New Look at Regional Variation in Health Care Spending." *American Economic Journal: Economic Policy* 11, no. 1 (Feb. 2019): 192–221. doi.org/10.1257/pol.20150421.

Cvach, M. "Monitor Alarm Fatigue: An Integrative Review." *Biomedical Instrumentation and Technology* 46, no. 4 (July–Aug. 2012): 268–77. doi.org/10.2345/0899-8205-46.4.268.

Dahrouge, S., E. Seale, W. Hogg, G. Russell, J. Younger, E. Muggah, D. Ponka, and J. Mercer. "A Comprehensive Assessment of Family Physician Gender and Quality of Care: A Cross-Sectional Analysis in Ontario, Canada." *Medical Care* 54, no. 3 (March 2016): 277–86. doi.org/10.1097/MLR.0000000000000480.

Dalmacy, D. M., A. Diaz, M. Hyer, and T. M. Pawlik. "Age-Based Left-Digit Bias in the Management of Acute Cholecystitis." *Journal of Gastrointestinal Surgery* 25, no. 12 (Dec. 2021): 3239–41. doi.org/10.1007/s11605-021-05065-3.

Dehaene, S., E. Dupoux, and J. Mehler. "Is Numerical Comparison Digital? Analogical and Symbolic Effects in Two-Digit Number Comparison." *Journal of Experimental Psychology: Human Perception and Performance* 16, no. 3 (1990): 626–41. doi.org/10.1037/0096-1523.16.3.626.

Deryugina, T., G. Heutel, N. H. Miller, D. Molitor, and J. Reif. "The Mortality and Medical Costs of Air Pollution: Evidence from Changes in Wind Direction." *American Economic Review* 109, no. 12 (Dec. 2019): 4178–219. doi.org/10.1257/aer.20180279.

Dhaliwal, G. "A Piece of My Mind. The Mechanics of Reasoning." *JAMA* 306, no. 9 (2011): 918–19. doi.org/10.1001/jama.2011.1027.

Dhuey, E., David F., K. Karbownik, and J. Roth. "School Starting Age and Cognitive Development." *Journal of Policy Analysis and Management* 38, no. 3 (2019): 538–78. doi.org/10.1002/pam.22135.

Dixon-Roman, E. J., H. T. Everson, and J. J. McArdle. "Race, Poverty, and SAT Scores: Modeling the Influences of Family Income on Black and White High School Students' SAT Performance." *Teachers College Record: The Voice of Scholarship in Education* 115, no. 4 (2013): 1–33. doi.org/10.1177/016146811311500406.

Doctor, J. N., A. Nguyen, R. Lev, J. Lucas, T. Knight, H. Zhao, and M.

Menchine. "Opioid Prescribing Decreases After Learning of a Patient's Fatal Overdose." *Science* 361, no. 6402 (2018): 588–90. doi.org/10.1126/science.aat4595.

Donabedian, A. "Evaluating the Quality of Medical Care." *Milbank Memorial Fund Quarterly* 44, no. 3 (July 1966): S166—S206. www.ncbi.nlm.nih.gov/pubmed/5338568.

———. *An Introduction to Quality Assurance in Health Care.* Oxford: Oxford University Press, 2002.

Donaldson, M. S., J. M. Corrigan, and L. T. Kohn. *To Err Is Human: Building a Safer Health System.* Washington, D.C.: National Academies Press, 2000. doi.org/10.17226/9728.

Dossa, F., D. Zeltzer, R. Sutradhar, A. N. Simpson, and N. N. Baxter. "Sex Differences in the Pattern of Patient Referrals to Male and Female Surgeons." *JAMA Surgery* 157, no. 2 (2022): 95–103. doi.org/10.1001/jamasurg.2021.5784.

Eckmanns, T., J. Bessert, M. Behnke, P. Gastmeier, and H. Ruden. "Compliance with Antiseptic Hand Rub Use in Intensive Care Units: The Hawthorne Effect." *Infection Control and Hospital Epidemiology* 27, no. 9 (Sept. 2006): 931–34. doi.org/10.1086/507294.

Elder, T. E. "The Importance of Relative Standards in ADHD Diagnoses: Evidence Based on Exact Birth Dates." *Journal of Health Economics* 29, no. 5 (Sept. 2010): 641–56. doi.org/10.1016/j.jhealeco.2010.06.003.

Elmore, J. G., et al. "Effect of Prior Diagnoses on Dermatopathologists' Interpretations of Melanocytic Lesions: A Randomized Controlled Trial." *JAMA Dermatology* 158, no. 9 (2022): 1040–47. doi.org/10.1001/jamadermatol.2022.2932.

Emory Woodruff Health Sciences Center. "CARES Fact Sheet." mycares.net.

Evans, W. N., M. S. Morrill, and S. T. Parente. "Measuring Inappropriate Medical Diagnosis and Treatment in Survey Data: The Case of ADHD Among School-Age Children." *Journal of Health Economics* 29, no. 5 (Sept. 2010): 657–73. doi.org/10.1016/j.jhealeco.2010.07.005.

Events Industry Council. *Global Economic Significance of Business Events.* 2018. insights.eventscouncil.org.

Federal Aviation Administration. "FAA TV: The History of CRM." U.S. Department of Transportation, 2012. www.faa.gov.

Feinstein, A. R. "The 'Chagrin Factor' and Qualitative Decision Analysis." *Archives of Internal Medicine* 145, no. 7 (1985): 1257. doi.org/10.1001/archinte.1985.00360070137023.

Fine, P. R. "The Saving of the President." 1982. www.youtube.com/watch?v=P2Wr3UPR5CU.

Fonarow, G. C., et al. "Influence of a Performance-Improvement Initiative on

Quality of Care for Patients Hospitalized with Heart Failure: Results of the Organized Program to Initiate Lifesaving Treatment in Hospitalized Patients with Heart Failure (OPTIMIZE-HF)." *Archives of Internal Medicine* 167, no. 14 (2007): 1493–502. doi.org/10.1001/archinte.167.14.1493.

Frakes, M., J. Gruber, and A. B. Jena. "Is Great Information Good Enough? Evidence from Physicians as Patients." *Journal of Health Economics* 75 (2021): 102406. www.sciencedirect.com.

Freakonomics, M.D. "Bad News—It's Your Surgeon's Birthday." Podcast, episode 36, May 5, 2022. freakonomics.com.

Freakonomics Radio. "How Many Doctors Does It Take to Start a Healthcare Revolution?" Podcast, episode 202, April 9, 2015. freakonomics.com.

Fridman, A., R. Gershon, and A. Gneezy. "COVID-19 and Vaccine Hesitancy: A Longitudinal Study." *PLOS One* 16, no. 4 (2021): e0250123. doi.org/10.1371/journal.pone.0250123.

Furuya, E. Y., A. Dick, E. N. Perencevich, M. Pogorzelska, D. Goldmann, and P. W. Stone. "Central Line Bundle Implementation in US Intensive Care Units and Impact on Bloodstream Infections." *PLOS One* 6, no. 1 (2011): e15452. doi.org/10.1371/journal.pone.0015452.

Gallup. "Confidence in U.S. Institutions Down; Average at New Low." July 5, 2022. news.gallup.com.

Ganguli, I., B. Sheridan, J. Gray, M. Chernew, M. B. Rosenthal, and H. Neprash. "Physician Work Hours and the Gender Pay Gap—Evidence from Primary Care." *New England Journal of Medicine* 383, no. 14 (2020): 1349–57. doi.org/10.1056/nejmsa2013804.

Gawande, A. "The Checklist." *New Yorker,* Dec. 2, 2007. www.newyorker.com.

———. "Why Boston's Hospitals Were Ready." *New Yorker,* April 17, 2013. www.newyorker.com.

Gilman, M., J. M. Hockenberry, E. K. Adams, A. S. Milstein, I. B. Wilson, and E. R. Becker. "The Financial Effect of Value-Based Purchasing and the Hospital Readmissions Reduction Program on Safety-Net Hospitals in 2014: A Cohort Study." *Annals of Internal Medicine* 163, no. 6 (2015): 427–36. doi.org/10.7326/M14-2813.

Glied, S. "The Credibility Revolution in Economics and How It Has Changed Health Policy." *JAMA Health Forum* 2, no. 11 (2021): e214335. doi.org/10.1001/jamahealthforum.2021.4335.

Gonyea, D. "From the Start, Obama Struggled with Fallout from a Kind of Fake News." NPR, Jan. 10, 2017. www.npr.org.

Goodstein, L. "Schiavo Case Highlights Catholic-Evangelical Alliance." *New York Times,* March 24, 2005. www.nytimes.com.

Grady, D., and R. F. Redberg. "Less Is More: How Less Health Care Can

Result in Better Health." *Archives of Internal Medicine* 170, no. 9 (2010): 749–50. doi.org/10.1001/archinternmed.2010.90.

Grunau, B., et al. "Association of Intra-arrest Transport vs. Continued On-Scene Resuscitation with Survival to Hospital Discharge Among Patients with Out-of-Hospital Cardiac Arrest." *JAMA* 324, no. 11 (2020): 1058–67. doi.org/10.1001/jama.2020.14185.

Hasselqvist-Ax, I., et al. "Early Cardiopulmonary Resuscitation in Out-of-Hospital Cardiac Arrest." *New England Journal of Medicine* 372, no. 24 (2015): 2307–15. doi.org/10.1056/NEJMoa1405796.

Heller, J. "Black Men Untreated in Tuskegee Syphilis Study." Associated Press, July 25, 1972. apnews.com.

Helmreich, R. L., A. C. Merritt, and J. A. Wilhelm. "The Evolution of Crew Resource Management Training in Commercial Aviation." In *Human Error in Aviation,* edited by R. Key Dismukes, 275–88. London: Routledge, 2017.

Helsen, W. F., J. van Winckel, and M. A. Williams. "The Relative Age Effect in Youth Soccer Across Europe." *Journal of Sports Sciences* 23, no. 6 (2007): 629–36. doi.org/10.1080/02640410400021310.

Hersh, E. D., and M. N. Goldenberg. "Democratic and Republican Physicians Provide Different Care on Politicized Health Issues." *Proceedings of the National Academy of Sciences* 113, no. 42 (2016): 11811–16. doi.org/10.1073/pnas.1606609113.

Hetsroni, A. "If You Must Be Hospitalized, Television Is Not the Place: Diagnoses, Survival Rates, and Demographic Characteristics of Patients in TV Hospital Dramas." *Communication Research Reports* 26, no. 4 (2009): 311–22. doi.org/10.1080/08824090903293585.

Hiatt, H. H., et al. "A Study of Medical Injury and Medical Malpractice." *New England Journal of Medicine* 321, no. 7 (1989): 480–84. doi.org/10.1056/NEJM198908173210725.

Hill, E. L., D. J. G. Slusky, and D. K. Ginther. "Reproductive Health Care in Catholic-Owned Hospitals." *Journal of Health Economics* 65 (2019): 48–62. doi.org/10.1016/j.jhealeco.2019.02.005.

Hillis, L. D., et al. "2011 ACCF/AHA Guideline for Coronary Artery Bypass Graft Surgery: A Report of the American College of Cardiology Foundation/American Heart Association Task Force on Practice Guidelines, Developed in Collaboration with the American Association for Thoracic Surgery, Society of Cardiovascular Anesthesiologists, and Society of Thoracic Surgeons." *Journal of the American College of Cardiology* 58, no. 24 (2011): e123–e210. doi.org/10.1016/j.jacc.2011.08.009.

Hinrichs, J. V., D. S. Yurko, and J. Hu. "Two-Digit Number Comparison: Use of Place Information." *Journal of Experimental Psychology: Human*

Perception and Performance 7, no. 4 (1981): 890–901. doi.org/10.1037/0096 -1523.7.4.890.

Hughes, A. "5 Facts About U.S. Political Donations." Pew Research Center, May 17, 2017. www.pewresearch.org.

Hurwitz, E. S., M. Haber, A. Chang, T. Shope, S. T. Teo, J. S. Giesick, M. M. Ginsberg, and N. J. Cox. "Studies of the 1996–1997 Inactivated Influenza Vaccine Among Children Attending Day Care: Immunologic Response, Protection Against Infection, and Clinical Effectiveness." *Journal of Infectious Diseases* 182, no. 4 (Oct. 2000): 1218–21. doi.org/10.1086/ 315820.

Hurwitz, E. S., M. Haber, A. Chang, T. Shope, S. Teo, M. Ginsberg, N. Waecker, and N. J. Cox. "Effectiveness of Influenza Vaccination of Day Care Children in Reducing Influenza-Related Morbidity Among Household Contacts." *JAMA* 284, no. 13 (2000): 1677–82. doi.org/10.1001/jama .284.13.1677.

Husain, S. A., K. L. King, and S. Mohan. "Left-Digit Bias and Deceased Donor Kidney Utilization." *Clinical Transplantation* 35, no. 6 (June 2021): e14284. doi.org/10.1111/ctr.14284.

IHI Multimedia Team. "Like Magic? ('Every System Is Perfectly Designed . . .')." Institute for Healthcare Improvement, Aug. 21, 2015. www.ihi.org.

Institute of Medicine. *Crossing the Quality Chasm: A New Health System for the 21st Century.* Washington, D.C.: National Academies Press, 2001. doi: 10.17226/10027.

Jacobson, C. E., C. S. Brown, K. H. Sheetz, and S. A. Waits. "Left Digit Bias in Selection and Acceptance of Deceased Donor Organs." *American Journal of Surgery* 224, no. 4 (2022). doi.org/10.1016/j.amjsurg.2022.03.039.

Jaiswal, J., and P. N. Halkitis. "Towards a More Inclusive and Dynamic Understanding of Medical Mistrust Informed by Science." *Behavioral Medicine* 45, no. 2 (2019): 79–85. doi.org/10.1080/08964289.2019.1619511.

James, J. T. "A New, Evidence-Based Estimate of Patient Harms Associated with Hospital Care." *Journal of Patient Safety* 9, no. 3 (Sept. 2013): 122–28. doi.org/10.1097/PTS.0b013e3182948a69.

Jangi, S. "Under the Medical Tent at the Boston Marathon." *New England Journal of Medicine* 368, no. 21 (2013): 1953–55. doi.org/10.1056/ NEJMp1305299.

Jena, A. B., D. P. Goldman, and S. A. Seabury. "Incidence of Sexually Transmitted Infections After Human Papillomavirus Vaccination Among Adolescent Females." *JAMA Internal Medicine* 175, no. 4 (2015): 617. doi.org/ 10.1001/jamainternmed.2014.7886.

Jena, A. B., N. C. Mann, L. N. Wedlund, and A. Olenski. "Delays in Emergency Care and Mortality During Major U.S. Marathons." *New England Journal of Medicine* 376, no. 15 (2017): 1441–50. doi.org/10.1056/NEJMsa1614073.

Jena, A. B., A. R. Olenski, and D. M. Blumenthal. "Sex Differences in Physician Salary in US Public Medical Schools." *JAMA Internal Medicine* 176, no. 9 (2016): 1294. doi.org/10.1001/jamainternmed.2016.3284.

Jena, A. B., A. R. Olenski, D. M. Blumenthal, R. W. Yeh, D. P. Goldman, and J. Romley. "Acute Myocardial Infarction Mortality During Dates of National Interventional Cardiology Meetings." *Journal of the American Heart Association* 7, no. 6 (2018): e008230. doi.org/10.1161/JAHA.117.008230.

Jena, A. B., A. R. Olenski, D. Khullar, A. Bonica, and H. Rosenthal. "Physicians' Political Preferences and the Delivery of End of Life Care in the United States: Retrospective Observational Study." *BMJ* 361 (2018): k1161. doi.org/10.1136/bmj.k1161.

Jena, A. B., V. Prasad, D. P. Goldman, and J. Romley. "Mortality and Treatment Patterns Among Patients Hospitalized with Acute Cardiovascular Conditions During Dates of National Cardiology Meetings." *JAMA Internal Medicine* 175, no. 2 (2015): 237. doi.org/10.1001/jamainternmed.2014.6781.

Jenkins, L. "Self-Made Man." *Sports Illustrated,* Jan. 31, 2008. www.si.com.

Jerant, A., K. D. Bertakis, J. J. Fenton, and P. Franks. "Gender of Physician as the Usual Source of Care and Patient Health Care Utilization and Mortality." *Journal of the American Board of Family Medicine* 26, no. 2 (2013): 138–48. doi.org/10.3122/jabfm.2013.02.120198.

Joint Commission. "All Accreditation Programs Survey Activity Guide." 2022. www.jointcommission.org.

———. "The Universal Protocol for Preventing Wrong Site, Wrong Procedure, and Wrong Person Surgery." Accessed 2022. www.jointcommission.org.

Jolly, S., K. A. Griffith, R. DeCastro, A. Stewart, P. Ubel, and R. Jagsi. "Gender Differences in Time Spent on Parenting and Domestic Responsibilities by High-Achieving Young Physician-Researchers." *Annals of Internal Medicine* 160, no. 5 (2014): 344–53. doi.org/10.7326/M13-0974.

Jones, S. R. G. "Was There a Hawthorne Effect?" *American Journal of Sociology* 98, no. 3 (1992): 451–68. doi.org/10.1086/230046.

Kaiser Family Foundation. "The Red/Blue Divide in COVID-19 Vaccination Rates." Sept. 14, 2021. www.kff.org.

———. "Unvaccinated Adults Are Now More Than Three Times as Likely to Lean Republican Than Democratic." Nov. 16, 2021. www.kff.org.

Kalwij, A. "The Effects of Competition Outcomes on Health: Evidence from the Lifespans of U.S. Olympic Medalists." *Economics and Human Biology* 31 (Sept. 2018): 276–86. doi.org/10.1016/j.ehb.2018.10.001.

Kato, H., A. B. Jena, and Y. Tsugawa. "Patient Mortality After Surgery on the Surgeon's Birthday: Observational Study." *BMJ* 371 (2020): m4381. doi.org/10.1136/bmj.m4381.

Kazda, L., K. Bell, R. Thomas, K. McGeechan, R. Sims, and A. Barratt. "Overdiagnosis of Attention-Deficit/Hyperactivity Disorder in Children and Adolescents." *JAMA Network Open* 4, no. 4 (2021): e215335. doi.org/10.1001/jamanetworkopen.2021.5335.

Keeley, E. C., J. A. Boura, and C. L. Grines. "Primary Angioplasty Versus Intravenous Thrombolytic Therapy for Acute Myocardial Infarction: A Quantitative Review of 23 Randomised Trials." *Lancet* 361, no. 9351 (2003): 13–20. doi.org/10.1016/S0140-6736(03)12113-7.

Keillor, G. "The News from Lake Wobegon." Accessed Nov. 12, 2022. www.garrisonkeillor.com.

Kelley Blue Book. "What Are Kelley Blue Book Values?" March 7, 2019. www.kbb.com.

Kim, J. H., et al. "Cardiac Arrest During Long-Distance Running Races." *New England Journal of Medicine* 366, no. 2 (2012): 130–40. doi.org/10.1056/NEJMoa1106468.

King, J. C., Jr., J. J. Stoddard, M. J. Gaglani, K. A. Moore, L. Magder, E. McClure, J. D. Rubin, J. A. Englund, and K. Neuzil. "Effectiveness of School-Based Influenza Vaccination." *New England Journal of Medicine* 355, no. 24 (2006): 2523–32. doi.org/10.1056/NEJMoa055414.

Koplewitz, G., D. M. Blumenthal, N. Gross, T. Hicks, and A. B. Jena. "Golf Habits Among Physicians and Surgeons: Observational Cohort Study." *BMJ* 363 (2018): k4859. doi.org/10.1136/bmj.k4859.

Kostis, W. J., K. Demissie, S. W. Marcella, Y. H. Shao, A. C. Wilson, A. E. Moreyra, and Group Myocardial Infarction Data Acquisition System Study. "Weekend Versus Weekday Admission and Mortality from Myocardial Infarction." *New England Journal of Medicine* 356, no. 11 (2007): 1099–109. doi.org/10.1056/NEJMoa063355.

Krabbe, E. E., E. D. Thoutenhoofd, M. Conradi, S. J. Pijl, and L. Batstra. "Birth Month as Predictor of ADHD Medication Use in Dutch School Classes." *European Journal of Special Needs Education* 29, no. 4 (2014): 571–78. doi.org/10.1080/08856257.2014.943564.

Kruger, J. "Lake Wobegon Be Gone! The 'Below-Average Effect' and the Egocentric Nature of Comparative Ability Judgments." *Journal of Personality and Social Psychology* 77, no. 2 (1999): 221–32. doi.org/10.1037/0022-3514.77.2.221.

Lacetera, N., D. G. Pope, and J. R. Sydnor. "Heuristic Thinking and Limited Attention in the Car Market." *American Economic Review* 102, no. 5 (2012): 2206–36. doi.org/10.1257/aer.102.5.2206.

Landhuis, E. "Scientific Literature: Information Overload." *Nature* 535, no. 7612 (2016): 457–58. doi.org/10.1038/nj7612-457a.

Lau, E. S., S. N. Hayes, A. S. Volgman, K. Lindley, C. J. Pepine, M. J. Wood, and American College of Cardiology Cardiovascular Disease in Women Section. "Does Patient-Physician Gender Concordance Influence Patient Perceptions or Outcomes?" *Journal of the American College of Cardiology* 77, no. 8 (2021): 1135–38. doi.org/10.1016/j.jacc.2020.12.031.

Lautenberger, D. M., and V. M. Dandar. *The State of Women in Academic Medicine, 2018–2019: Exploring Pathways to Equity.* Washington, D.C.: American Association of Medical Colleges, 2020. store.aamc.org.

LaVeist, T. A., L. A. Isaac, and K. P. Williams. "Mistrust of Health Care Organizations Is Associated with Underutilization of Health Services." *Health Services Research* 44, no. 6 (Dec. 2009): 2093–105. doi.org/10.1111/j.1475-6773.2009.01017.x.

Law, A. C., D. Peterson, A. J. Walkey, and N. A. Bosch. "Lottery-Based Incentives and COVID-19 Vaccination Rates in the US." *JAMA Internal Medicine* 182, no. 2 (2022): 235. doi.org/10.1001/jamainternmed.2021.7052.

Lawton, J. S., et al. "2021 ACC/AHA/SCAI Guideline for Coronary Artery Revascularization: A Report of the American College of Cardiology/American Heart Association Joint Committee on Clinical Practice Guidelines." *Journal of the American College of Cardiology* 79, no. 2 (2022): 197–215. doi.org/10.1016/j.jacc.2021.09.006.

Layton, T. J., M. L. Barnett, T. R. Hicks, and A. B. Jena. "Attention Deficit-Hyperactivity Disorder and Month of School Enrollment." *New England Journal of Medicine* 379, no. 22 (2018): 2122–30. doi.org/10.1056/NEJMoa1806828.

Lazar, K. "Threats of Termination Convince Many Hesitant Hospital Workers to Get COVID Vaccine, but Thousands of Holdouts Remain." *Boston Globe,* updated Oct. 15, 2021. www.bostonglobe.com.

Lerner, E. B., C. D. Newgard, and N. C. Mann. "Effect of the Coronavirus Disease 2019 (COVID-19) Pandemic on the U.S. Emergency Medical Services System: A Preliminary Report." *Academic Emergency Medicine* 27, no. 8 (Aug. 2020): 693–99. doi.org/10.1111/acem.14051.

Levitt, S. D., and J. A. List. "Was There Really a Hawthorne Effect at the Hawthorne Plant? An Analysis of the Original Illumination Experiments." *American Economic Journal: Applied Economics* 3, no. 1 (2011): 224–38. doi.org/10.1257/app.3.1.224.

Li, S., and S. Leader. "Economic Burden and Absenteeism from Influenza-

Like Illness in Healthy Households with Children (5–17 Years) in the US." *Respiratory Medicine* 101, no. 6 (June 2007): 1244–50. doi.org/10.1016/j .rmed.2006.10.022.

Lim, W. H., C. Wong, S. R. Jain, C. H. Ng, C. H. Tai, M. K. Devi, D. D. Samarasekera, S. G. Iyer, and C. S. Chong. "The Unspoken Reality of Gender Bias in Surgery: A Qualitative Systematic Review." *PLOS One* 16, no. 2 (2021): e0246420. doi.org/10.1371/journal.pone.0246420.

Lovell, J. A. " 'Houston, We've Had a Problem': A Crippled Bird Limps Safely Home." In *Apollo Expeditions to the Moon*, edited by E. M. Cortright, 247–63. Washington, D.C.: Scientific and Technical Information Office, National Aeronautics and Space Administration, 1975.

Lucas, J. A. "A History of the Marathon Race—490 B.C. to 1975." *Journal of Sport History* 3, no. 2 (1976): 120–38. www.jstor.org/stable/43609156.

Ly, D. P. "The Influence of the Availability Heuristic on Physicians in the Emergency Department." *Annals of Emergency Medicine* 78, no. 5 (Nov. 2021): 650–57. doi.org/10.1016/j.annemergmed.2021.06.012.

MacDonald, N. E., and Sage Working Group on Vaccine Hesitancy. "Vaccine Hesitancy: Definition, Scope, and Determinants." *Vaccine* 33, no. 34 (2015): 4161–64. doi.org/10.1016/j.vaccine.2015.04.036.

Matulevicius, S. A., K. A. Kho, J. Reisch, and H. Yin. "Academic Medicine Faculty Perceptions of Work-Life Balance Before and Since the COVID-19 Pandemic." *JAMA Network Open* 4, no. 6 (2021): e2113539. doi.org/10 .1001/jamanetworkopen.2021.13539.

McCambridge, J., J. Witton, and D. R. Elbourne. "Systematic Review of the Hawthorne Effect: New Concepts Are Needed to Study Research Participation Effects." *Journal of Clinical Epidemiology* 67, no. 3 (2014): 267–77. doi.org/10.1016/j.jclinepi.2013.08.015.

McClellan, M. "Does More Intensive Treatment of Acute Myocardial Infarction in the Elderly Reduce Mortality?" *JAMA* 272, no. 11 (1994): 859. doi .org/10.1001/jama.1994.03520110039026.

McNally, B., et al. "Out-of-Hospital Cardiac Arrest Surveillance—Cardiac Arrest Registry to Enhance Survival (CARES), United States, Oct. 1, 2005—Dec. 31, 2010." *Morbidity and Mortality Weekly Report: Surveillance Summaries* 60, no. 8 (2011): 1–19. www.ncbi.nlm.nih.gov/pubmed/ 21796098.

McWilliams, J. M. "Professionalism Revealed: Rethinking Quality Improvement in the Wake of a Pandemic." *NEJM Catalyst* 1, no. 5 (2020). doi.org/ 10.1056/cat.20.0226.

Melucci, A. D., A. Loria, E. Ramsdale, L. K. Temple, F. J. Fleming, and C. T. Aquina. "An Assessment of Left-Digit Bias in the Treatment of

Older Patients with Potentially Curable Rectal Cancer." *Surgery* 172, no. 3 (2022). doi.org/10.1016/j.surg.2022.04.038.

Merson, L.-O. *Le soldat de Marathon*. Oil on canvas. Private collection, 1869. commons.wikimedia.org.

Milkman, K. L., et al. "A Citywide Experiment Testing the Impact of Geographically Targeted, High-Pay-Off Vaccine Lotteries." *Nature Human Behaviour,* Sept. 1, 2022. doi.org/10.1038/s41562-022-01437-0.

Mitchell, A., M. Jurkowitz, J. B. Oliphant, and E. Shearer. "How Americans Navigated the News in 2020: A Tumultuous Year in Review: 5. Republicans' Views on COVID-19 Shifted over Course of 2020; Democrats' Hardly Budged." Pew Research Center, Feb. 22, 2021. www.pewresearch .org.

Mitchell, P., M. Wynia, R. Golden, B. McNellis, S. Okun, C. E. Webb, V. Rohrbach, and I. Von Kohorn. "Core Principles & Values of Effective Team-Based Health Care." *NAM Perspectives* (Oct. 2012). www.nam.edu.

Mohammad, M. A., et al. "Association of Weather with Day-to-Day Incidence of Myocardial Infarction: A Swedeheart Nationwide Observational Study." *JAMA Cardiology* 3, no. 11 (2018): 1081–89. doi.org/10.1001/ jamacardio.2018.3466.

Morrow, R. L., E. J. Garland, J. M. Wright, M. Maclure, S. Taylor, and C. R. Dormuth. "Influence of Relative Age on Diagnosis and Treatment of Attention-Deficit/Hyperactivity Disorder in Children." *CMAJ* 184, no. 7 (2012): 755–62. doi.org/10.1503/cmaj.111619.

NBC News. "United Airlines CEO Discusses Holiday Crowds, Vaccine Mandates, Air Rage." Nov. 23, 2021. www.today.com.

Neprash, H. T., B. Sheridan, A. B. Jena, Y. H. Grad, and M. L. Barnett. "Evidence of Respiratory Infection Transmission Within Physician Offices Could Inform Outpatient Infection Control." *Health Affairs* 40, no. 8 (Aug. 2021): 1321–27. doi.org/10.1377/hlthaff.2020.01594.

Nilsson, J., and M. R. Warren. "The Fight for Women Doctors." *Saturday Evening Post,* Jan. 14, 2016. www.saturdayeveningpost.com.

Nowak, M., and K. Sigmund. "A Strategy of Win-Stay, Lose-Shift That Outperforms Tit-for-Tat in the Prisoner's Dilemma Game." *Nature* 364, no. 6432 (1993): 56–58. doi.org/10.1038/364056a0.

Obermeyer, Z., B. Cohn, M. Wilson, A. B. Jena, and D. M. Cutler. "Early Death After Discharge from Emergency Departments: Analysis of National US Insurance Claims Data." *BMJ* 356 (2017): j239. doi.org/10 .1136/bmj.j239.

O'Connor, J. J. "Pressure Groups Are Increasingly Putting the Heat on TV." *New York Times,* Oct. 6, 1974, D19. www.nytimes.com.

Olenski, A. R., M. V. Abola, and A. B. Jena. "Do Heads of Government Age More Quickly? Observational Study Comparing Mortality Between Elected Leaders and Runners-Up in National Elections of 17 Countries." *BMJ* 351 (2015): h6424. doi.org/10.1136/bmj.h6424.

Olenski, A. R., A. Zimerman, S. Coussens, and A. B. Jena. "Behavioral Heuristics in Coronary-Artery Bypass Graft Surgery." *New England Journal of Medicine* 382, no. 8 (2020): 778–79. doi.org/10.1056/NEJMc191 1289.

Oliveira, D. F. M., Y. Ma, T. K. Woodruff, and B. Uzzi. "Comparison of National Institutes of Health Grant Amounts to First-Time Male and Female Principal Investigators." *JAMA* 321, no. 9 (2019): 898–900. doi .org/10.1001/jama.2018.21944.

Oster, E. *The Family Firm: A Data-Driven Guide to Better Decision Making in the Early School Years.* New York: Penguin Press, 2021.

Park, K. C. "Interview with a Quality Leader: Dr. Ashish Jha." *Journal for Healthcare Quality* 32, no. 5 (Sept. 2010): 10–11. doi.org/10.1111/j.1945-1474 .2010.00112.x.

Parker, M. M., A. Fernández, H. H. Moffet, R. W. Grant, A. Torreblanca, and A. J. Karter. "Association of Patient-Physician Language Concordance and Glycemic Control for Limited–English Proficiency Latinos with Type 2 Diabetes." *JAMA Internal Medicine* 177, no. 3 (2017): 380. doi.org/10 .1001/jamainternmed.2016.8648.

Peabody, F. W. "The Care of the Patient." *Journal of the American Medical Association* 88, no. 12 (1927): 877. doi.org/10.1001/jama.1927.02680380001001.

Pekkanen, J. "The Saving of the President." *Washingtonian,* March 10, 2011. www.washingtonian.com.

Perlmutter, E. M. "The Pittsburgh Marathon: 'Playing Weather Roulette.'" *Physician and Sportsmedicine* 14, no. 8 (Aug. 1986): 132–38. doi.org/10 .1080/00913847.1986.11709154.

Perry, J. E., L. R. Churchill, and H. S. Kirshner. "The Terri Schiavo Case: Legal, Ethical, and Medical Perspectives." *Annals of Internal Medicine* 143, no. 10 (2005): 744–48. doi.org/10.7326/0003-4819-143-10 -200511150-00012.

Pew Research Center. "Republicans, Democrats Move Even Further Apart in Coronavirus Concerns." June 25, 2020. www.pewresearch.org.

Porter, M. E. "What Is Value in Health Care?" *New England Journal of Medicine* 363, no. 26 (2010): 2477–81. doi.org/10.1056/NEJMp1011024.

Prescott, H. C., and T. W. Rice. "Corticosteroids in COVID-19 ARDS." *JAMA* 324, no. 13 (2020): 1292. doi.org/10.1001/jama.2020.16747.

Principi, N., S. Esposito, P. Marchisio, R. Gasparini, and P. Crovari. "Socio-economic Impact of Influenza on Healthy Children and Their Families."

Pediatric Infectious Disease Journal 22, no. 10 (Oct. 2003): S207–S210. doi .org/10.1097/01.inf.0000092188.48726.e4.

Pronovost, P., et al. "An Intervention to Decrease Catheter-Related Bloodstream Infections in the ICU." *New England Journal of Medicine* 355, no. 26 (2006): 2725–32. doi.org/10.1056/NEJMoa061115.

Putri, W. C. W. S., D. J. Muscatello, M. S. Stockwell, and A. T. Newall. "Economic Burden of Seasonal Influenza in the United States." *Vaccine* 36, no. 27 (2018): 3960–66. doi.org/10.1016/j.vaccine.2018.05.057.

Racine, E., R. Amaram, M. Seidler, M. Karczewska, and J. Illes. "Media Coverage of the Persistent Vegetative State and End-of-Life Decision-Making." *Neurology* 71, no. 13 (2008): 1027–32. doi.org/10.1212/01.wnl.0000320507 .64683.ee.

Ramos, L. V. "The Effects of On-Hold Telephone Music on the Number of Premature Disconnections to a Statewide Protective Services Abuse Hot Line." *Journal of Music Therapy* 30, no. 2 (1993): 119–29. doi.org/10.1093/ jmt/30.2.119.

Reardon, S. "Flawed Ivermectin Preprint Highlights Challenges of COVID Drug Studies." *Nature* 596, no. 7871 (Aug. 2021): 173–74. doi.org/10.1038/ d41586-021-02081-w.

Recovery Collaborative Group. "Dexamethasone in Hospitalized Patients with Covid-19." *New England Journal of Medicine* 384, no. 8 (2021): 693– 704. doi.org/10.1056/nejmoa2021436.

———. "Effect of Hydroxychloroquine in Hospitalized Patients with Covid-19." *New England Journal of Medicine* 383, no. 21 (2020): 2030–40. doi .org/10.1056/nejmoa2022926.

Redberg, R. F. "Cardiac Patient Outcomes During National Cardiology Meetings." *JAMA Internal Medicine* 175, no. 2 (Feb. 2015): 245. doi.org/10 .1001/jamainternmed.2014.6801.

Reichert, T. A., N. Sugaya, D. S. Fedson, W. P. Glezen, L. Simonsen, and M. Tashiro. "The Japanese Experience with Vaccinating Schoolchildren Against Influenza." *New England Journal of Medicine* 344, no. 12 (2001): 889–96. doi.org/10.1056/NEJM200103223441204.

Ring, D. C., J. H. Herndon, and G. S. Meyer. "Case Records of the Massachusetts General Hospital: Case 34-2010: A 65-Year-Old Woman with an Incorrect Operation on the Left Hand." *New England Journal of Medicine* 363, no. 20 (2010): 1950–57. doi.org/10.1056/NEJMcpc1007085.

Ringh, M., et al. "Mobile-Phone Dispatch of Laypersons for CPR in Out-of-Hospital Cardiac Arrest." *New England Journal of Medicine* 372, no. 24 (2015): 2316–25. doi.org/10.1056/NEJMoa1406038.

Rizo, C. A. "What's a Good Doctor and How Do You Make One?" *BMJ* 325, no. 7366 (2002): 711–11. doi.org/10.1136/bmj.325.7366.711.

Rodwin, B. A., V. P. Bilan, N. B. Merchant, C. G. Steffens, A. A. Grimshaw, L. A. Bastian, and C. G. Gunderson. "Rate of Preventable Mortality in Hospitalized Patients: A Systematic Review and Meta-analysis." *Journal of General Internal Medicine* 35 (July 2020): 2099–106. doi.org/10.1007/s11606-019-05592-5.

Roethlisberger, F. J., and W. J. Dickson. *Management and the Worker: An Account of a Research Program Conducted by the Western Electric Company, Hawthorne Works, Chicago.* With H. A. Wright. Cambridge, Mass.: Harvard University Press, 1939.

Root, A., J. P. Brown, H. J. Forbes, K. Bhaskaran, J. Hayes, L. Smeeth, and I. J. Douglas. "Association of Relative Age in the School Year with Diagnosis of Intellectual Disability, Attention-Deficit/Hyperactivity Disorder, and Depression." *JAMA Pediatrics* 173 (2019). doi.org/10.1001/jamapediatrics.2019.3194.

Rosenbaum, L. "The Less-Is-More Crusade—Are We Overmedicalizing or Oversimplifying?" *New England Journal of Medicine* 377, no. 24 (2017): 2392–97. doi.org/10.1056/NEJMms1713248.

———. "Reassessing Quality Assessment—the Flawed System for Fixing a Flawed System." *New England Journal of Medicine* 386, no. 17 (2022): 1663–67. doi.org/10.1056/NEJMms2200976.

Rosenberg, E. S., et al. "Association of Treatment with Hydroxychloroquine or Azithromycin with In-Hospital Mortality in Patients with COVID-19 in New York State." *JAMA* 323, no. 24 (2020): 2493. doi.org/10.1001/jama.2020.8630.

Roter, D. L., J. A. Hall, and Y. Aoki. "Physician Gender Effects in Medical Communication." *JAMA* 288, no. 6 (2002): 756. doi.org/10.1001/jama.288.6.756.

Roter, D. L., M. Lipkin Jr., and A. Korsgaard. "Sex Differences in Patients' and Physicians' Communication During Primary Care Medical Visits." *Medical Care* 29, no. 11 (Nov. 1991): 1083–93. doi.org/10.1097/00005650-199111000-00002.

Rui, P., and K. Kang. *National Hospital Ambulatory Medical Care Survey: 2017 Emergency Department Summary Tables.* National Center for Health Statistics, Centers for Disease Control and Prevention, U.S. Department of Health and Human Services. www.cdc.gov.

Saha, S., and M. C. Beach. "Impact of Physician Race on Patient Decision-Making and Ratings of Physicians: A Randomized Experiment Using Video Vignettes." *Journal of General Internal Medicine* 35, no. 4 (2020): 1084–91. doi.org/10.1007/s11606-020-05646-z.

Salles, A., M. Awad, L. Goldin, K. Krus, J. V. Lee, M. T. Schwabe, and C. K. Lai. "Estimating Implicit and Explicit Gender Bias Among Health

Care Professionals and Surgeons." *JAMA Network Open* 2, no. 7 (2019): e196545. doi.org/10.1001/jamanetworkopen.2019.6545.

Samuel, L. "Patients Fare Worse with Older Doctors, Study Finds." *Stat,* May 16, 2017. www.statnews.com.

Sanghavi, P., A. B. Jena, J. P. Newhouse, and A. M. Zaslavsky. "Outcomes After Out-of-Hospital Cardiac Arrest Treated by Basic vs. Advanced Life Support." *JAMA Internal Medicine* 175, no. 2 (Feb. 2015): 196–204. doi .org/10.1001/jamainternmed.2014.5420.

———. "Outcomes of Basic Versus Advanced Life Support for Out-of-Hospital Medical Emergencies." *Annals of Internal Medicine* 163, no. 9 (2015): 681–90. doi.org/10.7326/M15-0557.

Sarsons, H. "Interpreting Signals in the Labor Market: Evidence from Medical Referrals." Working paper, Nov. 28, 2017.

Sasson, C., D. J. Magid, P. Chan, E. D. Root, B. F. McNally, A. L. Kellermann, J. S. Haukoos, and CARES Surveillance Group. "Association of Neighborhood Characteristics with Bystander-Initiated CPR." *New England Journal of Medicine* 367, no. 17 (2012): 1607–15. doi.org/10.1056/ NEJMoa1110700.

Schmidt, H. G., and R. M. Rikers. "How Expertise Develops in Medicine: Knowledge Encapsulation and Illness Script Formation." *Medical Education* 41, no. 12 (Dec. 2007): 1133–39. doi.org/10.1111/j.1365-2923.2007 .02915.x.

Schneider, E. C., A. Shah, M. M. Doty, R. Tikkanen, K. Fields, and R. D. Williams II. *Mirror, Mirror 2021: Reflecting Poorly: Health Care in the U.S. Compared to Other High-Income Countries.* Commonwealth Fund (2021).

Schoenberg, S. "Look Inside the Security Headquarters for the 2019 Boston Marathon." *MassLive,* April 15, 2019. www.masslive.com.

Self, W. H., et al. "Effect of Hydroxychloroquine on Clinical Status at 14 Days in Hospitalized Patients with COVID-19." *JAMA* 324, no. 21 (2020): 2165. doi.org/10.1001/jama.2020.22240.

Senate Homeland Security and Governmental Affairs Committee. "Medical Response to COVID-19." C-SPAN, Dec. 8, 2020. www.c-span.org.

Shahian, D. M., et al. "Predictors of Long-Term Survival After Coronary Artery Bypass Grafting Surgery: Results from the Society of Thoracic Surgeons Adult Cardiac Surgery Database (the ASCERT Study)." *Circulation* 125, no. 12 (2012): 1491–500. doi.org/10.1161/CIRCULATIONAHA.111 .066902.

Shapiro, R. A., and T. Berland. "Noise in the Operating Room." *New England Journal of Medicine* 287, no. 24 (1972): 1236–38. doi.org/10.1056/ NEJM197212142872407.

Shen, M. J., E. B. Peterson, R. Costas-Muñiz, M. H. Hernandez, S. T. Jewell, K. Matsoukas, and C. L. Bylund. "The Effects of Race and Racial Concordance on Patient-Physician Communication: A Systematic Review of the Literature." *Journal of Racial and Ethnic Health Disparities* 5, no. 1 (2018): 117–40. doi.org/10.1007/s40615-017-0350-4.

Shi, Z., M. L. Barnett, A. B. Jena, K. N. Ray, K. P. Fox, and A. Mehrotra. "Association of a Clinician's Antibiotic-Prescribing Rate with Patients' Future Likelihood of Seeking Care and Receipt of Antibiotics." *Clinical Infectious Diseases* 73, no. 7 (2021): e1672—e79. doi.org/10.1093/cid/ciaa1173.

Siemieniuk, R. A. C., et al. "Drug Treatments for Covid-19: Living Systematic Review and Network Meta-analysis." *BMJ* 370 (2020): m2980. doi.org/10.1136/bmj.m2980.

Singh, M. "Heuristics in the Delivery Room." *Science* 374, no. 6565 (2021): 324–29. doi.org/10.1126/science.abc9818.

Skipper, C. P., et al. "Hydroxychloroquine in Nonhospitalized Adults with Early COVID-19: A Randomized Trial." *Annals of Internal Medicine* 173, no. 8 (2020): 623–31. doi.org/10.7326/M20-4207.

Slater, P. E., and P. Ever-Hadani. "Mortality in Jerusalem During the 1983 Doctors' Strike." *Lancet* 322, no. 8362 (1983): 1306. doi.org/10.1016/s0140-6736(83)91181-9.

Smith, A. W., et al. "U.S. Primary Care Physicians' Diet-, Physical Activity—, and Weight-Related Care of Adult Patients." *American Journal of Preventive Medicine* 41, no. 1 (July 2011): 33–42. doi.org/10.1016/j.amepre.2011.03.017.

Snow, J. *On the Mode of Communication of Cholera.* London: John Churchill, 1855.

Stamp, N. "I'm a Female Surgeon. I Feel Uncomfortable Telling Girls They Can Be One, Too." *Washington Post,* July 29, 2019. www.washingtonpost.com.

Stevens, J. P., D. J. Nyweide, S. Maresh, L. A. Hatfield, M. D. Howell, and B. E. Landon. "Comparison of Hospital Resource Use and Outcomes Among Hospitalists, Primary Care Physicians, and Other Generalists." *JAMA Internal Medicine* 177, no. 12 (2017): 1781. doi.org/10.1001/jamainternmed.2017.5824.

Stiegler, M. P., J. P. Neelankavil, C. Canales, and A. Dhillon. "Cognitive Errors Detected in Anaesthesiology: A Literature Review and Pilot Study." *British Journal of Anaesthesia* 108, no. 2 (Feb. 2012): 229–35. doi.org/10.1093/bja/aer387.

Stucky, C. H., and M. J. De Jong. "Surgical Team Familiarity: An Integrative Review." *AORN Journal* 113, no. 1 (2021): 64–75. doi.org/10.1002/aorn.13281.

Swamy, L., C. Worsham, M. J. Bialas, C. Wertz, D. Thornton, A. Breu, and

M. Ronan. "The 60-Minute Root Cause Analysis: A Workshop to Engage Interdisciplinary Clinicians in Quality Improvement." *MedEdPORTAL,* Feb. 15, 2018, 10685. doi.org/10.15766/mep_2374-8265.10685.

Tapper, E. B. "Doctors on Display: The Evolution of Television's Doctors." *Baylor University Medical Center Proceedings* 23, no. 4 (2010): 393–99. doi .org/10.1080/08998280.2010.11928659.

Temel, J. S., et al. "Early Palliative Care for Patients with Metastatic Non-small-cell Lung Cancer." *New England Journal of Medicine* 363, no. 8 (2010): 733–42. doi.org/10.1056/NEJMoa1000678.

Thaler, R. H., and C. R. Sunstein. *Nudge: Improving Decisions About Health, Wealth, and Happiness.* New Haven, Conn.: Yale University Press, 2008.

Thomas, M., and V. Morwitz. "Penny Wise and Pound Foolish: The Left-Digit Effect in Price Cognition." *Journal of Consumer Research* 32, no. 1 (2005): 54–64. doi.org/10.1086/429600.

Thompson, A. H., R. H. Barnsley, and R. J. Dyck. "A New Factor in Youth Suicide: The Relative Age Effect." *Canadian Journal of Psychiatry* 44, no. 1 (1998): 82–85. doi.org/10.1177/070674379904400111.

Thompson, A. H., R. H. Barnsley, and G. Stebelsky. " 'Born to Play Ball': The Relative Age Effect and Major League Baseball." *Sociology of Sport Journal* 8, no. 2 (1991): 146–51. doi.org/10.1123/ssj.8.2.146.

Towers, S., and Z. Feng. "Social Contact Patterns and Control Strategies for Influenza in the Elderly." *Mathematical Biosciences* 240, no. 2 (Dec. 2012): 241–49. doi.org/10.1016/j.mbs.2012.07.007.

Treisman, R. " 'A Disaster Within a Disaster': Carbon Monoxide Poisoning Cases Are Surging in Texas." NPR, Feb. 18, 2021. www.npr.org.

Trump, D. "Remarks by President Trump in a Meeting with U.S. Tech Workers and Signing of an Executive Order on Hiring American." Aug. 3, 2020. U.S. National Archives.

Tsugawa, Y., D. M. Blumenthal, A. K. Jha, E. J. Orav, and A. B. Jena. "Association Between Physician *U.S. News & World Report* Medical School Ranking and Patient Outcomes and Costs of Care: Observational Study." *BMJ* 362 (2018): k3640. doi.org/10.1136/bmj.k3640.

Tsugawa, Y., A. B. Jena, J. F. Figueroa, E. J. Orav, D. M. Blumenthal, and A. K. Jha. "Comparison of Hospital Mortality and Readmission Rates for Medicare Patients Treated by Male vs. Female Physicians." *JAMA Internal Medicine* 177, no. 2 (2017): 206–13. doi.org/10.1001/jamainternmed.2016 .7875.

Tsugawa, Y., A. B. Jena, E. J. Orav, D. M. Blumenthal, T. C. Tsai, W. T. Mehtsun, and A. K. Jha. "Age and Sex of Surgeons and Mortality of Older Surgical Patients: Observational Study." *BMJ* 361 (2018): k1343. doi.org/ 10.1136/bmj.k1343.

Tsugawa, Y., A. B. Jena, E. J. Orav, and A. K. Jha. "Quality of Care Delivered by General Internists in US Hospitals Who Graduated from Foreign Versus US Medical Schools: Observational Study." *BMJ* 356 (2017): j273. doi.org/10.1136/bmj.j273.

Tsugawa, Y., J. P. Newhouse, A. M. Zaslavsky, D. M. Blumenthal, and A. B. Jena. "Physician Age and Outcomes in Elderly Patients in Hospital in the US: Observational Study." *BMJ* 357 (2017): j1797. doi.org/10.1136/bmj.j1797.

Tversky, A., and D. Kahneman. "Availability: A Heuristic for Judging Frequency and Probability." *Cognitive Psychology* 5, no. 2 (1973): 207–32. doi.org/10.1016/0010-0285(73)90033-9.

———. "Judgment Under Uncertainty: Heuristics and Biases." *Science* 185, no. 4157 (1974): 1124–31. doi.org/10.1126/science.185.4157.1124.

Ulbricht, A., J. Fernandez-Fernandez, A. Mendez-Villanueva, and A. Ferrauti. "The Relative Age Effect and Physical Fitness Characteristics in German Male Tennis Players." *Journal of Sports Science and Medicine* 14, no. 3 (Sept. 2015): 634–42. www.ncbi.nlm.nih.gov/pubmed/26336351.

Umscheid, C. A., J. Betesh, C. VanZandbergen, A. Hanish, G. Tait, M. E. Mikkelsen, B. French, and B. D. Fuchs. "Development, Implementation, and Impact of an Automated Early Warning and Response System for Sepsis." *Journal of Hospital Medicine* 10, no. 1 (Jan. 2015): 26–31. doi.org/10.1002/jhm.2259.

U.S. News & World Report. "Methodology: 2023 Best Medical Schools Rankings." March 28, 2022. www.usnews.com.

U.S. Preventive Services Task Force. "Screening for Colorectal Cancer: US Preventive Services Task Force Recommendation Statement." *JAMA* 325, no. 19 (2021): 1965–77. doi.org/10.1001/jama.2021.6238.

———. "Screening for Lung Cancer: US Preventive Services Task Force Recommendation Statement." *JAMA* 325, no. 10 (2021): 962–70. doi.org/10.1001/jama.2021.1117.

Venkataramani, A. S., M. Gandhavadi, and A. B. Jena. "Association Between Playing American Football in the National Football League and Long-Term Mortality." *JAMA* 319, no. 8 (2018): 800–806. doi.org/10.1001/jama.2018.0140.

Viglianti, E. M., A. L. Oliverio, and L. M. Meeks. "Sexual Harassment and Abuse: When the Patient Is the Perpetrator." *Lancet* 392, no. 10145 (2018): 368–70. doi.org/10.1016/s0140-6736(18)31502-2.

Vincent, M. J., E. Bergeron, S. Benjannet, B. R. Erickson, P. E. Rollin, T. G. Ksiazek, N. G. Seidah, and S. T. Nichol. "Chloroquine Is a Potent Inhibitor of SARS Coronavirus Infection and Spread." *Virology Journal* 2, no. 1 (2005): 69. doi.org/10.1186/1743-422x-2-69.

Wallace, J., P. Goldsmith-Pinkham, and J. Schwartz. "Excess Death Rates for Republicans and Democrats During the COVID-19 Pandemic." National Bureau of Economic Research, Working Paper 30512, Sept. 2022. doi:10.3386/w30512.

Wallis, C. J. D., et al. "Association of Surgeon-Patient Sex Concordance with Postoperative Outcomes." *JAMA Surgery* 157, no. 2 (2022): 146. doi.org/10.1001/jamasurg.2021.6339.

Wallis, C. J. D., B. Ravi, N. Coburn, R. K. Nam, A. S. Detsky, and R. Satkunasivam. "Comparison of Postoperative Outcomes Among Patients Treated by Male and Female Surgeons: A Population Based Matched Cohort Study." *BMJ* 359 (2017): j4366. doi.org/10.1136/bmj.j4366.

Whaley, C. M., J. Cantor, M. Pera, and A. B. Jena. "Assessing the Association Between Social Gatherings and COVID-19 Risk Using Birthdays." *JAMA Internal Medicine* 181, no. 8 (2021): 1090. doi.org/10.1001/jamainternmed.2021.2915.

Whaley, C. M., T. Koo, V. M. Arora, I. Ganguli, N. Gross, and A. B. Jena. "Female Physicians Earn an Estimated $2 Million Less Than Male Physicians over a Simulated 40-Year Career." *Health Affairs* 40, no. 12 (Dec. 2021): 1856–64. doi.org/10.1377/hlthaff.2021.00461.

Wickström, G., and T. Bendix. "Commentary." *Scandinavian Journal of Work, Environment, and Health* 26, no. 4 (2000): 363–67. doi.org/10.5271/sjweh.555.

Williamson, T. "The Goals of Care—Is There a (Black) Doctor in the House?" *New England Journal of Medicine* 383, no. 6 (2020): e43. doi.org/10.1056/nejmpv2024338.

Wolraich, M. L., et al. "Clinical Practice Guideline for the Diagnosis, Evaluation, and Treatment of Attention-Deficit/Hyperactivity Disorder in Children and Adolescents." *Pediatrics* 144, no. 4 (Oct. 2019): e20192528. doi.org/10.1542/peds.2019-2528.

Worsham, C. M., and A. B. Jena. "The 'Successful Failures' of Apollo 13 and Covid-19 Vaccination." *Stat,* April 11, 2022. www.statnews.com.

Worsham, C. M., J. Woo, and A. B. Jena. "Birth Month and Influenza Vaccination in Children." *New England Journal of Medicine* 383, no. 2 (2020): 184–85. doi.org/10.1056/NEJMc2005928.

Worsham, C. M., J. Woo, A. B. Jena, and M. L. Barnett. "Adverse Events and Emergency Department Opioid Prescriptions in Adolescents." *Health Affairs* 40, no. 6 (June 2021): 970–78. doi.org/10.1377/hlthaff.2020.01762.

Worsham, C. M., J. Woo, M. J. Kearney, C. F. Bray, and A. B. Jena. "Carbon Monoxide Poisoning During Major U.S. Power Outages." *New England Journal of Medicine* 386, no. 2 (2022): 191–92. doi.org/10.1056/nejmc2113554.

Worsham, C. M., J. Woo, A. Zimerman, C. F. Bray, and A. B. Jena. "Association of Maternal Cervical Disease with Human Papillomavirus Vaccination Among Offspring." *JAMA Network Open* 4, no. 12 (2021): e2134566. doi.org/10.1001/jamanetworkopen.2021.34566.

Zimerman, A., C. M. Worsham, J. Woo, and A. B. Jena. "The Need for Speed: Observational Study of Physician Driving Behaviors." *BMJ* 367 (2019): l6354. doi.org/10.1136/bmj.l6354.

INDEX

Page numbers in *italics* refer to figures and illustrations.